Africanism and Authenticity in African-American Women's Novels

Amy K. Levin

University Press of Florida

Gainesville · Tallahassee · Tampa · Boca Raton
Pensacola · Orlando · Miami · Jacksonville · Ft. Myers

08 07 06 05 04 03   6 5 4 3 2 1

Library of Congress Cataloging-in-Publication Data
Levin, Amy K., 1957–.
Africanism and authenticity in African-American women's novels /
Amy K. Levin
p. cm.
Includes bibliographical references and index.
ISBN 0-8130-2631-8 (acid-free paper)
1. American fiction—African American authors—History and
criticism. 2. Women and literature—United States—History—20th
century. 3. American fiction—Women authors—History and criticism.
4. American fiction—20th century—History and criticism. 5. African
American women—Intellectual life. 6. American fiction—African
influences. 7. African American women in literature. 8. African
Americans in literature. 9. Africa—In literature. I. Title.
PS374.N4L48 2003
813'.5099287'08996073—dc21 2003040190

The University Press of Florida is the scholarly publishing agency
for the State University System of Florida, comprising Florida A&M
University, Florida Atlantic University, Florida Gulf Coast University,
Florida International University, Florida State University, University
of Central Florida, University of Florida, University of North Florida,
University of South Florida, and University of West Florida.

University Press of Florida
15 Northwest 15th Street
Gainesville, FL 32611–2079
http://www.upf.com

for Eric, with love and thanks
for sharing our first year of marriage
with this book

Contents

Acknowledgments

The sources of this work have been as varied and international as the influences I have sought to describe. To begin, I wish to thank Patterson Williams of the Denver Art Museum's Education Department for encouraging me almost twenty years ago to develop children's workshops in the African art galleries. This experience instigated not only my appreciation of African art, but also my interest in West African women's secret societies, such as Sande.

As a Ford Foundation fellow at the Center for the Study of Black Literature and Culture at the University of Pennsylvania in the summer of 1992, I had opportunities to refine the ideas presented in the second half of this book. I am grateful to John Roberts, who continually asked tough, thought-provoking questions, and to Houston Baker, who offered support in my work on ghostwriting.

Versions of two chapters appeared in collections of articles that have already been published and are being reprinted with permission from the publishers. Chapter 2, on Gloria Naylor, was first published as "Metaphor and Maternity in *Mama Day*," in *Gloria Naylor's Early Novels*, edited by Margot Anne Kelley (Gainesville: University Press of Florida, 1999). Maryemma Graham included material from chapter 6, on *Jubilee*, as an article titled "The Violation of Voice, Revising the Slave Narrative" in her edited collection, *Fields Watered with Blood: Critical Essays on Margaret Walker* (Athens: University of Georgia Press, 2001). In both cases, the editors' comments were invaluable in revising the chapters and shaping them into their final form.

Most of all, I wish to thank Mickie Grover, who read long sections of the manuscript over twelve years, sometimes repeatedly, continually offering encouragement, advice, and love. I am grateful, too, to my parents, Eugene and Barbara Levin, for introducing me to the world beyond the United States.

A Note on the Text

The decision whether to use African diacritical marks in this text posed a significant dilemma. Since one of the central points of this book is the need to respect Africanisms, I initially intended to use the markings that would best indicate African pronunciation. However, the task soon proved to be daunting.

Most works of Africanist literary criticism cited in the book omit African diacritical marks, as does some anthropological work published in the United States. Many American journals and certain book publishers actively discourage authors from using the marks. Consequently, when I quote African literary criticism and some anthropology, the terms are unmarked. Other anthropological works focusing exclusively on Africa use the diacritical marks, though not always consistently. For instance, Margaret Drewal and Babatunde Lawal mark Gelede differently.

Ultimately, I decided to be guided by two principles. When quoting other works, I have retained the original orthography. Elsewhere in the text, I have omitted the diacritics in order to achieve as much consistency as possible. I continue to value African languages and the cultures from which they spring, as the rest of this book will show.

1

Otherness and the Black Mask

In Gloria Naylor's *Mama Day*, the old family homestead, which is vacant, is referred to as the "other place." Situated at the far end of the island of Willow Springs, the homestead is reached after crossing woods rumored to be haunted, as well as a graveyard, the family's history inscribed on its stone tablets. The "other place" is special in a number of ways: only Mama Day, the matriarch and local healer, goes there with any regularity; the house is encircled by a lush and overgrown garden; intricately carved cabinets line the kitchen. Most of all, Mama Day repeatedly implies that the "other place" is the locus of magical events and powerful secrets. Residents of the island refer to the "other place" in hushed, awed tones, aware of its mysteries. Like the former slave Sapphira Wade, one of the first inhabitants, it does not "live in the part of our memory we can use to form words" (4). Shaded, silent, and gloomy, the "other place" is linked to death (the "other side") and the unconscious, even as it links Africa and America, the legacies of slavery and the hopes of freedom.

In opening this book with "the other place," I pay homage to Naylor's enchanting novel, a text that has delighted me repeatedly and led to critical "other places" that I will explore in the following chapters. I, too, will be using the term in a number of ways that may be extrapolated from Naylor's work. On the surface, the "other place" is an abandoned Eden, the origin of the family whose lineage is traced at the beginning of the novel, just as Adam's descendants are listed in Genesis. Naylor revises or "signifies" (to borrow a useful term from *The Signifying Monkey: A Theory of African-American Literary Criticism*, by Henry Louis Gates, Jr.) on the story of Eden, making her Eve the slave girl Sapphira who killed her master, Bascombe Wade, abandoned her seven sons, and walked over a cliff. Tempting as it might be to read Naylor's story as a version of

Adam and Eve, this interpretation would not fully capture the resonances of the "other place," the magic and otherness of the spot. To refer to the spot as an Eden is to read "white," by emphasizing the text's Western European influences instead of its distinctively African or African-American qualities.

Another, more suggestive reading of the "other place" is to consider it in light of the numerous critical discussions of otherness. French feminists, including Luce Irigaray, have defined otherness as being at the core of women's self-understanding; critics of African-American literature, such as Gates and W. Lawrence Hogue, have noted that in the past, much literary analysis has treated blacks as other (Gates, *Figures in Black* xxxii; Hogue 24). In contrast, these contemporary critics seek to center what is African-American. Clearly, the other is defined and delimited by one's discursive universe; in terms of the two kinds of criticism mentioned above, texts by African-American women, including *Mama Day*, are doubly other, on account of race and gender. In her essay, "Variations on Negation," Michele Wallace refers to this kind of otherness as "the 'other' of the 'other'" (60), and she explains the difficulties of articulating theory from this "dangerously unspeakable" posture (60) of the doubly silenced.

In Naylor's universe, the island of Willow Springs, lying between two states but part of neither, and owned by blacks since before the Civil War, represents the otherness of blackness. It has its own laws and codes, both linguistic and behavioral. Within Willow Springs, the "other place" is the double otherness of the African-American female. Significantly, the "other place" is mysterious, frightening, and alluring—like the conventional stereotype of the black woman.

If race and gender render Naylor's heroines doubly other, then their "other place" must, of necessity, be defined by both these qualities; it must be at once African and female. Indeed, the "other place," reached through the graveyard but now largely unknown and unexplored, is a metonymic expression of the women's African legacy. It is no wonder that Mama Day, who has been initiated into its magic and fertility rites, is the only one who returns frequently. Younger people, including her great-niece Cocoa, experience the perpetual sense of loss and *atopia* that—for Houston Baker—characterize the blues and African-American art (*Blues, Ideology, and Afro-American Literature* 5). Cocoa's lack of connection to her roots is of major concern to Mama Day. More is at stake than the end of a family line; for Mama Day, the dwindling of the Days and the population of Willow Springs corresponds to the extinction of a long and hallowed tradition going back to Africa and the days preceding slavery. This tradition influences many of the characters' actions, giving the women strength and power. Its rituals and magic structure their lives.

Throughout this book, I wish to make a case for the Africanist "other place" as a presence in contemporary novels by African-American women. The legacy represented by the "other place" is derived in particular from traditional West African organizations, such as the Sande society of Mende women and the Gelede of the Yoruba. The other (mother) place is at once Africa and the location of women-centered society rituals. Even though their power was much reduced by the end of the twentieth century, such societies, both male and female, had existed in Africa for hundreds of years, since before the arrival of European colonists. It is therefore likely that enslaved Africans were aware of and may have participated in their traditions. Although societies vary, certain features remain constant, such as an emphasis on the use of dance in ritual ceremonies. The societies may also educate, regulate, and medicate. They are part of the governing structure in certain communities; in addition, much art is created for society rituals.

Strong and long-standing, special societies permeated almost every level of existence in parts of West Africa and, in some cases, continue to do so. The societies are often referred to as secret or closed organizations because certain knowledge or rituals are available only to initiates or those of higher rank. Many of the associations are also sources of powerful matriarchs, and they have generated their own kind of knowledge, which cannot always be spoken, let alone written. For example, in Sande, the leader adjudicates in marital disputes (Boone 38). According to Robert Farris Thompson, the Ejaghan people of Cameroon and Nigeria believe that woman was "the original bearer of civilizing gifts" (231), possessed of the secrets of Ngbe, the male society, before men learned them (236). Masked with feathers, monkey bones, and other signs of their power, members of the Nnimm female society present a daunting image of their sex as "a multitextured manifestation of potentialities, resisting the pigeonholing of women as purely instruments of labor" (235). Indeed, the secrecy and masking instigate such fear that they function as "checks against injustices . . . committed against them [members] by men or other women" (235). Ultimately then, secret societies provide some protection for women in cultures where they might otherwise be power-less. And the fenced enclosures of these societies, together with their se-crets, inscribe a private women's space within a larger patriarchy. Other groups, such as Gelede, are ruled by men but celebrate women's roles and respect female gods.

The leaders of closed societies wear distinctive ritual masks that mark their rank and express their power. Perhaps the most widely recognized is the black mask of Sande's *Sowei*. The highly polished surface of the wood draws attention to the beauty of her blackness, and her high, ornately carved hair, often topped by a carved bird, indicates her closeness to the sky and the natural world of animals. Most of all, the mask's tiny slits for eyes and mouth indicate the impenetrable secrets of its owner. From these mysteries spring her power; she reveals nothing unless it is her will. Within the context of secret societies, her silence may be protective and empowering.

If "Signifyin(g)" or an ironic kind of revision is the central trope in Gates's study of African-American literature, then the power and secrecy attributed to women in West African closed societies is a trope for rela-tionships and discourse in African-American novels by women. The black mask of the *Sowei* is a symbol for this mode of reading. The mask not only summarizes the qualities outlined above; it also indicates the way in which late-twentieth-century novels assume a mask or cover of references to European texts (as when Naylor alludes to Genesis in *Mama Day*). The mask functions as a protective and defensive strategy.

While secret societies and their leaders may celebrate certain aspects of women's lives, such as motherhood, all of them act to some extent as agencies of social control, regulating women. Some of the societies, in-cluding Sande, practice female excision, restricting women's abilities to experience sexual pleasure. Ignoring such practices would be intellectu-ally dishonest. Our picture of these societies must therefore be compli-cated and detailed enough to allow for their many facets. While it is im-portant to recognize the positive aspects of these associations, there are dangers in romanticizing them as part of an idealized vision of Africa or demonizing them as vestiges of an unenlightened dark culture. Femi Ojo-Ade addresses this paradox, noting that many African Americans have failed to recognize the diverse civilizations of Africa, portraying the nations as "primitive": "they have often sought refuge in an idyllic, in-nocent Africa. An African observer would admit that there is a tenuous

Africanness in it all, but its authenticity and depth are debatable" (9). These dilemmas will be discussed at greater length in the two chapters on Alice Walker, whose novels reveal the complexities of contemporary African-American women's relations with the continent of their ancestors.

"Tenuous" as some African references may be, it has not been that long since Africanisms were virtually ignored. Until recently, critics and other researchers discussed African-American culture as if it were purely a product of the "New" World, as if no African culture had survived the trip across Atlantic. Such attitudes, Gates suggests, fulfill certain ideological functions: "Common sense, in retrospect, argues that these retained elements of culture should have survived, that their complete annihilation would have been far more remarkable than their preservation. . . . The notion that the Middle Passage was so traumatic that it functioned to create in the African a tabula rasa of consciousness is as odd as it is a fiction, a fiction that has served several economic orders and their attendant ideologies" (*The Signifying Monkey* 4). The idea of a "tabula rasa" helped perpetuate notions of the superiority of Western cultures and encouraged researchers to seek explanations for traits of African-American culture almost exclusively in European and American traditions.

As a result, when Robert Farris Thompson's *Flash of the Spirit* appeared in the early 1980s, his arguments concerning Africanisms in American culture were novel to many Americans. Other scholars such as Joseph Holloway soon followed his lead. Taking a slightly different approach, Patricia Jones-Jackson's 1987 book, *When Roots Die,* compares the culture of the Sea Islands off Georgia and South Carolina to Nigerian traditions, finding extensive similarities not only in language but also in modes of storytelling and other aspects of culture. According to Jones-Jackson, the Sea Islands lend themselves especially well to a study of remnants of African traditions among black Americans; their "remoteness . . . contributed to the continuation of the African-derived culture" (1). Africanisms are also visible in the various forms of conjure known as hoodoo, voodoo, and obeah found among black people of the Americas; many of their potions and spells include items that have special significance among African peoples: for instance, parts of chickens, chalk or grave dust, and serpent skins. Traces of an African heritage may be less apparent in other sectors of American society, but they exist nevertheless, as indicated by an increasing range of scholars from a variety of disciplines, including medicine, anthropology, music, dance, art, and religion. In fact, during the past fifteen years, the existence of Africanisms in contemporary African-American culture has become accepted as a truism. The woman healer possessed with knowledge of herbal remedies has become a commonplace in discussions of African-American culture. Americans of all races are aware that popular music is driven by African-derived elements, that rituals in black churches are underscored by African traditions such as call and response, and that voodoo as seen (and often distorted) in film integrates elements of African practices.

At the same time, these Americans can rarely point to the specific African traditions from which these cultural manifestations are derived. This is mainly because of a lack of knowledge, but also because with the slave trade, individuals from different regions of West Africa and belonging to a range of societies were thrown together, their cultures and habits mingling and often becoming indistinguishable. This hybridity is evident when Robert Farris Thompson notes that voodoo in Haiti, Louisiana, and elsewhere incorporates Yoruba practices as well as other African influences and elements of Catholicism (163).

Novels about African-American women reflect a similar mixture of African traditions, complicating the task of distinguishing references to particular societies or rituals. For example, fictional characters including Charles Chesnutt's conjure woman and Naylor's Mama Day are familiar with occult lore and herbal remedies resembling those found in West Africa. In her essay "In Search of Our Mothers' Gardens," Alice Walker recognizes the conflicts experienced by Phillis Wheatley, torn from Africa and taken into slavery in America. Later in the essay, Walker dares to imagine an earlier, African version of her mother, loving beauty and telling stories. Yet this act of imagination is not creation out of nothing. Rather, it is an act of recuperation, the result of love and longing. It is no wonder that in her *The Temple of My Familiar*, Walker invests several characters with mystical, psychic powers and endows one of her heroines, Lissie, with the ability to remember her many pasts, including her life in African communities of women. Lissie's memories at once call attention to and bridge the discontinuities in the history of African Americans. In *The Daughter's Return*, Caroline Rody defines such figures as "mothers-of-history," the objects of characters' and authors' fantasies of return to a time before slavery and colonial oppression: "Staging dramatic, often fantastic encounters with the past, they [the authors] foreground the mother-daughter relationship as the site of transhistorical contact" (3).

In late-twentieth-century novels by African-American women, a strain of lyricism and magic competes with the often grim realities of characters' lives. In *Beloved,* graphic scenes of violence against slaves are juxtaposed with episodes in which a ghost rises from the water or is banished by the communal voices of women. Part of *Mama Day* is set on the bustling streets of Manhattan; yet on the coastal island of Willow Springs, a cruel woman named Ruby is able nearly to kill another merely by rubbing an ointment in her hair. These ominous eruptions of magic and the supernatural are rarely experienced by whites in the novels. On the rare occasions when they are accessible to whites, they are horrifying and incomprehensible. In *Jubilee,* although Margaret Walker strives for historical accuracy in telling the story of her great-grandmother, an eerie, extraordinarily large rooster stares down and terrifies the slave owner. Disrupting the quotidian order of life in America, such visions are reminders of the "other place," Africa. While some of these connections initially appear coincidental or superficial—as when chickens, considered by the Mende protectors of women, attack the male hero/intruder in *Mama Day*—others are deep and radically affect one's reading. As a result, careful study of African beliefs is necessary to understand this literature fully, to widen our definition of the term *tradition* to include what is black and female.

Gendered Africanisms are now resurfacing in what has been variously interpreted as the mystery and magic of novels by such contemporary authors as Gloria Naylor, Toni Morrison, and Alice Walker. In the mid-1980s, Marjorie Pryse described such writers as "metaphorical conjure women . . . who make it possible for their readers and for each other to recognize their common literary ancestors (gardeners, quilt makers, grandmothers, rootworkers, and women who wrote autobiographies) and to name each other as a community of inheritors. By their combined recognition and mutual naming, based on magic, oral inheritance, and the need to struggle against oppression, black women writers . . . [are] transforming silence into speech" (5). Often these magical qualities and heritages are particularly evident in female characters who are leaders, many of whom possess special skills for healing the spirit or body. Their appearances are so frequent that Houston Baker argues, "a poetics of Afro-

American women's writing is, in many ways, a phenomenology of conjure" (*Workings of the Spirit* 66): "The poetry of *conjure* as an image resides in the secrecy and mysteriousness of its sources of power, in its connection to ancient African sources syncretized by a community of diasporic believers with Christian scriptures" (89). It is one aim of the first part of this book to render the "secrecy and mysteriousness" of Africanisms more accessible to readers. Yet Caroline Rody argues that "fictional magic is not simply an efflorescence of the anti-rational elements of an indigenous culture or region; neither does a narrative mix of magic and realism merely imitate a strange cultural encounter" (64).[1] For her, magic in the novels is linked to colonialism and postcolonialism, too; "magic works to figure the shaping persistence of colonial history in the postcolonial present . . . breaks down the realist barriers that would keep such potent history at a distance" (65). The second half of this book will be more concerned with the latter type of magic as contemporary authors confront ghosts of colonial as well as African history.

A study of traditional African secret societies and their female leaders also demystifies certain aspects of late-twentieth-century novels. For example, it is common among West African women's secret societies for young women to undergo an initiation, just as boys are initiated into male societies. In the process, the girls are said to die; they are reborn as women, cognizant of the secrets of adulthood and of the closed society itself. The secrecy of the sodalities has been compared with the hidden depths of rivers (Boone 50), and when girls reappear in public after their initiation, they are said to have risen from the waters (Butt-Thompson 210). Sande women mark their "property" (initiates as well as physical objects) by daubing it with white clay from river beds (Boone 18), and annual retreats to the female enclosure are compared with being immersed in cleansing waters (Boone 50). The *aje*, a woman whose powers resemble witchcraft, is of critical importance in Gelede, and she is often connected to birds and night creatures.[2]

Contemporary novels by African-American women also repeatedly link initiation, rebirth, flight, and water, so often that the similarities appear more than coincidental. Although these may be interpreted as references to Christian baptism and other Western rituals, in our reading, which centers African traditions, this imagery yields other meanings. In Toni Morrison's *Beloved*, for instance, two crucial immersions occur, and both lend themselves to interpretations other than allusions to baptism.

First, Sethe practically drowns when she is escaping her master and in labor with her daughter Denver. This episode marks the death of her slave self, as well as her initiation into the world of free blacks. Later, Sethe slashes the throat of her daughter Beloved rather than return her to slavery. At this time, Beloved is initiated into the cruelties of racism; significantly, her ghost later surfaces from the river, covered in mud.

In *Mama Day*, three drownings occur. The slave girl Sapphira walks over the cliff into the ocean. Later, Ophelia, Mama Day's mother, follows Sapphira after her daughter Peace drowns in a well. These drownings reflect the isolation of the characters; they cannot be reborn into a society of women. Years later, their descendant Cocoa (also named Ophelia) becomes victim to a cruel spell, the severity of which becomes apparent when Cocoa showers. Cocoa's recovery is contingent on the death of her husband because he draws her away from Willow Springs, both physically and intellectually; he is a strict materialist and rationalist who places little faith in Mama Day's sorcery and medicine. If Cocoa were to return to Manhattan with the strong-willed George, she, too, would be isolated, and she would be unable to take her place as successor to Mama Day. For Cocoa, the shower is part of a process that ultimately binds her to the community of women; it marks a stage in her initiation. Significantly, her second marriage, to a mild-mannered man, takes her only as far as Charleston, from which she frequently visits Willow Springs.

In Jamaica Kincaid's novels, water is equally important. In *Annie John*, the heroine is virtually reborn after a long illness that culminates in a protracted cleansing rain storm. Images of women beckoning out of the water appear repeatedly in her novels and short stories, where mothers are associated with obeah and the supernatural. These visions mark the separation of the heroine from her mother and her African heritage.

The uses of water in *Mama Day, Beloved,* and *Annie John* are only a few examples of connections between African practices and events in contemporary novels. Along with the importance of African traditions, cultural dislocation is a recurrent theme in the works discussed in this book. In Toni Morrison's novels, it appears in the heroines' uneasy relationships with the communities in which they live. Jamaica Kincaid's characters, on the other hand, experience *atopia* despite being confined to small islands, and Alice Walker deals increasingly with the tensions experienced by Africans and African Americans when they come into contact. Interestingly, few authors have written novels exploring the original point of contact between cultures, chronicling the slaves' landing in the Americas, but in recent years many have examined the experience of slavery and the near extinction of Africanisms. They understand how important this time was in contributing to the cultural dislocation experienced by people of African descent across the diaspora. Therefore, even as it is essential to record Africanisms in late-twentieth-century novels by African-American women and to develop this awareness into a way of reading, I have found it equally important to analyze the novels that document slavery and the suppression of African culture.

Another theme that accompanies Africanisms in novels by African-American women is motherhood, especially as it has been constructed by the nineteenth-century cult of true womanhood, the twentieth-century narratives of psychoanalysis, and the Moynihan report with its pathologizing of African-American families. In the past, discussions of mother figures in novels by African-American women have often focused on the destructive aspects of such matriarchs as Eva Peace in Toni Morrison's *Sula* and Silla Boyce in Paule Marshall's *Brown Girl, Brownstones*. Characters such as Sethe in Morrison's *Beloved* or Mattie Michael in Naylor's *Women of Brewster Place* are also penalized for not living up to white norms of motherhood, even though these standards are not appropriate to their circumstances. These literary critiques based on dominant ideologies fail to account for the complexities of African-American women's novels and women's full range of experience. Instead, they tend to essentialize motherhood and womanhood in ways that privilege white norms. Yet West African secret societies are governed by strong, quiet women who are respected and feared by the men around them. These leaders offer a different, more affirmative model for the maternal figures in the contemporary novels I will analyze.

A third theme concerns temporality and spatiality: when we study Africanisms in American cultures, we treat Africa as if it existed out of time and as if its various regions were indistinguishable. This tendency makes it easier to idealize Africa, because scholars do not have to confront the complicated realities of the continent. In analyzing traditions transmitted through the Middle Passage, however, scholars need to be aware of African cultures of that era. As Patricia Jones-Jackson has indicated, the African practices among people of the Sea Islands are several hundred years old, and not current, since America's coastal population has had little contact with Africa since the end of the slave trade. Societies such as

Sande are rapidly losing power, particularly in urban areas of contemporary Africa. Consequently, in studying Alice Walker's depictions of contemporary Africa, one must be acquainted with African modernity as well. Kadiatu Kanneh's book *African Identities* is particularly important in situating Africa against temporal and spatial axes, thus resisting further essentialisms.

Finally, studying Africanisms takes researchers away from a focus on certain Western institutions, such as Christianity, that remain extremely important to African Americans today. Ojo-Ade argues that "the Christianization of Blacks in America is a force of de-Africanization" (11), which may be true in some ways, but does not account for the many black churches in the United States that have incorporated African rituals such as call and response into their worship. Throughout my readings, especially in the second half of this book, therefore, I will concentrate on what happens when the Africanisms come into contact with Christianity. Discussion of neo-slave narratives, such as Margaret Walker's *Jubilee*, will be especially useful in this context. A significant number of these recent works, including not only *Beloved* but also *Dessa Rose* by Sherley Anne Williams and *Family* by J. California Cooper, have much in common with nineteenth-century slave narratives as well. These works are important because they record the coming into contact of African traditions and European domination, and they explore what happens to Africanisms under oppression.

Reading for the marks of Africa in this manner has involved assuming otherness for myself and taking the societies and African-American women for my center. I have attempted not to appropriate or essentialize the other (a tendency which is all too easy for many white feminists), but rather to appreciate and celebrate it. By definition, the secrecy of the societies also makes it difficult for the outsider to learn about them. I have therefore been forced to rely on the work of anthropologists and scholars who have spent long periods of time among African peoples. When I am aware of significant variations in society practices, I will discuss how these differences affect readings of literary texts. At the same time, I have been aware of the irony of my position and sought to keep in mind Michele Wallace's warning, "not only is it necessary that we focus on difference rather than on sameness or universality, but also, at every conceivable moment, we must choose and take responsibility for what we will emphasize in ourselves and others" (66). A crucial step in assuming this "responsibility" must be an awareness that "Ordinarily, accounts of art, literature, and culture fail to acknowledge their governing theories; further, they invariably conceal the *inventive* character of such theories" (Baker, *Blues, Ideology, and Afro-American Literature* 9). By rendering my "governing theories" explicit and by recognizing other approaches, I hope to keep myself and my audience aware of the ideological choices critics constantly make.

Foremost in my mind is the notion that literary theory as it is practiced in most universities is an invention of Western academia. Theory that appears in journals and academic monographs is a genre with conventions no less evident than those governing novels and poems. It is little wonder, then, that most criticism of works by African Americans turns to Eurocentric themes and images. Such criticism is an example of the extent to which white values are taken as normative as well as of the tendency to appropriate, render invisible, or invalidate what fails to fit the dominant paradigms. In more extreme cases, critics may argue that a work not grounded in Western culture has *no* theory, as if Western literary theory were the only possible kind of theory. Instead, Houston Baker asserts, "We are always embroiled with theory—even when the word itself is absent. It is an illusion to suppose that a non-theoretical subject position is possible. . . . Theoretical models are always partial and shifting, tentative and reflexive, always hybrid installments on understanding" (*Workings of the Spirit* 1).

I therefore remain aware that the mode of reading I am recommending is only one of many angles, one that, like any other critical perspective, must be limited by its own particular blind spots, by its ideology and discursive formations. Such choices are never truly "innocent," and they are followed by a host of consequences. By concentrating on the African strands in the texts I discuss, I am in the first part of this work especially choosing not to focus primarily on the American part of the African-American appellation. I am concerning myself with allusions to other white European or American texts mostly to show the contrast between Eurocentric and Afrocentric modes of reading and not to distract readers from the centrality of African traditions.

In adopting this method, I have been inspired by Paula Gunn Allen's article, "Kochinnenako in Academe," which offers comparative readings of a Native American myth. By contrasting white feminist, Keres, and feminist Keres interpretations of the same story, Allen draws attention to the different emphases, inclusions, and exclusions of each approach. Her Keres readings are particularly illuminating for mainstream audiences who lack an appropriate cultural context and are unable to recognize the importance of certain symbols. Because Eurocentric readings of African-American novels are abundant, it is unnecessary for me to discuss such interpretations in depth (as Allen does), but it is important to follow her lead in offering readings based on appropriate cultural traditions.

In briefly reminding my readers of the prevalence of other critical approaches, I also wish to pose questions that have preoccupied me throughout this study: why have the majority of critics focused so insistently on what is typically female or typically African-American in works by black women writers, to the exclusion of what is derived from African women? Why the silence? Is the double otherness of the "other place" still erased in the "unrelenting logic of dualism" (Wallace 60), which values whiteness and masculinity over blackness and femininity? What of the strong traditions of West African women's sodalities? Have these, too, been lost in a construction of tradition that excludes what is both black and female? And what is it about literary study in the past decade that has led to an increase in study of Africanisms?

As Hortense Spillers argues, "'tradition' for [the] black women's writing community is a matrix of literary *discontinuities* that partially articulate various periods of consciousness in the history of an Afro-American people" ("Cross-Currents, Discontinuities: Black Women's Fiction" 251). The discontinuous, that which remains inarticulate, must be recovered. The reasons for this exclusion become clearer in a review of common critical perspectives. Feminism, the first approach I will discuss, acknowledges the otherness of gender, identifying and privileging what is distinctively female about a given text. Such criticism often discusses works by black and white authors simultaneously and seeks commonalities. While this approach initially appears sound, in practice it often flattens differences, erasing the otherness of black women writers' works by reading "white," or focusing exclusively on Western influences.

Specifically, because so many African-American women's novels concern maternity, they seem to lend themselves to discussion by white feminists, such as Marianne Hirsch in *The Mother/Daughter Plot*. Hirsch traces the depictions of mother figures in novels by Alice Walker, Toni Morrison, and others back to Greek myths without alluding to African influences. She refers to a separate "feminist tradition" (4), but never explicitly to the possibility of an African tradition. This exclusion affects Hirsch's reading significantly. She proposes to recover the mother's voice, to view the mother as a frequently powerless figure who may also be frightening. In failing to consider the African roots of texts by African Americans, she neglects the possibility that maternal figures are based on the powerful leaders of secret societies, women who choose silence instead of having it imposed on them. For them, silence is a way to retain mystery and hence power. Their complex relations with their daughters and younger women in the society may reflect concern with finding a worthy successor rather than merely reflecting European and American psychoanalytic theories.

The difficulty with the feminist interpretations offered by Hirsch and others is that they continue to rely on a presumption of a universal mythology or set of archetypes based on European models. As recently as 2001, Shirley Stave's edited collection on Gloria Naylor contains an article by R. Mark Hall referring to Joseph Campbell's *Hero With a Thousand Faces* and James Frazer's *Golden Bough*. The same article refers only generally and briefly to John S. Mbiti's *African Religion and Philosophy* (77–96). Stave's own contribution to the collection focuses primarily on how Naylor's work revises the Bible (97–117). The continuing dominance of these Eurocentric approaches is daunting in a country that increasingly claims to value diversity. Marion Kraft draws an analogy that aptly indicates the inappropriateness of such approaches: "Why do we still need constructs of (European) universal monomyths to reconstruct African mythology, re-visions and re-inventions in African-American culture? To my knowledge, there are no European analyses of European literature, myths and mythology that underscore, e.g., the trope of the African trickster as a 'tempting pattern' for a white writer 'interested in myth and folklore'" (232). In fact, while many critics consider nothing odd about interpreting African-American literature solely from a Eurocentric perspective, they would find the reverse at best bizarre and at worst ridiculous. Consider, for instance, the possibilities of reading F. Scott Fitzgerald's *Great Gatsby* in terms of African closed societies or Kate Chopin's *Awakening* using African symbols of birds and flight.

While the feminist critics I have cited are Americans, Gayatri Spivak has noted that many French feminists are "self-centered" (158). In her dismantling of French feminist appropriations of the culture and history of Third World women, Spivak attacks Julia Kristeva in particular. According to Spivak, Kristeva romanticizes a Chinese matrilineal system whose existence is dubious at best, because this notion of matrilineage serves Kristeva's ideology (159–60). Further, Spivak suggests that Kristeva offers solutions to Third World women that are available only to the relatively privileged white female academic (158). In the end, she argues that "The difference between 'French' and 'Anglo-American' feminism is superficial." Instead, "there has to be a simultaneous other focus: not merely who am I? but who is the other woman? How am I naming her? How does she name me?" (179). Although Spivak directs her discussion and questions primarily at French critics' treatment of Asian women, her points are equally applicable to Africa and African women's traditions.

While feminist theory has emphasized gender over race, critics of black American literature have for the most part preoccupied themselves with identifying a distinctively African-American aesthetic, based on the influences of slavery and oppression. For instance, Houston Baker's *Blues, Ideology, and Afro-American Literature* re-reads American literary history to "reveal profoundly brilliant economic expressive strategies designed by Africans in the New World and the Old to negotiate the dwarfing spaces and paternally aberrant arrangements of western slavery" (31). This emphasis on slavery leads Baker to focus on the economic subtext in Olaudah Equiano's slave narrative rather than on African influences. Ultimately, then, Baker's study concentrates primarily on the "New" World.

Baker's reading of literary history is not based merely on economy; it focuses on "expressive strategies" as well. In this emphasis on rhetoric and language, Baker refers repeatedly to Foucault and others. Foucault is also crucial to W. Lawrence Hogue's *Discourse and the Other,* a study of political, economic and cultural influences on African-American writing. Yet Hogue's and Baker's reliance on European theory reveals another reason why it is difficult to find criticism that treats a continuity between African and African-American cultures. As Foucault himself suggests in defining his archaeologies of knowledge, ideology and discursive formations determine the nature of one's knowledge. Presumably, if one relies too heavily on Foucault or other European critics, one's focus is shaped by their theories, and one risks overlooking what is distinctively African.

Wole Soyinka has pointed to the problematic nature of this trend, emphasizing that "what remains permanently contestable is the *universality* of concepts and values" (48)—that is, that "concepts and values" drawn from Euro-American works, whether they be critical essays or myths, do not apply to other cultures. In fact, Soyinka issues a strong warning that it is "a serious academic lapse to transfer the entirety of that [European] language of criticism to any literature which, while undeniably cognizant of other world literatures, nevertheless consciously explores the world-view of its own societies" (44). For the critic who has been steeped in European and American criticism, a different, more African, critical language must be found, one with its own metaphors and metonyms.

As the field of African-American literary criticism grows, authors are in fact turning to a serious and methodical consideration of African influences in texts by black Americans. Initially, such concerns were mentioned in passing, as when Barbara Smith noted in "Towards a Black Feminist Criticism" that "Zora Neale Hurston, Margaret Walker, Toni Morrison, and Alice Walker incorporate the traditional Black female activities of rootworking, herbal medicine, conjure, and midwifery into the fabric of their stories" (174). Barbara Christian also addresses gender issues in her article, "An Angle of Seeing: Motherhood in Buchi Emecheta's *The Joys of Motherhood* and Alice Walker's *Meridian* (1984)." The essay, included in *Black Feminist Criticism*, opens with a study of "the ideology of motherhood in early twentieth century Nigeria" (213), which she later applies to Walker's and Emecheta's novels. In her discussion of the "many-sidedness of African women's status" (215), Christian mentions secret societies and their initiations but does not include a detailed description of their influences and power. Her focus on motherhood is a valuable "angle" of reading; yet, as Christian herself indicates, "This essay is a beginning inquiry rather than a conclusive one" (211), leaving space for additional research on the institution of motherhood as well as on West African women.

The Signifying Monkey, by Henry Louis Gates, Jr., differs significantly from Christian's work because it focuses directly on specific traditions. Gates takes Esu-Elegbara, the master trickster and messenger of the gods in Yoruba culture, as "a figure for . . . interpretation and double-voiced utterance" (xxi) as well as "indeterminacy" (21) in his "fiction of origins" of an African-American rhetorical tradition. The first half of his study is devoted to establishing Esu-Elegbara (Legba in Fon mythology) and the signifying monkey of African-American folklore as central figures in his rhetoric. In the second half, he applies his theory to several novels, including *Their Eyes Were Watching God*. Gates's study is groundbreaking in many ways, including its systematic and assertive approach to the question of the transmission of a distinctively African tradition. He perceives the "black vernacular tradition" as a "signpost, at that liminal crossroads of culture contact and ensuing difference at which Africa meets Afro-America" (4). Like others, he seeks African traditions through American cultural manifestations such as voodoo and obeah, offering readers an understanding of how African traditions might have been transmitted through the centuries.

Thorough as this study may be, Gates is not entirely convincing on the applicability of his trope and theories to women. Initially, he claims that Esu is associated with the phallus, and he quotes Robert Pelton's *Trickster in West Africa* in noting that Esu is the "living copula" (27). Later, though, he monkeys around with this interpretation, invoking Esu's doubleness and claiming that Esu may be "genderless, or of dual gender . . . despite his remarkable penis feats" (29). Gates takes this figure as a sign that "Fon and Yoruba discourse is truly genderless, offering feminist literary critics a unique opportunity to examine a field of texts, a discursive universe, that escaped the trap of sexism inherent in Western discourse. This is not to attempt to argue that African men and women are not sexist, but to argue that the Yoruba discursive and hermeneutical universes are not" (30). In view of the intricate and inextricable connections between discourse and the men and women who use it, it is unlikely that Fon and Yoruba discourse is "truly genderless." Moreover, a study of West African associations, male and female, indicates that they have their own discursive practices that define and distinguish them.

Since the publication of *The Signifying Monkey*, many critics have adopted an Africanist perspective in works on African-American literature in general as well as on specific texts. Books such as Joseph Holloway's *Africanisms in American Culture* offer interdisciplinary perspectives, while Gay Wilentz's *Binding Cultures* compares contemporary novels by African and African-American women. In *From Folklore to Fiction: A Study of Folk Heroes and Rituals in the Black American Novel*, H. Nigel Thomas traces the development of fictional heroes from African folk stories, conjuring, and spells as well as from Christian beliefs and from African-American forms, such as the dozens. In addition, he acknowledges the importance of secret societies in setting linguistic traditions that ultimately led to colorful yet cryptic jive expressions (38).

Similarly, in *From Trickster to Badman,* John Roberts recognizes the importance of African conventions and rites. His book, which concentrates more on folklore than on novels, begins with the thesis that "Black culture building in America . . . represents an extension of African culture building and not European as it has so often been conceptualized" (4). While both of these works point in useful directions, they do not concentrate on gender issues, and therefore, they cannot consistently uncover the distinctive traces of an African women's tradition.

Indeed, given the increasing quantities of feminist texts, it is surprising that the preponderance of articles and books refer to West African male and female cultures and their myths as if they were the same. In *Mythmaking and Metaphor in Black Women's Fiction,* Jacqueline de Weever alludes to the story of the male farmer Ananse. This tale is useful in interpreting texts such as Morrison's *Tar Baby,* but does not yield insights into distinctively female West African traditions. Although Lindsey Tucker deals extensively with conjure women in "Recovering the Conjure Woman: Texts and Contexts in Gloria Naylor's *Mama Day,*" she compares Mama Day with Esu-Elegbara instead of with female leaders or mythical characters. Other articles speak in such general terms about magical realism or African influences that gendering is not discernible. In her analysis of *Mama Day,* Elizabeth Hayes suggests that the Africanisms are manifestations of an early animism, failing to account for gender.

Womanism, as defined by Alice Walker, recognizes the unique heritage of African-American women, but it does not always conceptualize an African heritage in concrete, particular terms. Significantly, Walker's definition fails to mention Africa explicitly, although she refers to blackness and to folk wisdom (*In Search of Our Mothers' Gardens* xi–xii). This omission reflects the complicated nature of gendered Africanisms in Walker's novels. Her works deal with Africa much more directly than novels by such authors as Gloria Naylor and Sherley Anne Williams, but they have aroused considerable critical controversy because of the ways in which they represent Africa, alternately romanticizing the continent and reifying images of it as a primitive place.

Africana womanism is less problematic, since it acknowledges an African heritage more consistently, but literary criticism based on this theory may have shortcomings as well. In "Africana Womanist Revision in Gloria Naylor's *Mama Day* and *Bailey's Cafe,*" Dorothy Perry Thompson indicates that the "Africana womanist widens the circle to be more inclusive of cultural elements that (re)member the past—Africa, creating a connectedness for diasporic women in their secondary cultures" (91). But the article then attempts in approximately twenty pages to cover all of the following: "Regarding content, these elements include the ancestor/goddess of African tradition, necromancy, ritual, spiritual exploration/investigation, communalism, and general celebration of culture. Regarding discursive strategy the characteristic elements are multiple-voiced narration, conflation of temporal and spatial realities (part of African worldview), linguistic appropriateness (frequently, a speakerly text), and a matricentric focus" (92). This article is extremely important in outlining these directions, but it cannot possibly treat the sources of all of the African cultural elements to which it refers.

Articles and books that attempt to account more comprehensively for Africanisms in contemporary works by African-American women are beginning to appear with increasing frequency. *Black Feminist Thought* by Patricia Hill Collins is built on the premise that Africans in America gained some authority by "retaining significant elements of West African culture" (10) and that "the knowledge produced in Black communities was hidden from and suppressed by the dominant group" (10). Throughout the book, Collins traces black American women's West African heritage, considering the importance of "othermothers" and strong maternal leaders (115–23). She asserts that female bonding is further evident in an "ethic of caring" (215) derived from African traditions. Yet these qualities of African-American women's lives are often absent from contemporary cultural products; in particular, Collins decries the effects of "controlling images," such as the mammy and Jezebel, that "form a nexus of elite white male interpretations . . . meshing smoothly with systems of race, class, and gender oppression" (78). Collins argues that "controlling images" should be replaced by an "Afrocentric feminist aesthetic for beauty" (88); indeed, by developing *Mama Day* around strong women who are influenced by African traditions, Gloria Naylor succeeds in presenting an alternative to the dominant culture's stereotypes of black women.[3]

Other critics refer even more explicitly to African traditions. Sharon Holland's "*Bakulu* Discourse: The Language of the Margin in Toni Morrison's *Beloved*," suggests that the ghost in Morrison's novel is an "African retention" (92), linked to the Yoruba river goddess Osun. Likewise,

Carole Boyce Davies refers to the Yoruba *abiku*, children who die young and return to trouble their mothers (3, 55). Such works are truly ground-breaking because they point readers directly to African retentions, so that the resemblances between contemporary novels and African traditions no longer seem fuzzy or coincidental, and they focus on traditions that specifically affect women. These new directions need further exploration and extension, and it is my intent to begin that process in this book.

In the first part of *Africanism and Authenticity*, I will offer readings of four of the most prominent African-American women authors to-day—Gloria Naylor, Toni Morrison, Jamaica Kincaid, and Alice Walker (Kincaid was born in the Caribbean, but her continued residence and publication in the United States warrants her inclusion in the book). Throughout, I have taken a dual approach to Africanisms in these authors' novels. In tracing resemblances between West African women's rituals and the lives of women characters, I illustrate the continuing importance of a heritage that is black, female, and African. I have also focused on another aspect of African influences: how they permeate the novels' structures and styles.

Each of the four authors uses Africanisms in ways that are appropriate to her aesthetic and thematic goals. In Naylor's *Mama Day*, the community of Willow Springs reflects the values and power relations evident in West African women's societies. Allusions to Africa are indirect and appear through metonyms and metaphors. Moreover, despite their contiguity, Naylor emphasizes the underlying dissimilarities between island and mainland cultures. In stressing the essential otherness of Willow Springs, Naylor implies that these differences reflect the conflicts between those who value their African heritage and those who desire to be assimilated into American culture.

While reference to art historian Sylvia Ardyn Boone helps illuminate Africanisms in Naylor's work, my reading of Toni Morrison's texts will draw on the writings of cultural anthropologist Victor Turner, particularly his works on social drama and ritual, as well as on the Gelede society of the Yoruba. Through allusions to Turner, I will demonstrate how rites of initiation and liminality, similar to those found in West Africa, are central in Morrison's novels. Morrison focuses primarily on characters who exist in an indeterminate space between cultures, races, or life stages rather than on difference or otherness. This emphasis on indeterminacy is reflected in Morrison's fluid, poetic style as well.

In my study of Jamaica Kincaid's work, I will examine the transmission of Africanisms in the Caribbean, not only through obeah and medicine, but also through rituals and symbols. Recent theory on region and geography will be used explain how the claustrophobic nature of the islands arises from the layering of three cultural traditions: indigenous, African, and European colonial. Because the heroines' relations with their mothers or mother figures enact the conflicts among cultures, these older women become reflections of the heroine's dislocation. In contrast to the "mother-of-history" described earlier, these figures are described by Caroline Rody as "mothers-of-forgetting," in a "historyless condition" (110).

Alice Walker's *Possessing the Secret of Joy* takes a more direct approach to African influences, considering what happens when a twentieth-century West African woman moves to the United States. In doing so, Walker questions the survival of such rituals as genital excision, which oppress West African women. She also suggests a continuity in the suffering of black women on both continents. Once again, the structure of the novel takes root in the cultures it represents; the multivocal, fragmented narrative reflects the disruption of African women's worlds.

By offering four different approaches to Africanisms in contemporary novels by African-American women, I hope to illustrate not only the variety in their works, but also the complexities and richness lent by African influences. Specifically, Africa means something different in each author's works. Because of the indirect transmission of traditional influences and the unwritten history of many African women, these writers must combine imagination, (re)memory, and knowledge in representing Africa. Consequently, their texts almost inevitably invoke questions of authenticity and appropriation.

Moreover, any understanding of the role of Africanisms in African-American women's writing would be incomplete if it failed to take into account the effects of the imposition of European culture on African women in the New World. Thus, the second half of this book examines how authors develop narrative strategies to authorize oppressed African-American women as the tellers of their own stories. Even as these authors' works incorporate direct or indirect allusions to Africa, they turn repeatedly to (re)telling the stories of their female ancestors following the infamous Middle Passage. As a result, in such novels as *Jubilee, Be-*

loved, Dessa Rose, and *Family,* Margaret Walker, Toni Morrison, Sherley Anne Williams, and J. California Cooper respectively seem more concerned with slavery, the Civil War, and freedom than with Africa.

How is it that such narratives are burgeoning even as fiction reflects a heightened focus on the importance of an African heritage? What is the connection between Africanisms and the theme of appropriation found so frequently in novels about slavery and its aftermath? Answers to these questions may be found in the texts listed above, as well as in an exploration of Alice Walker's works, which chart a return to Africa through their examination of ritual genital excision. A central premise of this section of *Africanism and Authenticity* is that late-twentieth-century women writers turn repeatedly to writing about slavery and its consequences. The antebellum era was a time in which European culture was inflicted on Africans, often violently. In writing about this period, authors illustrate what happens to African traditions when they come into contact with European conventions. They demonstrate how black women's bodies become texts expressing cultural violations. Thus, Africanisms and appropriation are intricately (and inextricably) connected in novels such as *Jubilee, Beloved, Dessa Rose,* and *Family.*

The first chapter in part 2, "The Violation of Voice: Revising the Slave Narrative," focuses particularly on the connections between violence and voice through a comparison of Margaret Walker's *Jubilee* and a nineteenth-century slave narrative, *Incidents in the Life of a Slave Girl,* by Harriet Jacobs. Jacobs is concerned with establishing her authority as a writer in a society that looks down upon fugitive slaves. She uses a variety of rhetorical strategies and narrative discontinuities to protect herself. In retelling the story of a slave ancestress, Margaret Walker adopts many of Jacobs's techniques, with variations that empower—and give voice to—blacks. For instance, she inserts Africanisms as subtle markers of the continuing presence of an authentic, subversive black culture within the white slavocracy. She uses narrative discontinuities to indicate the weakening of the plantation system and the passivity of white women. In this way, Margaret Walker revises the story of her forebears, rendering it distinctively black, female, and African, as well as American.

The concern with authority and appropriation finds expression in different ways in Morrison's *Beloved* and Cooper's *Family.* These novels, set in the same period as *Jubilee,* may be characterized as ghostwritings. Not only do they concern ghosts, but they incorporate posthumous narratives, in which characters who have been brutalized speak about their experiences. On another level, the authors themselves stand in as ghostwriters or mediators, offering readers stories in the first person ostensibly by those who have been silenced. The role of the contemporary author as mediator raises new questions about authenticity, even as Morrison and Cooper, like Margaret Walker before them, are able to reappropriate the discourse of slavery.

In *Dessa Rose*, Sherley Anne Williams addresses these questions as well. Because her narrative opens with a white man's account of slavery, she, too, forces readers to consider the role of mediation in obscuring the voices of African-American women. At the same time, Williams's characters are able to signify on the conventions of the slave trade by selling themselves repeatedly for their own profit. In doing so, they invert dominant power relations, creating a space in which blacks can exert power and voice.

Similar issues arise in Alice Walker's *Possessing the Secret of Joy*, as well as her nonfiction text, *Warrior Marks: Female Genital Mutilation and the Sexual Blinding of Women*, written in collaboration with Pratibha Parmar. In these books, Alice Walker adopts the tropes and rhetorical strategies her colleagues and predecessors developed for reappropriating the discourse of slavery. Yet Walker and Parmar's position is more ambiguous, for they alternate between filling the roles of authors and editors. Like the writers of accounts of slavery, Alice Walker and Pratibha Parmar seek to authorize African women by authenticating their experiences. Their texts are multivocal, incorporating first person accounts as well as material from medical works and other sources. Thus the structure of *Warrior Marks* also resembles accounts by fugitive slaves, with Alice Walker and Pratibha Parmar standing in as editors and facilitators. Significantly, a key passage in *Warrior Marks* describes a visit to the House of Slaves on Gorée Island, from which Africans were shipped to the Americas.

Ultimately, Walker's and Parmar's texts constitute what Houston Baker would refer to as a journey back, a return to Africa, an attempt to reclaim the heritage of black women. This chapter of my book will show that every point of departure is also a place of return, as authors' imaginations and memories free the stories of black women.

In a way, then, this work presents a circular journey as it follows the experiences of women from Africa to America and back. What remains distinctive in both parts of the book is the attention paid to the importance of female African traditions and their role in the creation of African-American women's culture. That this task inevitably involves complex issues of mediation and appropriation is not surprising, given the history of violation and silencing that has influenced the lives of so many African-American women.

Part I

2

Metaphor and Maternity in *Mama Day*

The title of Gloria Naylor's third book, *Mama Day,* suggests that the novel will concern maternity. Yet Miranda Day, the title character, is *not* a biological mother. Instead, as the ruling matriarch of the Day family and of the island community of Willow Springs, as healer, advisor, midwife and conjurer *par excellence,* the old woman offers a model of mothering based not on biological kinship or the Freudian reading of the nuclear family, but on female solidarity and a vision of women's leadership that may be traced to West African women's cultures. Indeed, *Mama Day* harks back to distinctly female African rites, which must be acknowledged in order to gain a full understanding of the text. Her magic resembles the kind of conjure described by Houston Baker in the previous chapter rather than the postcolonial, revisionary magic delineated by Caroline Rody.

Recent critical discussions on mothers and motherhood in novels by African-American women writers have, for the most part, participated in a Eurocentric feminist dialogue. In *Reading from the Heart,* for instance, Suzanne Juhasz discusses *Mama Day* in a chapter titled "The Magic Circle: Fictions of the Good Mother" (181–205). Juhasz convincingly develops her ideas in the context of theories proposed by such psychologists as Nancy Chodorow, Jessica Benjamin, and D. W. Winnicott (14). Not all Eurocentric readings are so effective. The shortcomings of Eurocentric feminist discussions of motherhood in Toni Morrison's *Beloved* and Jamaica Kincaid's novels will be considered in later chapters. Still other critics have traced references to canonical works in African-American women's novels: for instance, when Catherine Ward compares Naylor's *Linden Hills* with Dante's *Inferno.* While some might argue that Naylor and her sister novelists reinforce the canon, Peter Erickson suggests that allusions to such "classics" as Shakespeare's *Hamlet* or *The Tempest* subvert the dominant paradigm: "Naylor's interest in Shakespeare neither translates into kinship nor supports a model of continuity; the main note is rather one of conflict and difference" (246).

Yet a growing number of discussions of maternity in African-American women's fiction have departed from European archetypes altogether, comparing fictional characters with mothers in actual African-American families and attributing their strength to economic, political, and cultural circumstances. Such critics as Celeste Fraser have taken this perspective on Gloria Naylor's first novel, *The Women of Brewster Place*, as well as on works by other authors, such as Paule Marshall. Yet in their more magical moments, many novels by African-American women reject both sociological mimeticism and reductive psychoanalytic theories. In Morrison's *Beloved*, Sethe, a silent woman, must resolve her relationship with the ghost of a daughter. And in *Mama Day*, the title character renders a woman fertile and saves her great-niece from a hideous curse.

Indeed, a multitude of writers diverge from the "realistic" mode with its negative depictions of maternity and dismal city housing. The portraits of mothers in urban poverty are balanced by those of women in rural communities and small towns. The latter often combine two elements: a positive model of maternity (or female leadership) and a trace of the supernatural.[1] Peter Erickson contends that magical places such as Willow Springs "take on an aspect of pastoral refuge . . . as a romantic avoidance of the present political crisis whose primary focus is urban." Ultimately, however, he asserts that *Mama Day* "is not simply escapist because it enacts another drama" (241). Helen Fiddyment Levy concurs, noting that "Naylor's career suggests that portrayals of black rural communities, even the ideal home place, represents [*sic*] more than a facile 'romantic' vision of the folk" because they "capture the distinctive experience of black history and community" (281). Indeed, works like Naylor's are not acts of avoidance (after all, Naylor comes face-to-face with urban existence in her two Brewster Place novels) but rather deliberate choices to confront a different crisis: a cultural one. The touch of the supernatural indicates that the authors' aesthetic interests are not limited to depicting the oppressive nature of urban life for many African Americans. Instead, surreal elements in novels may be read as signs of an African presence, while the mother figures may be viewed as expressions of a conception of female authority derived from West African women's traditions. Such a reading privileges what is distinctively female and Afri-

can. Dorothy Perry Thompson illustrates how Afrocentric and Eurocentric interpretations of the same tale will differ. First, she shows that a
Jungian reading of *Mama Day* would interpret the cane as a phallic symbol, and the chicken coop where the eggs are stored as a female symbol.
Yet, Thompson argues, chickens "are ever-present in the ritual drama of
the diaspora. As noted by Zora Neale Hurston, they are especially important in sacrificial rites of the Hoo Doo culture of the American South and
the Caribbean" (97), which in turn bears marks of African rites. And, as I
shall demonstrate, an Africanist reading also reveals that the cane is a
sign of leadership, a staff of office.

Barbara Christian's article, "An Angle of Seeing: Motherhood in Buchi
Emecheta's *The Joys of Motherhood* and Alice Walker's *Meridian*
(1984)," also provides a conceptual framework for reading *Mama Day*.
Christian traces the relationships between traditions of motherhood in
West Africa, and especially in Nigeria, and the behavior of characters in
two contemporary novels. Christian effectively summarizes the varied
and often contrasting views of motherhood in West Africa, noting
sources of women's subordination as well as of their power. She shows
how conventions that devalue women, such as the bride price, oppress
mothers. At the same time, she explains, women's organizations and
other traditional structures empower women, giving them support and
some measure of control over their lives (214–15).

Christian describes these exclusively female organizations, or secret
societies, as sisterhoods that "buttress" (215) women, providing friendship and the aid of peers. Yet these closed societies are also strongly hierarchical in their structure, repeating the ranking of women within families, from senior wives down to junior wives. The societies fulfill many
maternal functions, and their leaders act as surrogate mothers, educating
adolescent girls. If we expand our discussion of African traditions in contemporary women's novels beyond biological motherhood, we can include these leaders, thereby gaining useful insights into the magic of
such novels as *Mama Day*, as well as into *The Women of Brewster Place*,
where Mattie Michael provides a moral center for the women on her
street, and *Bailey's Cafe*, where Eve offers a refuge for outcast women.
Naylor's most recent book, *The Men of Brewster Place*, is less magical,
but deals with similar issues as they apply to men by focusing on definitions of manhood and male leadership in an environment detached from
African traditions and rituals, including initiation ceremonies.

West African women's secret societies with their female forms of leadership have existed for hundreds of years. Most likely, secret society beliefs and practices were transmitted directly and indirectly in a variety of forms, including folk medicine, superstitions, and tales about conjurers or tricksters. Some of the most obvious vestiges of secret society rituals are found in Caribbean voodoo; as Margaret Creel has shown in *"A Peculiar People": Slave Religion and Community-Culture among the Gullahs,* remnants of African traditions are equally apparent in practices in Gullah communities, which resemble Willow Springs in *Mama Day.* Similarly, Patricia Jones-Jackson argues that Gullah and African beliefs must be taken into account to understand African-American lore. She claims that "traditional theories [of folk tales] have posited the powerless being as the personification of the slave" and provides evidence instead "that physically insignificant creatures were revered for their intelligence in Africa" prior to the diaspora (113). A Gullah belief of African derivation critical in *Mama Day* is the notion that individuals *"cannot* die until all the children for whom they are responsible are grown and able to care for themselves, or until their responsibilities are delegated to someone else" (Jones-Jackson 24).

A close reading of *Mama Day* in the context of African beliefs and one particular women's secret society suggests ways of understanding the novel that go beyond surface allusions to canonical works, such as *The Tempest* and *Clarissa.* The superiors of West African women's societies offer a version of maternity not based exclusively on biological kinship or a catastrophic view of the family. This model emphasizes earned respect as well as a conception of the female community itself as a kind of family. The most obvious examples of this carryover in Naylor's works of this tradition are found not only in *Mama Day,* but also in *The Women of Brewster Place,* where "individual identity is shaped within the matrix of the community" (Fowler 26).

African secret associations differ, and in the next chapter, I will analyze Toni Morrison's work with reference to the Gelede society of the Yoruba. Linking the two authors' works to different societies will emphasize exactly why it is so important to discuss Africanisms in specific terms. An approach that focuses on Africanisms in a general way might elide women's roles or consider them against a male-derived standard. It might also lead to dangerous assumptions of a monologic, idealized African culture. Instead, a strategy that acknowledges the unique features of

women's lives in the varied cultures from which slaves were taken en-
riches our readings of contemporary texts by African-American women.
At the same time, I do not intend to imply that Naylor's work is only
affected by Mende rituals or that Morrison's novels reflect traces of
Yoruba traits exclusively. Nor do I plan to establish a one-to-one corre-
spondence between the works of individual authors and single African
communities. Just as slave culture in the United States evolved from an
amalgam of African societies, any given text reflects traditions of various
peoples. My selections are intended as examples, but I could just as easily
focus on Sande references in Morrison's texts (and to some extent, I do)
or on Gelede in Naylor's novels.

The traditions of the Sande society of Sierra Leone, the Ivory Coast,
and contiguous regions seem particularly pertinent to discussions of
Mama Day. As Margaret Creel has shown, many of the Gola slaves
brought to the coastal areas of South Carolina belonged to Sande or its
male counterpart, Poro (45–52). These societies were also common to the
Mende people, who were actively involved in the slave trade (41). Moreover, although information on all of the secret societies is difficult to ob-
tain, the practices and rituals of Sande are relatively well documented,
largely because of Sylvia Ardyn Boone's excellent book-length study of
the organization, *Radiance from the Waters: Ideals of Beauty in Mende
Art*. Boone's descriptions of Sande iconography are fundamental to understanding how the society's leadership may be used as a model for understanding maternity in *Mama Day*.

As Boone indicates, Sande is a society of women after puberty. Young
women are admitted following an initiation ceremony and an induction
period, during which they are taught the essentials of Sande medicine,
etiquette, and law. Only after their initiation are Sande women permitted
to marry; thus initiation is ordinarily a prerequisite for motherhood.
Moreover, while biological mothers play an important role in their
children's upbringing, Sande controls mothering by training pregnant
women in the necessary skills and by joining biological mothers in teach-
ing their daughters.

A critical structural feature of Sande is that it parallels the hierarchy
of women in the family, where a senior wife trains and supervises junior
wives. The head wife, like the local Sande leader or *Sowei*, is referred to as
"a mother and a mistress and [a junior wife] will call her *yie*, 'mother,' or
ma, 'lady'" (Boone 6). Encoded in Mama Day's very name is this meta-

phorical concept of maternity, which involves female leadership as well as the responsibilities associated with biological motherhood in European and American societies. Miranda Day is called *mama* because she is the "lady" or leader of the women in Willow Springs. While Europeans and Americans also use words for "mother" as names for older women (such as Old Mother Hubbard of nursery lore), the application of this term to such characters as Mama Day is different because, like Sande leaders, they command enormous respect and authority.

A summary of the duties of the Sande *Sowei,* or leader, reveals deeper similarities between her position and Mama Day's role in her community. The *Sowei* is a powerful woman who is elected to office. Much of her power is directly attributable to her knowledge of society secrets from which other members are excluded. Another distinguishing feature is the *Sowei*'s mastery of society practices. She knows its techniques of healing, she dances in its rituals, and she wears the black *Sowo* mask, the embodiment and articulation of the society's ideals. As Boone indicates, *Sowo* means expert (28), and, as such, the leader is responsible for supervising the education of initiates, perpetuating society traditions, and adjudicating in marital disputes. The *Sowei* oversees women's regular retreats to a special enclosure, where they gain further training and often fatten themselves to become more fertile. Finally, the *Sowei* is powerful because she is a liminal being. Monni Adams interprets the blackness of the *Sowei*'s wooden mask as a symbol of the mystery of the woods and the spirits that inhabit them. Worn into town by the leader of the society, the mask represents the taming and control of anarchic forest spirits. Thus the *Sowei* is one who links forest and village, the spirit realm and the human world, order and chaos (62).

Several other features of the female leaders of secret societies, and especially of Sande, are important to our discussion. In many societies, the leaders carry intricately carved staffs of office (Butt-Thompson 30–32). The societies have their own private words or languages and give their members special names that may indicate their rank (Butt-Thompson 33). Furthermore, many societies appoint an anti-leader who plays a complex but crucial role in the life of the community. In Sande, this figure is called *Gonde.* If the *Sowei* is expert in all the female arts, her mask an expression of the beauty of her soul, her small, slit eyes a sign of her mystery, *Gonde* is a vision of failure. Her clothing is torn and disreputable, her gait unsteady, her behavior frequently ridiculous. She "coaches" the initiates, but she is also "a funny, lovable character who lightens the gloom and reminds everyone that Sande is not always so deadly serious" (Boone 30).

According to Boone, *Gonde* is essential to the structure of Sande society: there are "two masks because it takes *both* to *express fully* the realities of the social milieu." *Gonde* is compared with one of the "rival chiefs who always struggle against each other publicly" even though they are "united in their basic aims and ideology." The two are "complementary" (Boone 39). While the *Sowei* represents and exercises control (Adams 62), *Gonde* resembles the woman who has "let herself go" (Boone 39–40). The ridicule heaped on *Gonde* minimizes the threat such a woman poses to the order and stability of the community, and especially to male power.

Other aspects of Sande offer explanations for important parts of *Mama Day* and are inextricable from Naylor's portrayal of maternity. First, hair-braiding is an important art form in Sande, where it is considered an expression of woman's beauty. Female hair, in its abundance, is seen as a sign of fertility, and is thus not to be handled casually. In fact, hair is so important that one should allow only a trusted associate to braid it, for "Offering to plait another woman's hair is a way of asking her to become your friend. A beautiful, distinctive style is considered a gift of love" (Boone 186). Conversely, "Conjurers commonly use strands of hair in various of their 'routines' designed to harm the person from whom the strands have been taken" (Harris 84), a belief common in Africa and among some blacks in the Americas.

Another important element of Sande is the chicken, woman's confidant and protector. The bird alerts women of approaching danger. But more than that, the chicken, which may accompany a woman in her daily tasks, is a sign of domesticity, of community: "The Mende word for chickens, *te*, and the word for town, *ta*, are the same in the definite, *tei*" (Boone 210). The chicken is associated with Sande in another way, too. Like the *Sowei*, the chicken is a liminal creature, capable of traveling on the ground or in the air, of perceiving internal and external realities. Frequently carved on the crown of the *Sowo* mask, a chicken signifies "clairvoyance" (Boone 208); in addition, "Chickens [are] able to see into the human heart" (Boone 210). The *Sowo* mask is also often topped with carvings of snakes, which may represent goodness; when they are combined with chickens or birds, "the theme seems to be the certainty and inevitability of struggle, and the probability of a stalemate at best" (Boone 215).[2]

These and other elements of Sande iconography are prominent in *Mama Day*. The connections between Sande and the novel permeate the very structure and texture of the narrative, deepening the portrayal of maternity therein. Mama Day functions as a *Sowei* in Willow Springs, controlling communication and the women in the community. Her arch-rival Ruby fulfills the role of *Gonde* and is integral to the working of the plot. The red chicken, like her counterparts in Sande, is an extension of the *Sowei*. And, just as much Sande activity revolves around the search for worthy successors to transmit society's values, the conflict in Naylor's plot may be derived from Miranda Day's hope that her great-niece (called Ophelia, Cocoa, or Baby Girl, depending on the context) will continue her traditions.

The importance of finding a female to succeed Mama Day as matriarch of Willow Springs is in part due to the weakness of the men in the community. The male inhabitants of Willow Springs are shadowy and passive, at best powerless and at worst ridiculous. Doctor Buzzard, who might be considered Mama Day's male conjurer counterpart, is a gambler who cheats at cards. His only medicine is the liquor he distills in the woods outside of town. Instead of confronting or controlling spirits, he is terrified by Mama Day's joking imitations of ghosts in the woods. The allusion to a feared scavenger bird in his name is as ironic as the fact that it is also the name of a popular conjurer in the Sea Islands (Jones-Jackson 25). Another man, the son of Reema, the hairdresser, is an anthropologist so obsessed with jargon that he has forgotten the language of the people around him. Ambush Duvall, despite his powerful name, is dominated by his mother, Pearl. And Junior Lee is a ridiculous figure, ruled by his wife, Ruby.

To all intents and purposes, then, Willow Springs is a matriarchal society, its roots going back to the slave girl Sapphira who murdered her master, Bascombe Wade, after he deeded her his land. Sapphira later walked over a cliff into the ocean, away from her seven sons. Yet Sapphira has lived on in the minds of her descendants, her death the subject of whispers. Her name comes to Mama Day in a dream after she has prayed to the "Father and Son as she'd been taught" (280), suggesting that Sapphira inhabits a powerful realm beyond the level of consciousness. She has become a mythical figure because of her strength and ruthlessness—after all, a man died because he loved her, and she abandoned seven sons. In fact, the African Sapphira is viewed as the "Great Mother" of Willow Springs, the first in a line of strong mother figures who can work conjure, of whom Mama Day is the latest. Sapphira herself is never named publicly (4), as if to name her were to invoke powers too awesome to face. Sapphira's death is commemorated in a local ritual called Candle Walk or "18 & 23 night," in which the inhabitants of Willow Springs march through the town carrying candles, singing and chanting, "Lead on with light, Great Mother" (111). Gifts are exchanged on the occasion; in particular, the villagers bring tokens of their respect to the current matriarch, thanking her for her beneficent offices during the year and paying homage to her magical abilities.

Significantly, Sapphira's sons and their descendants do not bear Wade's name, but one she chose—Day. Although the Day family has produced seven sons of seven sons, the line has run to women. The story of Sapphira who "could break a man's heart" (150) and leave her children has been repeated several times over the centuries as other women have drowned deliberately or accidentally, leaving their men to die for love and their children to grieve.

Despite the dwindling size of the family, the Days have remained influential in Willow Springs. As Trudier Harris notes, Mama Day revises the stereotype of the hideous, outcast conjurer in African-American culture (69). In fact, the female community, much like the earlier model of the Sande association, revolves around its leader's authority. Miranda Day's slight stature belies her strength. Within her family, she has taken her mother's place since the latter's death, helping to raise her siblings, their children, and grandchildren. Within the community, she has occupied a position of leadership. Her authority, like that of the *Sowei*, has various sources. First, she is associated with birth and fertility in a number of ways. As midwife, she has assisted at the births of most of the children on the island, having "Caught babies till it was too late to have my own" (89). Mama Day also possesses the secrets to enable other women to become fertile; when young Bernice Duvall fails to conceive, Mama Day works with her until she is pregnant.

Mama Day is the healer on the island, too. She cures Bernice Duvall's cysts and is expert at herbal remedies. As in Sande, Mama Day's remedies are as much spiritual as physical; she can remove a curse, and part of her remedy for Bernice's infertility involves planting seeds. Even though

Mama Day lacks formal medical training, she has gained the respect of Dr. Smithfield from the mainland as well as of the other townspeople.

But the greatest source of Miranda Day's power is her knowledge of family mysteries. Mama Day alone regularly traverses the graveyard to the other place, the old family homestead, repository of its secrets and African traditions. She goes there to work her magic with Bernice; the remedy for Ophelia's curse must be found after a journey to the other place as well. In fact, even though the other place was originally the plantation of Bascombe Wade, it has become equivalent to a female enclosure, visited by women on errands with Mama Day. Significantly, the only male who is allowed to enter the other place is doomed to die, because, like male visitors to the enclosures of West African women's societies, he presents a challenge to female authority.

In addition to ruling over the mysteries of the other place, Mama Day also possesses the power of divination, which goes beyond intuition. She knows when the weather is about to turn. She can see into her great-niece's heart and discover that Cocoa is in love. And most importantly, she senses the approach of evil and death.

Finally, Mama Day has linguistic power. She knows just how to phrase a letter to Cocoa to achieve a desired response. She knows how to persuade Bernice to trust her. She has used language as well as medical knowledge to gain the respect of the mainland doctor.

Mama Day's powers are accompanied by several of the marks of the *Sowei's* authority. The matriarch carries an intricately carved walking stick she has inherited from her father. This stick becomes associated with its bearer and functions as a staff of office. The snakes carved on the sides of the stick (88) could be read as symbols of Satan; however, a reading that centers the otherness of African women's societies emphasizes their beneficent aspects, and is more consistent with Mama Day's personality. Finally, Mama Day spends a great deal of time tending to her chickens, which are ultimately extensions of her will and protectors of the order on Willow Springs.

Just as the *Sowei* in Sande must preoccupy herself with the transmission of society's values, Mama Day must find a worthy successor. Cocoa is the last remaining Day, and she has the requisite strong will. As Mama Day indicates, "If I had known then what I was knowing all along, I woulda named her something else. Sapphira" (151). Cocoa has inherited the blackness of the *Sowo* mask, the darkness that indicates mystery and power over nature and people: "*the* Baby Girl brings back the great, grand Mother. We ain't seen 18 & 23 black from then till now. The black that can soak up all the light in the universe, can even swallow the sun" (48).

Yet Ophelia poses a problem in this respect. Cocoa has left Willow Springs for another island, Manhattan, where she has been quick to acquire a false polish, an odd dialect, and a disregard for family traditions. What really draws Ophelia away from Mama Day's influence, though, is her marriage to George Andrews, a strong, independent businessman. An engineer, George is associated with Western science rather than African forms of knowledge. Moreover, George's background is the antithesis of Willow Springs; an orphan, he knows little about his kin. His last name, inherited from the benefactor of the orphanage he attended, indicates no blood ties. Instead, it reminds readers of the way African-American slaves bore their owners' last names. As George himself comments to Cocoa, "You had more than a family, you had a history. And I didn't even have a real last name" (129).

Within the structure of Naylor's novel, George represents an African-American culture that has been torn from African traditions; he is ignorant of the identity of his mother, Mariam, an Ethiopian refugee (revealed in *Bailey's Cafe*). Thus, even though he is only a second-generation American, he is more deracinated than the inhabitants of Willow Springs. His scientific, rationalistic bias has failed to prepare him for the mystical nature of knowledge in Willow Springs, and his congenital heart defect is an expression of his emotional rigidity. Because of his personality, he draws Cocoa further away from her roots, making it unlikely that she will succeed Mama Day.[3] In fact, George refuses to accompany Cocoa to Willow Springs for her annual vacations, and he yields only under duress in the year in which most of the events in the novel occur.

George's much postponed visit to Willow Springs precipitates the climax of the narrative. The intrusion of a strong male in the matriarchal community of the coastal island immediately disrupts its order; the fact that this male is an engineer who is alienated from African culture, scoffing at magic and folk medicine, heightens the disruption. George underestimates Mama Day, believing he is "reasonable in expecting wrinkles, sagging skin, some trembling of the limbs" (175), and offending her pride. After Miranda leads him on an exhausting walk through the woods, though, he begins to respect her strength. She in turn is convinced of his limitations, which she treats somewhat humorously. But George threatens the matriarchy in another way as well. During the first half of the novel, Naylor stresses that George and Cocoa's relationship is based on a struggle for power, and by the time the two reach Willow Springs, this battle is being played out in George's desire to have a child. If George and Cocoa do conceive a baby, it will be even more unlikely that Cocoa will return to the women's community of Willow Springs. Therefore, much as she desires her niece's happiness, Mama Day has cause for wanting the relationship to fail. Although Lindsey Tucker suggests that George becomes an "initiate" (182), he must be removed from the island for the order of Willow Springs to be perpetuated. This creates a dilemma: as beneficent matriarch and loving great-aunt, Mama Day is not prepared to initiate the process.

Another woman on the island, Ruby, ultimately takes care of the problem for her. Ruby is presented as Mama Day's rival. She is a heavy, slatternly woman, her eyes "pressed into tiny slits" (134) resembling those on a Sande mask. For the most part, Ruby is a grotesque figure of fun and ridicule. Yet Ruby is extremely protective of her husband, Junior Lee, and will use magic to eliminate any rival. In fact, she has led Junior Lee's previous lover to her death. When Cocoa catches Junior Lee's eye, Ruby casts a spell to eradicate her new rival, a spell that ultimately has the effect of killing George. Thus although Ruby initially appears to be Mama Day's rival and opposite, an Afrocentric perspective enables us to see that Ruby functions as an extension of Mama Day, just as *Gonde* works in concert with the *Sowei*.

Together with Abigail, Mama Day and Ruby form a complete image of maternal leadership. Abigail offers an Americanized vision of womanhood. Although she assists Mama Day in nurturing and educating, she shows no desire for leadership. Her assimilation into the dominant culture is most evident in her exclusion from the secrets of Mama Day's medicine and her absence from the other place. She complements Mama Day and Ruby, who transcends ridiculous qualities to represent the sexual, angry aspects of womanhood. Ruby's energy is reflected in the disorder with which she is associated, while her power is apparent in the fact that Mama Day herself fears Ruby's spells.

Ruby's manner of placing a curse on Cocoa alludes to West African traditions, for she braids Cocoa's hair into an elaborate style. As she does so, she rubs Cocoa's scalp with a poisoned pomade. Cocoa, who has been away from the island and is not initiated into its secrets, cannot read Ruby's intentions, and this ignorance leads to disaster. Had she been living on the island, Cocoa would have known that Ruby has rubbed out other rivals in the past in a similar manner; she would have respected Ruby's power.

Instead, Cocoa is doomed to suffer a hideous illness that causes her physical and mental agony. For a time, her life is in danger. George finds himself frustrated and helpless. A storm seems to conspire with the women to cut the island off from the mainland, preventing him from rushing his wife to a doctor. He is thrown back on Mama Day's resources, provoking a confrontation between their opposing worldviews. It will take nothing less than recourse to magic to rescue Cocoa, recourse to magic that involves cutting off her braids and destroying Ruby's house. The remedies of the mainland doctor favored by George will not suffice.

If George is frustrated because he cannot rely on science to cure his wife, Mama Day is distressed because, "'It's gonna take a man to bring her [Cocoa] peace'—and all they had was that boy" (263). Miranda's choice of the stereotypical derogatory term for African-American males, "boy," indicates the extent of George's alienation from African culture, with its defining initiations into manhood. The two characters are so far apart that they do not speak the same language; as Mama Day says, "We ain't even got his kind of words to tell him what's going on" (267). Even the characters' definitions of the problem are different. George acknowledges a conflict between his rationalistic view of the world and Mama Day's intuitive, mystical knowledge. Mama Day has a broader perspective, which includes George's assessment of the conflict as well as the problem of finding a worthy successor. She knows that the real battle is over possession of Cocoa.

The resolution must weave together these different strands. It must preserve Cocoa; it must reduce Ruby's power; and it must eliminate George before he draws Cocoa away from Mama Day's influence permanently. Mama Day's design ultimately fulfills all of these objectives. She acts at once as judge, doctor, and guide.

Mama Day sends George to the old chicken coop with the family walking stick and ledger, ordering him to bring back whatever he finds under the nest of the old red hen. These are odd instructions, indeed, and they invoke the West African dimensions of mothering in the novel. In the walking stick, George is taking a reminder of Mama Day's rank and power. Bearing the family ledger, he carries its history by his side. And, as he enters the chicken coop, an enclosure at once rural and female, he is completely removed from all that is familiar to him. It is no wonder, then, that this setting has made him "decidedly uneasy" (Harris 97) from the start.

George is puzzled to find nothing under the hen's nest—and this discovery elicits a moment of insight: "But there was nothing to bring her. Bring me straight back whatever you find. Could it be that she wanted nothing but my hands?" (300). Still, George remains unsure about Miranda's purpose: "There was nothing that old woman could do with a pair of empty hands. . . . All of this wasted effort when these were *my* hands, and there was no way I was going to let you [Cocoa] go" (301). Unwittingly, George stumbles on the truth—that Mama Day wants him to offer all he has, to relinquish Cocoa.

The hen valiantly pecks away at this intruder in her realm, defending Mama Day's territory by attacking George. Her behavior is consistent with Sande iconography in several ways. Most obviously, she protects her owner and the community. Secondly, both Ruby (because of her name) and the rust-colored hen are associated with the color red. The chicken also shares Ruby's massive proportions, her thick neck, and her jealousy (300); in fact, the two are metaphorically related. The hen, like Ruby, ultimately functions as an agent or extension of Mama Day. Her pecking forces George to flee in such fear that his fragile heart gives out, and he dies.

George's death reconfirms Mama Day's influence over Ophelia, who admits that "one of my worlds" had ended (302). Miranda visits the other place a final time on the next Candle Walk night, knowing she will not return again because "the other place holds no more secrets that's left for her to find. The rest will lay in the hands of the Baby Girl—once she learns how to listen" (307). Like Bascombe Wade and some of his descendants, George has died because he has attempted to possess what man cannot own; he is "another one who broke his heart 'cause he couldn't let her go" (308). His death opens the path for Cocoa's initiation, for her learning to listen and to understand her heritage, "the beginning of the Days" (308).

Mama Day's victory is tempered by her understanding that Cocoa must "go away to come back to that kind of knowledge [about the Days]" (308) and the reasons for her husband's death. Just as the bird and snake together on the *Sowo* mask suggest the inevitability of conflict, the story that links the chicken and the snake-carved walking stick is one repeated over and over in a man's struggle to control one of the Day women.

The succession of the Days assured for the time being, Cocoa moves to Charleston. But Naylor makes clear that Charleston is not completely beyond the family's influence, for Cocoa walks "in the midst of familiar ground" there (308–9). Her new husband is "second-best" and does not try to alienate her from her native culture as George did (309). Cocoa eventually bears two sons, thus perpetuating the family and preparing for the struggle to be renewed in future generations. The closing scene of the novel shows Mama Day at peace in Willow Springs.

Mama Day may rest at the end of the novel because she has succeeded in finding someone to listen and carry on her traditions. She has fulfilled her role as leader on the island, curing the spiritually and physically infirm, working in concert with her protector, the hen, and her complement, Ruby.

In conclusion, our reading of the novel is deepened and complicated by reference to West African women's closed societies, which allows us to understand the workings of magic in the text as well as the role of such characters as Ruby who appear to be enemies of Mama Day, yet ultimately work their will. This angle of reading also allows us to understand how Mama Day can initially approve George's influence over the recalcitrant Cocoa but turn against him when he poses a threat to her own authority over Cocoa. Finally, this perspective helps us to accept Cocoa's second marriage, which we are encouraged to approve even though in many ways it represents a diminishment of the love and passion Cocoa experienced with George.

Similar visions of maternity, female leadership, and their relation to gender roles are evident in Naylor's other works as well, though the connections to African traditions are most evident in *Mama Day*. In *The Women of Brewster Place*, Eva leads the community of women, providing continuity with the past (103). Although Margaret Earley Whitt describes Eva as a trickster "Papa Legba figure" (23), in our female Africanist reading, she is more closely related to the Sande *Sowei*. Eva is followed as leader by Mattie Michael, who rocks Ciel through her grief after she loses her baby, and she dreams of unity at the end of the book. To some extent, her friend Etta Mae Johnson functions as a *Gonde* figure. Etta Mae Johnson is the picture of vibrant sexuality: "She stood out like a bright-red bird among the drab morality that dried up the breasts and formed rolls around the stomachs of the other church sisters. This woman was still dripping with the juices of a full-fleshed life" (67). Her physical appearance is only one manifestation of rebelliousness, for she is "a black woman who was not only unwilling to play by the rules, but whose spirit challenged the very right of the game to exist" (59). Her complementarity to Mattie is most evident when Mattie offers to bake a cake for Ciel's wedding and Etta Mae volunteers to dance at the event (178). Nevertheless, in the world of Brewster Place, Etta Mae is largely powerless, as is apparent when she comes home to Mattie after failing to marry the Reverend. Finally, while the pairing of Mattie and Etta Mae exemplifies Naylor's use of dual leaders, *The Women of Brewster Place* also offers a successor in Kiswana Browne, who adopts an African name, treasures the statue of a Yoruba god, and strives to unite the community in a tenants' association. Although Kiswana previously inhabited the community of Linden Hills, which assimilated the norms of mainstream white society, she is attempting to reconstruct or revive her heritage, and as a fledgling community leader, prepares to undertake the maternal aspects of the *Sowei*.

The street in *Bailey's Cafe* serves a function similar to Willow Springs. It is no accident that the owner's wife Nadine hails from the Sea Islands and resembles "an African goddess, plunked right down on the third row of bleachers at a Brooklyn Eagles game." Her hair is arranged royally, "in one thick crown of braids that circled her head. When my eyes moved down, the scenery got even better: one of those gazelle necks . . . and then what can only be described as a Bantu butt" (13–14). Yet even though Nadine is a living reminder of her African heritage, it is Eve who leads the women on the block. The Christian allusion implicit in her name is ironic because her house serves a function similar to a Sande enclosure, as Eve takes in women of all ages who have suffered as a result of their relations with men. This suffering acts as their initiation, a symbolic excision (and while many of them carry physical scars, one of them has actually been circumcised). Like Sande enclosures, Eve's home functions as a retreat; Mariam gives birth there, Jesse Bell goes through drug withdrawal in her room, and the flowers surrounding the house are evidence that it rests on fertile soil. Although male visitors are allowed into the house, they are required to follow Eve's regulations, or "they can stay away" (92). The only male member of the community is named Miss

Maple, and he wears female garments for a considerable portion of the year (not only does he find dresses cooler, but they come to represent his marginality in the white working class world). And Eve's house is surrounded by a certain mystery. Bailey, the narrator, cannot explain what makes a woman "ready" for Eve's or how Eve decides what to charge for rent (81). Others in the community gossip curiously about Eve's house, wondering whether it could be a "whorehouse," because they have no other way of categorizing the female household (81). Significantly, although Eve's is central in the book and most of the intertwined narratives focus on women, the novel's title refers to a male-owned space, a circumstance that indicates the liminal nature of the female society.

Naylor's fifth book, *The Men of Brewster Place*, also refers to a male space. While the book focuses on men, Naylor indicates that "there was always a Her in his story" (8), frequently delineating the role of a man. Like Naylor's first book about the same characters, *The Men of Brewster Place* is generally in a realistic mode, though Naylor performs some magic by reviving the character Ben, who died in *The Women of Brewster Place*. Part of Ben's story takes place on a plantation whose geographical location is as elusive as that of Willow Springs: "No point in looking for it on the map 'cause Richland only existed in the map of our minds" (11). And significantly, Ben, who traces the stories of the last generation of Brewster Place men, is named after the youngest of Jacob's sons.

An important scene is reminiscent of Mama Day frightening Dr. Buzzard in the forest by howling like a ghost; in this case, Reverend Moreland Woods (whose very name recalls the setting of the scene in *Mama Day*) is ridiculed at a church meeting for his pretensions of hearing the voice of God. Seymour, a young actor, hides, making sounds and calling the minister's name, thus mocking the call from God and exposing its falsity. Like Dr. Buzzard, Moreland is revealed to be a sham, using false magic to take advantage of others. And appropriately in this case, the tormentor is an actor, whose name indicates that he can "see more" than what is on the surface.

Beyond these allusions to other kinds of knowledge, *The Men of Brewster Place* explores what happens to men who are separated from their roots, while suggesting that initiations to racism, humiliation, and violence replace more traditional rituals of manhood. Ben presents the dilemmas in his initial account of his grandfather's childhood. The grandfather's sister dies after being raped by a white man, and when he objects to a minister's false piety at the funeral, his mother slaps him, saying, "Shut your mouth. Be a man" (16). From the beginning then, silence and manhood are equated.

Throughout the book, Naylor's characters question "What does it mean to be a man" (28), struggling with the way manhood is defined for them in America because of their race and class. Ben, for instance, comments that "We called ourselves boys even though in my late twenties I was the youngest one there" (19). Eugene's erratic behavior toward his wife is explained when readers learn that he is gay; his struggle comes out of the gap between "everything I [Eugene] believed a man should be" and his homosexuality (71). C. C. Baker, an antagonist in *The Women of Brewster Place,* kills his brother on orders from a drug lord known as the Man and thanks "God for giving him the courage to . . . be a man" (129). In contrast, Brother Jerome, named after the Biblical scholar, may be developmentally impaired, but he is able to make his "piano tell any story that he wanted. And it was *your* story if you listened real hard" (32). Where males are oppressed by normative white definitions of manhood, Jerome offers a hope and an irony—that the truth comes not from God, as father, or his representatives (Moreland Woods and the minister at the funeral) but from a perpetual child, one who communicates nonverbally. This irony has a certain appropriateness, since African males were often regarded as childlike by the European colonizers who "civilized" them, and it is Jerome's simplicity that allows him to tell suppressed stories.

The final episode of the text occurs in the male enclosure of a barbershop: "If those chairs could talk, they would be at it day and night with sadder and sadder stories" (161). Greasy, another character who is mentally impaired, keeps repeating "I am a Man." One day, he holds a razor to the barber's throat. When the men try to stop Greasy, he slits his own throat. "The garbage can to hold all our fears" (167), Greasy leaves the men feeling unsettled, and indeed, his death signals the demise of Brewster Place as well: "Max's place will be the last holdout. . . . This is the only place for us men to get together, to look into each other's eyes and see what we need to see—that we do more than just exist—we thrive and are alive" (167). The men's story ends in a pessimistic vein, rather than indicating the possibility of the transmission of traditions evident at the end of *Mama Day.* Ironically, the bleak ending reinforces the importance of those traditions, memorializing their passing.

Linden Hills is even more problematic in an Afrocentric context.

Mama Day herself surfaces to visit her relatives, and she brings recipes to make wayward men attend to their wives. A type of conjure is also evident in the formulas that Willa Nedeed discovers in the basement. These recipes, tested by one of her predecessors, point to a central theme of the novel: the disastrous consequences of the fragmentation and suppression of the Afrocentric female community with its assimilation into the American middle class. The possibility of women's leadership is simultaneously destroyed. Generations of Nedeed women have been obliterated or erased by their husbands, to the extent that one female is seen fading out of her own photographs. Other women in Linden Hills find themselves alone or unhappy, devoid of any female support. Lester Tilson's sister Roxanne affects an Afro, but refuses to assist in the liberation of Zimbabwe (57). Her prospective husband, Xavier, is deeply troubled about her dark color, and sees it as deleterious to his career. When Lycentia Parker dies, her husband has every trace of her removed from the house before her funeral; when Laurel Dumont divorces, she is also evicted from the community. Such alienation, which radically contrasts the strong network of female associations in *Mama Day*, indicates what happens to mainland women deprived of ties to a female community rooted in an African past. They are exiled from history, which in *Linden Hills* is told only in terms of male genealogies. Again, the women do not figure in the novel's title.

Thus, Naylor's other works—*The Women of Brewster Place, Linden Hills, Bailey's Cafe,* and *The Men of Brewster Place*—reinforce the importance of connections to an African model of female leadership, both directly and indirectly, by contrast. Naylor makes this point in a unique fashion, but it is nevertheless an iteration of a theme Carolyn Cooper finds increasingly common in works by black women globally: "In all of these feminist fictions of the African diaspora the central characters are challenged, however unwillingly, to reappropriate the 'discredited knowledge' of their collective history. The need of these women to remember their 'ancient properties' forces them, with varying degrees of success, to confront the contradiction of acculturation in societies where 'the press toward upward social mobility' represses Afrocentric cultural norms" (84).

Naylor particularly values independence for women, rather than their being controlled by men. She privileges women's connections to other women and establishes a model of family continuity in distinct opposition to the broken African-American families found in many other novels. In this positive vision of maternity, two sides of womanhood—the wise, beneficent matriarch and the angry, jealous sexual female—are shown to be inextricably connected. One side acts for the other. Finally, in *Mama Day*, Naylor asks us to hear as our own voice (10) the mystical knowledge of that other place where the rationalistic laws of the mainland "don't apply" (3). Reading the secrets of Mama Day, we, too, are initiated into her wisdom, so that ultimately the text reaches out to us, replicating the relationship between Mama Day and Cocoa in the bond between author and reader.

3

Clearing Space

Dramas of Liminality and Initiation in Morrison's Novels

My reading of Gloria Naylor's *Mama Day* was instigated by the otherness of the other place as metaphor and metonym for Africanisms in the community of Willow Springs. This reading was grounded in Sylvia Ardyn Boone's research on the Sande society and, in particular, in her description of its leaders. In discussing Toni Morrison's work, I will similarly seek allusions—direct and indirect, conscious and unconscious—to African women's traditions. However, there is a significant contrast between Morrison's fictional worlds and Naylor's island community. Although both writers are concerned with liminality, Naylor focuses primarily on otherness and difference. Instead of emphasizing Willow Springs's location between Africa and America, she stresses its opposition to mainland values, noting that strangers would not know how to understand events in the community, and calling the old homestead the other place. In contrast, Morrison concentrates on the complexities of the in between. Her treatment of margins or borders is multifaceted. Most obviously, her novels turn repeatedly to young women who undergo varieties of initiatory experiences, from Pecola Breedlove in *The Bluest Eye* to Dorcas Manfred in *Jazz*. Works such as *Beloved* and *Tar Baby* explore the distinctions between myth and history, life and death, the physical and metaphysical. Correspondingly, characters consistently inhabit or undergo transformative experiences in marginal spaces—the Clearing in *Beloved*, Isle des Chevaliers in *Tar Baby*, "outdoors" in *The Bluest Eye*, Pilate's home in *Song of Solomon*, and the Convent in *Paradise*. More specifically, in *Beloved*, Sethe gives birth in a secluded spot between dense woods and the Ohio River. As she struggles, she thinks of the baby as an antelope within her, which in turn mingles with images of her African mother dancing like an antelope. Even though Sethe has never seen an antelope, she has access to her African legacy in this marginal setting (30–31).

Liminality in Morrison's work is not merely a thematic quality, but also a characteristic of the author's style, which shifts from oral to written expression, from prose to poetry, from univocal to multivocal narrative. Even the recurrent images in her novels are of liminal creatures, such as birds, that can survive in two elements. Because all these aspects of liminality are most apparent in *Sula* and *Paradise,* and because other critics have explored Africanisms in *Song of Solomon* at length, the following discussion will focus primarily on the former two novels with brief reference to Morrison's other works.

This notion of liminality has arisen repeatedly in recent works by prominent critics of African-American literature. For instance, in *The Signifying Monkey,* when Henry Louis Gates, Jr., develops a major portion of his thesis from the doubleness of Esu-Elegbara, he points out that Esu-Elegbara is the West African guardian of thresholds and a trickster (29–30). In *Moorings & Metaphors,* Karla Holloway characterizes "shift" as a cultural "space" between subjectivity and objectivity, or what "happens when the textual language 'bends' in an acknowledgment of 'experience and value' that is not Western" (62). For her, as for Gates, liminality includes acknowledging the African. In *Blues, Ideology, and Afro-American Literature,* Houston Baker invokes this concept as well in his comparison of "mythic and literary acts" (116). In developing their theories, both Holloway and Baker allude to Victor Turner's work on ritual, which, in turn, is based in part on Arnold Van Genepp's analysis of rites of passage.

Other critics have applied Turner's and Van Genepp's theories specifically to Morrison's novels. For instance, in "Roadblocks and Relatives: Critical Revision in Toni Morrison's *The Bluest Eye,*" Michael Awkward alludes to Turner and marginality when he suggests that Claudia MacTeer is preparing for initiation into adult society (60). Doreatha Drummond Mbalia refers to Van Genepp in discussing how Milkman Dead passes through a "liminal stage" in *Song of Solomon* (56–59). Wilfrid Samuels, too, applies Van Genepp's theories to *Song of Solomon,* contending that Milkman is essentially an initiate going through a liminal phase (61), while Linda Krumholz alludes to Turner in making a similar contention regarding Milkman (558–59).

Such analyses, though useful, have so far been restricted to brief sections of longer studies or to the analysis of the male character Milkman. In discussing Morrison's work, I, too, will draw on Turner's definitions of rituals, and particularly initiatory ceremonies, as creating spaces of indeterminacy and liminality. But by consistently bringing his theories together with specific and appropriate rituals among women in West Africa, I intend to demonstrate the extent to which Morrison's work is permeated by gendered Africanisms. Awareness of the broader theories as well as of the specific rites can therefore deepen and enhance readers' experiences with Morrison's texts. Ultimately, Morrison's body of work enacts liminality as it bridges two cultures.

Turner's work is especially apposite because in *The Ritual Process*, he draws on his experiences in Africa, his knowledge of European cultures, and other anthropologists' research to describe liminality. Above all, he claims that ambiguity is a necessary condition. Liminal beings cannot be categorized because "these persons elude or slip through the network of classifications that normally locate states and positions in cultural space. . . . their ambiguous and indeterminate attributes are expressed by a rich variety of symbols in the many societies that ritualize social and cultural transitions" (95). The linkage of liminality and symbolism lends itself to literature. As noted in the previous chapter, certain animals are connected with liminality in African cultures; the frequency with which they appear in novels by African Americans seems more than coincidental. Among the Mende, these animals include "snakes operating between earth and water, birds between earth and air" (Boone 201), and especially chickens. For the Bambara, antelopes, which range the earth but have horns that reach for the sky, are liminal creatures, and it is therefore appropriate that Sethe envisions the antelope in a marginal setting. Similarly, other African peoples view spiders, which can climb from the ground to the sky, as liminal beings. Such Africanisms resurface in slightly different forms in African-American lore such as the stories of Tar Baby and the Flying African.

Liminality extends beyond symbols to particular conditions and places. Both Boone (45) and Turner (*The Ritual Process* 95) view initiates as liminal beings, existing between childhood and adulthood. In Sande and other societies, initiation is characterized as a death and rebirth (Boone 65; Turner, *The Ritual Process* 100); hence, initiates often take new names. In addition, because of the extensive lore surrounding initiation in African societies, certain places and rites become associated with liminality. Enclosures for initiatory retreats fall into this category, as they are often on the edges of towns or in a "sacred . . . grove, a world apart" (Boone 45), like the other place. More frequently, "The village and the wilderness . . . are by necessity interdependent; each defines the other. The boundaries between the two realms are usually flexible, and they are joined by a transitional zone in which work and some ritual activities can take place. The boundaries must continually be crossed—both literally . . . and figuratively, through ritual" ("Wild Spirits" 4–5).

In various African cultures, the forest, with its deep, dark pools, is "a place of potential fortune and of danger, . . . inhabited by spirits who are normally invisible. If one were to meet a forest spirit there, one would undergo some kind of transformation" (Adams 62). Untamed, such spirits are "capable of causing barrenness and death" (Uchendu 98). Thus, to contain and control these anarchic spirits, members of Sande and other societies bring them into the village through liminal rituals involving dances and masks (Adams 62). Mama Day plays off similar fears of the forest when she pretends she is a "haint" and scares Dr. Buzzard (81).

As mentioned in the introduction, water is linked with initiation and liminality. Besides the pools in the forest, Boone cites the proximity of streams to sacred enclosures and notes that Sande initiates are daubed with *hojo*, white clay from river bottoms, to signify their closeness to the spiritual and religion. The whiteness of the clay has another symbolic function, too. According to Turner, liminality is linked to a kind of blankness; neophytes "may be represented as possessing nothing" (*The Ritual Process* 95), and they "must be a *tabula rasa*, a blank slate, on which is inscribed the knowledge and wisdom of the group. . . . They have to be shown that in themselves they are clay or dust, mere matter, whose form is impressed upon them by society" (*The Ritual Process* 103). In particular, Turner associates whiteness with this state (*The Ritual Process* 104). The white clay used in Sande expresses these qualities: an "appreciation of white implies the Mende preference for cut ground, cleared spaces, shorn growths; white is 'empty,' clear, free of everything extraneous. So it is bright and visible, with nothing hidden" (Boone 21).

This "emptiness" of initiates has a social dimension as well. Neophytes relinquish all rank, kinship, or social status in their transition from childhood to adulthood. Thus, Boone characterizes the phase as "a disorienting *vie à l'envers*" (45). In general, the liminal phase during initiations or other rituals is socially subversive, even "dangerous and anarchical" (Turner, *The Ritual Process* 109), because "In liminality, the underling comes uppermost" (*The Ritual Process* 102). It follows, then, that individuals passing through a liminal phase exhibit the following attributes: "they are persons or principles that (1) fall in the interstices of social structure, (2) are on its margins, or (3) occupy its lowest rungs" (*The Ritual Process* 125).

Liminal beings may be associated with the religious and supernatural as well; according to Turner, novices may be compared with "ghosts, gods, or priests" (*From Ritual to Theatre* 27), as they participate in rituals of "effacement" (*From Ritual to Theatre* 26). In *The Ritual Process*, Turner elaborates, "liminality is frequently likened to death, to being in the womb, to invisibility, to darkness, to bisexuality, to the wilderness, and to an eclipse of the sun or moon" (95). During their liminal phase, creatures are perceived essentially as spirits, neither alive nor dead (in *Mama Day*, when Cocoa is ill and close to death, she might be considered to be in a liminal phase).

Additionally, liminal creatures, outside the structures of society and in transition, may temporarily form a *communitas* of equals (Turner, *The Ritual Process* 106–8), which is less hierarchical than a formal community. Turner asserts that such *communitas* generally emerges, but Boone's and Bledsoe's studies of Sande initiates indicate that, in fact, rank continues to exist as rituals become increasingly structured by conventions (Boone 63; Bledsoe 459–62).

The symbolic, religious, and social qualities of liminality offer insights into Morrison's works. But additional reference must be made to Turner's arguments about social drama, for repeatedly, Morrison's novels enact the four phases Turner outlines: "breach, crisis, redress, and *either* reintegration *or* recognition of schism" (*From Ritual to Theatre* 69). Turner uses his research among the Ndembu of Zambia to explain how such social dramas give narrative shape to events.

A breach creates antagonism and may challenge authority, until it provokes a crisis. In turn, the crisis "exposes the pattern of current factional struggle within the relevant social group, be it village or world community; and beneath it there becomes slowly visible the less plastic, more durable, but nevertheless gradually changing basic social structure, made up of relations which are relatively constant and consistent" (*From Ritual to Theatre* 70). Redress may take a variety of forms, ranging from legal solutions to "the performance of public ritual" (70). These rituals involve a scapegoat or sacrifice (71), and involve "reflexivity" or increased self-consciousness (75). It is the redressive phase that Turner characterizes as "a liminal time, . . . when an interpretation . . . is constructed to give the appearance of sense and order to the events leading up to and constituting the crisis" (75). Redress is usually followed by reintegration of the group, although the larger community will have been changed by the breach. In some cases, where no resolution is possible, the society will acknowledge an "irreparable breach between the contesting parties, sometimes leading to their spatial separation" (71). The latter is the most common outcome in Morrison's works and, often, the scapegoating of one or more women still leaves its marks on the community.

Significantly, these phases resemble Van Genepp's description of rites of passage, which he "divides into rites of separation, threshold rites, and rites of re-aggregation, for which he also employs the terms preliminal, liminal, and postliminal" (Turner, *From Ritual to Theatre* 80). Because Morrison's works explore rites of passage, and especially of initiation, even as they enact social dramas among African-American communities, Van Genepp's and Turner's theories provide an appropriate critical framework. They are also consistent with Wole Soyinka's description of the Yoruba "Fourth Stage" in which human beings "bridge the gulf between themselves and the deities as well as the ancestors, the gulf between the unborn, and present time" (Ischinger 138). In addition to clarifying the thematic content of Morrison's works, these theories describe the narrative structure of her novels. Turner's definition of social drama as public ritual offers useful insights into the shifting relationships between individuals and communities. Viewing Morrison's works as performances enables readers better to understand her exploration of transitions between oral and written expression, past and present. Finally, these theories illuminate Morrison's unique bridging of European and African cultures.

Although Turner's work, based as it is on research with African cultures, seems particularly relevant in studying Morrison's use of Africanisms, it does not focus primarily on women. Nor does most of the recent literary criticism based on Turner's work seek to identify the allusions to distinctively female and African rituals of liminality in Morrison's fiction. Therefore, continued reference must be made to other scholars, not only Boone, but also more recent authors and critics of her work. These references enable readers to recognize the influences of African women's initiations and other liminal rites or spaces.

Current research on the Gelede society of the Yoruba, for instance, deepens and complicates our understanding of the importance of liminality in Morrison's work, especially *Paradise*. Gelede rituals include masked men dancing through town, and certain kinds of knowledge are available only to insiders (Lawal xix), as in Sande. However, gender relations are somewhat different in the Yoruba society. Babatunde Lawal's 1996 study of the Gelede emphasizes male dominance in the community, to the extent that the dancers are men dressed as women. Yet despite the existence of male kings, the Gelede society sees women as complex, capable of combining beneficence and evil in one person: "There are two main reasons for this pro-female stance. One is that the preservation of humanity depends on the role of the female as mother; the other has to do with the linking of motherhood to a special power, akin to witchcraft, that can be used for good and evil" (xiv). The nurturing female role is linked to the Great Mother, and the dancers serve to educate the community to the "virtues of social living and good citizenship" (xiv). While medicine men are responsible for protecting the community, the *aje*, a kind of witch, is not always a power for good: "The *àjẹ̀* stereotype is an old woman who wields astonishing telepathic powers. She is thought to conceal the source of her power in a closed calabash containing a bird. Hence the nickname . . . wielder of bird power. At night, her soul enters the bird and flies away to attend meetings or to suck the blood of unsuspecting victims, who eventually die of some undiagnosable disease. Because of a mysterious object that lies in her stomach, the *àjẹ̀* does not require any other medicine to accomplish her objectives. She needs only to dream or wish evil, either consciously or unconsciously, and evil will happen! She operates invisibly, hears the slightest whisper, and possesses a kind of 'x-ray' eyes" (Lawal 3).

Like Sande, Gelede is headed by a woman who functions as a liaison between the Great Mother and the community. According to Lawal, the priestess is frequently considered a good *aje* (82). The *aje* possess mystical qualities similar to those attributed to powerful women in European cultures, and, because many negative occurrences are blamed on them, they are often scapegoats. Their doubleness makes them liminal creatures, at once cherished and feared.

Babatunde Lawal discusses the position of Gelede within a male-oriented community and posits that the attribution of special powers, both good and bad, to the *aje* is a way to exert social control. Women have been acculturated to accept the negative images of the *aje* and the accompanying perception that the *aje* is linked to dissension among co-wives (33). Yet not all women are endowed with the potential for such strength and mystery; they must undergo an initiation to become an *aje* (33). At the same time, according to Lawal, females are conscious that men recognize their power, and they know how to use this circumstance to their benefit (34). Thus the masked male dancers "humble themselves," their ritual performances designed to "appease women" in special ceremonies (Lawal 79), without disrupting the social order of everyday life. The society, instead of valuing combativeness, promotes harmony through its performances, and emphasizes reform rather than punishment for social breaches (79). Finally, Gelede is rooted in the people's myths of origins and is thus associated with ancestors.

While Morrison makes no explicit references to the Gelede society, she has commented in a variety of contexts on the importance of the African "ancestor" (see for instance, "Rootedness: The Ancestor as Foundation"). In "City Limits, Village Voices," she argues that "the benevolent, protective, wise Black ancestor is imagined as surviving in the village but not in the city" (39), reinforcing commonplaces about the differences between the two locales. Larger communities, including those in *The Bluest Eye, Sula*, and *Jazz*, are further detached from their roots. In *Paradise*, Morrison depicts the tragic consequences of a small town adopting "city values": "the absence or presence of an ancestor determines the success of the protagonists. For the ancestor is not only wise; he or she values racial connection, racial memory over individual fulfillment. Fighting the ancestor frequently occurs, but the devastation of the protagonist never takes place unless he succeeds in ignoring or annihilating the ancestor" ("City Limits, Village Values" 43). In such cases, there can be no restoration or reintegration; says Morrison, "if we don't keep in touch with the ancestor . . . we are, in fact, lost" and "When you kill the ancestor, you kill yourself" ("Rootedness: The Ancestor as Foundation" 344). Over and over, her novels reenact this drama, so that the "true ancestor is frequently a social or secret outlaw" (Morrison, "City Limits, Village Voices" 43), rather than an assimilated member of the community.

These allusions are apparent even in Morrison's first published novel, *The Bluest Eye*. Throughout, Pecola Breedlove is excluded from the social structures of her community. While Claudia and Frieda offer Pecola some companionship, they are children, and they cannot provide the support and leadership that would be available from a society of women. Pecola's own mother pushes her away in preference for the little white girl, and the MacTeers house her only temporarily. Pecola lacks a spiritual as well as a physical home; as Claudia's mother would say, she is "outdoors" (17). In this novel, "outdoors" functions as an expression of liminality; it is a space occupied by individuals, such as Cholly Breedlove, who exist on the peripheries of "approved" society.[1]

The prostitutes, all three of whom are, significantly, named after places, provide the closest analogue to a women's society. With their bottles tossed over the rail, they show an utter disregard for the rules of propriety Mrs. MacTeer has inculcated in her daughters. Their household, however, forms not a community, but *communitas*, a temporary gathering of equals on the margins of society. Moreover, it is dependent on men—whom the women detest—for survival. The *communitas* lacks both the power and leadership of West African women's societies. Although the inhabitants can in some ways educate the girls, they have no effective means of aiding them. Ultimately, because of its disarray and sterility (its sex is most decidedly not for procreation), the prostitutes' household may be read as an ironic signification on African women's associations, a comment on what has evolved from the capitalistic economy that spawned slavery and colonialism.

Read in terms of social drama, Pecola's premature puberty, together with her homelessness, creates a breach in the community, which literally has no place for the youngster's physical precocity and unattractiveness. Pecola's desire for blue eyes challenges authority and the implicit rule that only little white girls with blonde curls may be loved. But it is Pecola's pregnancy that creates a crisis. Her condition excludes her from categorization: she can no longer be merely "daughter" or "child." Her swelling belly offers proof of the violation of social norms. It also marks the community's failure to protect those who make visible its spiritual ugliness; the liminal is defined by and in turn defines the surrounding society.

Pecola's visit to Soaphead Church is an attempt at redress, which involves the hideous sacrifice of the dog, and ends in the complete scapegoating of Pecola after her descent into madness. Clearly, no reintegration is possible, only "irreparable breach" (Turner, *From Ritual to Theatre* 71). The failure of reintegration is most apparent in Claudia's effort to construct a narrative of the social drama, an effort that remains fractured by the prose of the primary school reader, which constructs a world of white normativity.

In depicting the devastating effects of the absence of a cohesive and regulated community of women, Morrison emphasizes its importance. By showing the weakness of women without their own society, she indicates the power of sorority and the need for historically based bonds and traditions. In *Sula*, her second novel, Morrison complicates her depiction of female communities, as well as her study of liminality and initiation. In the black neighborhood of the Bottom, all the households, with the exception of Shadrack's, which is aberrant, are female. The men are deracinated, mostly wandering the streets and populating pool halls, whistling at women, drinking, and gossiping. Ajax and Jude seem to drop in for brief sexual interludes; BoyBoy is put out by Eva; Plum is killed for his desire to return metaphorically to the womb; and the Deweys are as inconsequential as they are indistinguishable. Even Nel's father is a "seaman . . . in port only three days out of every sixteen" (17).

The Bottom is not just any community of female-run households, however. Numerous events and circumstances in the novel are tinged with metaphor and magic, even though plausible explanations are offered: Chicken Little's flight through the air and death, Shadrack's madness, Eva Peace's missing leg, Sula's facial marking, and the plague of robins. The novel constantly crosses and recrosses the boundaries of realism, so that liminality becomes a quality of the narrative itself. The natural and supernatural coexist, indicating the simultaneity of an American present and African ancestry. In turn, that simultaneity generates the central conflict in the plot—Sula's otherness or Africanism in an increasingly Eurocentric community. These qualities are essential aspects of Morrison's later novels as well.

Indeed, even as the magical and logical coexist in Medallion, the Bottom contains two kinds of female households. The first, like Nel's home, is conventional. Its inhabitants compete in propriety and submit to the norms of white America. The second, like the Peace household, is subversive, mysterious, and, at times, dangerous. These two types of families embody competing visions of womanhood. The latter still shows traces of its African heritage. On the other hand, the rapidity with which the members of the proper households follow Shadrack to their deaths reflects their gradual but deliberate acquiescence to the annihilation of their past, the crushing of their spirit.

Although Vashti Crutcher Lewis argues that Helene Wright understands her African roots (95), Nel's mother is one of the most conforming black women in Medallion. She forces her daughter to wear a clothespin on the tip of her nose so that it will lose the flatness reminiscent of her African heritage (55). Helene Wright's "apology for living" (20), as evident in the "oppressive neatness" of her home (29), eventually forces "her daughter's imagination underground" (18) until Nel wakes one day to discover that her marriage has died. As Sula says, "Now Nel was one of *them*. . . . Nel belonged to the town and all of its ways" (120).

While Nel "belongs" to the town, Sula's family ignores the community's dictates and displays distinct traces of West African women's traditions. The Peace homestead is a magical building, warm and nurturing, in contrast to the rigid order of other houses: "As for Nel, she preferred Sula's woolly house, where a pot of something was always cooking on the stove; where the mother, Hannah, never scolded or gave directions; where all sorts of people dropped in; where newspapers were stacked in the hallway, and dirty dishes left for hours at a time in the sink, and where a one-legged grandmother named Eva handed you goobers from deep inside her pockets or read you a dream" (29). The Peace household contradicts all the Bottom's strictures.[2] It is "woolly," in opposition to the neatly pressed hair of others in the town; it is "slack" because the mother never gives orders; it has no respect for history, allowing newspapers to accumulate; and it disregards rules for household management with its piles of dishes. This is not to suggest that everything African is disordered; rather, Morrison questions Eurocentric definitions of order. Finally, it is evident that the Peaces are not ashamed of their African roots, as Eva dispenses peanuts, a staple in many African cultures. Candy, on the other hand, is associated with white culture throughout Morrison's oeuvre, especially in *The Bluest Eye*, where the rich child can afford candy, and sweets rot Pecola's mother's teeth, as well as in *Tar Baby*, where the white owners of the candy factory adopt the heroine.

The contrast between the Peace household and the larger community reveals an important quality in several of Morrison's novels—that there is no unified, monologic African-American community. Morrison consistently distinguishes between the two kinds of blacks and then illustrates how their conflicts give rise to individuals like Sula or Pecola. These characters are caught, often tragically, between the two cultures and their values.

While it seems that "positive values are associated with specific practices of West African culture" in Morrison's "interrogation of dominant cultural values" (Sitter 19), Eva Peace embodies a model of womanhood that embraces the extremes of the Gelede *aje*. Almost everything about Eva is ambiguous. Eva's name is at once appropriate and ironic. Although she is the matriarch of the clan, she refers back to African as well as European and Christian origins. Her mysterious missing leg, like Sula's snipped finger, makes her more—rather than less—of a woman. This sign of suffering functions metaphorically as an act of excision.

Although Eva is the matriarch or leader of the Peace household, her role is more complicated than Mama Day's. To begin with, her jurisdiction is smaller and more restricted. Eva Peace presides over a marginal household scorned by the other women in the town. Despite its hierarchy, it resembles *communitas,* because it challenges the authority and structure of the larger community.

The Peace household also bears multiple resemblances to West African women's societies. Similar to the *Sowei* and other female leaders, Eva is responsible for educating other women in the household. Moreover, her home seems to generate fecundity in its inhabitants: "It was manlove [sic] that Eva bequeathed her daughters" (41). Hannah and Sula reject monogamy by taking multiple lovers, including men who are married to other women; in this way, they accept a model analogous to the African family with its multiple wives, one that is contrary to the mores of the "good" women of town.

At the same time, Eva appears more menacing than Mama Day. Like the enclosures of African women's organizations, her home is dangerous to male intruders, such as Plum. The Deweys hover in perpetual childhood, and Tar Baby is a drunk. Like the leaders of African women's societies, Eva determines the fates of others under her sway. She decides that her husband must depart and her son must die. Her ruthlessness in eliminating her son is balanced in part by her attempt to save Hannah. It is obvious, nevertheless, why Eva cannot answer the simple question of whether she loves her children. Her role is to lead, not to love.

Sula inherits many of Eva's qualities, including her potential for ruthlessness. She watches her mother burn, and she has Eva hospitalized, knowing that her grandmother is the only human being who understands her. But Morrison's portrait of Sula is more complicated than her picture of Eva. While her grandmother refuses to leave home after she loses her leg, Sula has a life in the larger world. In fact, she is one of the few characters in the novel who willingly moves from the Bottom, and when she returns she is never fully incorporated into the community. Existing on the margins of the Bottom's society, Sula is a liminal being whose closest analogue is Shadrack. Ultimately, Sula is torn between the two worlds she inhabits; as Morrison says, she is "formless" and inconsistent (53), like fire and water, the two elements with which she is constantly associated.

Sula's birthmark testifies to her multiplicity; like it, she can be read in many ways. At times, the mark appears to be a rose, its thorns indicating Sula's dangerous nature. Later, it resembles a copperhead or rattlesnake, at once poisonous, strong, and beautiful, like its bearer. Moreover, as noted previously, in the context of West African iconography, the snake is a liminal being, capable of moving along and under the ground, and when linked with birds (such as the plague of robins that herald Sula's return), it signifies the certainty of strife (Boone 215). Toward the end of the novel, Shadrack describes the mark as a tadpole, a creature, like Sula, in transition and ultimately capable of surviving in two elements. Karla Holloway elaborates on the meaning of the birthmark as a sign of Sula's difference: "Sula embodies the essential African archetypes of fire, water, and ground. The thorny, fire-color of her rose, the watery tadpole, the earthbound snake that are variously seen in the tattoo on Sula's forehead are physical manifestations of these African archetypes. . . . If Morrison warns us against women like these, it is because Sula carries these archetypes in a hostile land" ("Acknowledgment of Womanself" 69–70).

While Sula is associated with a range of liminal creatures, and especially snakes, Nel is compared with spiders, "whose only thought was the next rung of the web, who dangled in dark dry places suspended by their own spittle, more terrified of the free fall than the snake's breath below" (120). From an Africanist perspective, this quotation alludes to the myth of Ananse. Ananse, a greedy farmer, steals from his family, but is caught when they trap him with a rubbery tar baby. Then, "Ashamed, Ananse changes himself into a spider, spins his thread, and flees to the ceiling of his hut" (de Weever 36). Nel's concentration on "the next rung of the web" resembles Ananse's desperate need to survive. She, too, is willing to transform herself to escape the "free fall," or the blackness from which her mother spent years trying to extricate her family.

Although Nel attempts to avoid the dangerous "free fall" as well as confrontations with her African nature, in Sula's life, struggle is inevitable. As Karla Holloway suggests, Sula is a reminder of a freer, Afrocentric womanhood, in contrast to the restricted lives of the women around her. The difference between the two women is most apparent when one compares their initiations, the episodes when it becomes clear that they are separate individuals preparing for adulthood. Nel's awareness develops immediately after her trip to New Orleans with her mother. Nel is horrified and changed by her mother's submissiveness to whites as well as her rejection of the sensual Creole life: "she had gone on a real trip, and now she was different" (28). Her realization, which renders her physical travels a metaphor for her spiritual journey, occurs as she gazes into the mirror:

> "I'm me," she whispered. "Me."
> Nel didn't know quite what she meant, but on the other hand she knew exactly what she meant.
> "I'm me. I'm not their daughter. I'm not Nel. I'm me. Me."
> Each time she said the word *me* there was a gathering in her like power, like joy, like fear. (28)

Nel's "discovery" (28) is mixed. Not only is she confused by its significance, but in her rejection of the name given by her parents, a diminutive of her mother's Helene, she takes not a name with spiritual significance, as in an African initiation, but the word *me*, which is at once anonymous and universal. In choosing such an anonymous name, Nel becomes an indistinguishable part of the mainstream community of the Bottom. Significantly, the trip "was the last as well as the first time she was ever to leave Medallion" (29). It is appropriate, then, that what she feels is neither power, joy, nor fear, but "like" all three. Although she has detached herself from her parents, she is not to know herself as an individual.

More importantly, Nel's moment of self-awareness (such as it is) occurs as she gazes at her reflection in the mirror. Her "discovery" alludes to European cultures, reverberating as it does against the myth of Narcissus, developmental psychology, and Lacanian theory of the mirror stage of development. By framing Nel's reflection in this manner, Morrison implies that her character is being initiated into a society dominated by whites. Further, she indicates that, like a mirror image, this moment goes no further than the surface. Nel generates not genuine emotions, but their simulacra, for in essence, she performs them.

While Nel is socialized to fear the taunts of white boys and creates increasingly "elaborate" (54) routes home, Sula faces the hooligans with a blade in hand. Instead of attacking them with the knife, she slashes off the tip of her own finger. In doing so, Sula asserts her inviolable selfhood, her unwillingness to submit, even at the risk of self-destruction. Had Sula's aim not been "inaccurate," the narrator says, she might have done herself more damage (54). It is a gesture that goes directly to the self, not its reflection, one that confirms a breach between Sula and the larger community.

Sula's sacrificial act is also metaphorically equivalent to (but not the same as) female excision or clitoridectomy. She has cut off a "scrap of flesh, like a button mushroom, curling in the cherry blood" (54), a particle soft and pink as a clitoris. Initially, this dramatic gesture seems to reinforce the boys' power, just as genital excision, though frequently performed by women, originates in and confirms men's desire for control. After all, if the boys had not menaced the girls, Sula would never have resorted to self-mutilation. However, when Sula challenges, "If I can do that to myself, what you suppose I'll do to you?" (54–55), she is not threatening merely to castrate the boys. Her assertive language causes the boys to back off in fear and admiration, because it establishes her verbal authority and violates the communal norm of women's submissiveness. Sula's response inspires Nel's respect as well, though it is clearly beyond the bounds of sanctioned behavior. Sula's sacrifice thus leads not to redress and reintegration, but to continued breach.

The episode of the death of Chicken Little is similarly initiatory; it, too, forms part of a social drama. The episode is preceded by the girls' retreat into the forest. Nel and Sula walk past families and boys into a space enclosed by four trees, like the retreat of a female society. There, they rehearse their budding sexuality with twigs, grass, and debris. The wordless, prelinguistic ritual of liminality is interrupted by Chicken Little. Like male intruders in African women's enclosures, the boy is doomed to punishment at Sula's hands. This is no protective chicken like those in Sande iconography; it is a young boy whose name alludes to a folktale, and whose fate will invert his namesake's prediction, "the sky is falling." More importantly, in dropping into the water, Chicken Little indicates that for the submissive society of Medallion, the story of the Flying African is only a myth. The incident foreshadows the town's collective burial as well as Sula's predatory behavior toward men. Shadrack's admonitory "Always" to Sula (62) seals her separation from the society around her, creating a breach that becomes a full-fledged crisis when Sula returns to Medallion as an adult.

The "plague of robins" that "accompanies" (89) Sula's return is a sign that she brings an Africanist presence back into town. The birds are reminiscent of the *aje*'s night flights. As such, Sula—and her harbingers— unsettle the community and especially Nel, stirring her childhood ambivalence toward the town's values, her preference for Sula's home over her own. It is no wonder, then, that Nel comments, "it was like getting the use of an eye back, having a cataract removed," for Sula "helped others define themselves" (95). In regaining the use of her "eye," Nel has also regained an "I," her childhood self.

Paradoxically, Sula's presence forces Africanisms to the surface of the community as they seek "counter-conjure" (113). Odd events begin to appear ominous and to take on significance beyond their appearances. During the "evil days" (89), the populace of the Bottom cannot fully deny its African roots: "Sula, like most of the outsiders in Morrison's fictions, also represents aspects of the community that it does not wish to confront, namely, its own essence, its own unconscious, for Sula is a part of every member, a part of an idea of blackness itself" (Rigney 55). The community binds together in combating this threat to their carefully performed propriety; in short, Sula gives "them leave to protect and love one another" (117). The irony of Sula's position is best explained by Morrison herself in an interview with Thomas LeClair: "the community in *Sula* let her stay. They wouldn't wash or bury her. They protected themselves from her, but she was part of the community" (28). To the very end, Sula remains on the margins, excluded from the essential rites of burial within the community, yet a significant and necessary influence, reinforcing the importance of the African in defining African America. The irony that the outcast is essential to the community's self-definition is a common motif in Morrison's novels, including *The Bluest Eye, Beloved,* and *Paradise.*

What Sula lacks is that most Eurocentric of notions, an ego (119), for "she had no center, no speck around which to grow" (119). The contrast between her and others not only draws the community together, but it acts as a rebuke, calling attention to the fact that their selves, like pearls, form around "specks," bits of dirt and refuse. She is dangerous because, in opposition to the birds that die around town or Chicken Little, she is capable of the "free fall" (120). Having nothing to lose, she also resembles "the artist with no art form" (121). This comparison has been interpreted variously by critics since the book appeared, but it takes on new significance in an Africanist context. Sula lacks an art form not merely because she is a black woman in an oppressive society, but because her own culture has been deracinated and largely forgotten. She has been separated from the indigenous art forms of African peoples; since life itself is a form of creation, she cannot shape even her own life. Torn briefly by her love for Ajax, whose name, derived from a Greek warrior, indicates her split between European and African cultures, it is no wonder she is doomed to "disintegration" (147).

If Sula's return and affair with Ajax create a crisis in the community of the Bottom, her death is essentially a sacrifice that brings some redress to the community. For Sula herself, as for Pecola Breedlove, no reintegration is possible at this point. Later, however, Eva is the instrument of Nel and Sula's reconciliation, when she points out that, underneath, the two women are "just alike" (169). Nel tries to deny this truth, asserting that Eva is an evil old woman. Yet in the end, Nel needs Sula, calling her name, the sound making "circles of sorrow" (174). Ritual, which has structured the narrative, is now revealed as an inevitable part of the women's lives; Nel's cries resemble an endless circle dance with an invisible partner or an interrupted call and response.

In this way, Morrison reasserts the importance of solidarity, and she indicates that there is some kinship between the two apparently different kinds of African-American women. They share their loss of a common culture, the destruction of a way of living together as women. This kinship must be recognized, for those who follow blindly without acknowledging African influences die on National Suicide Day. Thus, whereas the end of The Bluest Eye is pessimistic, with Pecola mad and alone, the conclusion of Sula establishes some possibility of community and continuity despite the uprooting of African cultures.

This theme resurfaces in Morrison's next novel, *Song of Solomon*, where the author contrasts the appropriately named household of Dead women, who are sterile and fear men, with Pilate's fertile female community. Pilate combines the power of an *aje* with the qualities of a family historian, carrying her father's bones in a sack that recalls the medicine bags or *minkisi* carried by Kongo conjurers (*nganga*). The similarity is apparent when one notes that *minkisi* hold various curatives, such as white clay (a symbol of the white skin of the dead), earth from graves, and other relics (MacGaffey 62). Yet for most of the narrative, Milkman is cut off from this past, and his imagination is limited to supposing that the treasure in Pilate's sack must be material wealth.

Milkman can fulfill the story of the Flying African only after he has acknowledged his heritage and, particularly, the power and influence of his female ancestors. Before that, he is responsible for Hagar's thoroughly Europeanized shopping spree and death. In the end, when he accepts Circe, who represents a European heritage, and Pilate, who retains elements of her African culture, he comes to terms with his past. Africanisms in the novel have been amply analyzed in numerous books and articles, including "Creative African Memory: Some Oral Sources of Toni Morrison's *Song of Solomon*" by Ousseynou Traore, *Binding Cultures* by Gay Wilentz, and *Mythmaking and Metaphor in Black Women's Fiction* by Jacqueline de Weever. However, because the main character is male, this novel offers fewer opportunities than *Sula* for studying women's participation in distinctively female rites derived from African traditions.

It is difficult, too, to offer an extensive Afrocentric and gendered reading of *Tar Baby*. In this novel, Morrison again establishes a contrast in forms of womanhood, comparing the terrifying vision of the wild women in the forest and the Europeanized Jadine, who is last seen literally in the air, flying to Paris, capital of a former colonial power, and not to Africa. The wild women are a reminder of the African past, from which Jadine has divorced herself. As she sinks into the mud below them like a tar baby, it is as if she were sinking into her own color; instead of enjoying its nurturing humectants, she perceives it only as filth and waste. Her attitude thus resembles Nel's fear of the "free fall." Her affair with the tar-black Son is therefore doomed, as she flies off to resume life with a white man. In essence, Jade is rejecting a liminal or initiatory experience offered by the earth women. She cannot understand the significance of the offer, because her "formal education has provided her with no knowledge of her own culture and history" (Ryan 80). Although the narrative records a social drama, its conclusion is ambiguous. The primary female character is (re)integrated into white society with her return to Paris; at the same time, her departure confirms a continuing breach between Jadine and the African-American community.

In *Beloved,* which will be discussed as a type of slave narrative in chapter 7, Morrison extends her study of the black female community. Baby Suggs, the matriarch of the household at 124 Bluestone Road, leads the women of the community, indeed, the community as a whole, in their meetings in the Clearing, which resonates with allusions to African ritual. The Clearing, an empty place in the woods, operates as a liminal space between the domestic and wild, the white community and the black, between the past and present, the spirit and the body that is its conduit. As Monni Adams has indicated, in African cultures such places offer an opportunity for the community to control dangerous forest spirits through ritual and dance (62). Anything can happen in such spots, and they are therefore especially suitable for the ritual of initiation, the ceremony of passage from childhood to adulthood.

Yet Baby Suggs creates a breach in the community when she is perceived as displaying the eminently Christian sin of pride. She serves too many pies at the celebration of Sethe's freedom. Immediately afterward, the community divides, the bulk of it retreating into a Europeanized civilization, and refuses to warn Sethe of the approach of the slave catchers. The majority of the community becomes, by an act of omission, collaborators with white Southerners. This breach is only partly healed when the ghost is banished.

In contrast, Baby Suggs's house, like the Peace household, remains affected by African culture. It is a marginal, female space, as Sethe's husband never reappears, and her two sons leave. Even Paul D is menaced by the ghost and forced to depart until the novel's close. The ease with which the ghost becomes pregnant indicates that it is also a nurturing place, one that generates fertility. Like the other place in Naylor's novel, 124 Bluestone Road is ruled by its own probabilities and possibilities. Events that could never happen or be believed elsewhere in the town, such as furniture flying through the air or the appearance of a succubus, seem reasonable within this space. The presence, first invisible, then visible, of the ghost, indicates the existence of the past within the present.

The incarnation of the ghost after Paul D's appearance creates a crisis. With it, the present of the narrative, the immediate past of slavery, and the more distant past of African cultures collapse into one. All three inhabit the same physical space in the house as well as the same narrative space within the text. Temporal order is thrown into disarray, resembling the circularity of an African world view rather than Eurocentric chronology. A kind of *communitas* emerges as well. This *communitas* is not apparent merely in the temporal shift, but also in a reversal in power relations, as Denver begins to care for her mother, Sethe.

In fact, the plot may be read as a story of community and initiation gone wrong. Beloved, a ghost, hovering between life and death, is clearly a liminal being. Moreover, her pallid appearance as she rises from the water, dressed in white, reverberates against Sylvia Ardyn Boone's and others' descriptions of female African initiates being associated with water spirits and dressing in white. In a way, Beloved's slit throat functions as the excision requisite for the initiation into an African society; similar to initiates, she is "reborn" as a grown woman. Dressed in white, also the color of death and ancestors in many African societies, Beloved is closely connected to the past. In this context, Beloved's surfacing may be read as an ironic signification not only on the Christian ritual of baptism but also on West African initiations, for she is being initiated into the cruelty and savagery of a racist American society. The Africanisms continue after Beloved's incarnation. The enclosures of African women's societies function as "fattening houses" where women retreat to gain weight and become more fertile; so too, does Beloved develop a voracious appetite at 124 Bluestone Road in preparation for her pregnancy.

Alternatively, the apparition may be viewed as a Yoruba spirit child or *abiku*. According to William Handley, Morrison herself discussed *Beloved* in terms of African spirit children in a British television interview (689, n.6). Indeed, Gelede, with its focus on motherhood, contains numerous rites to combat *abiku* or infant mortality. Margaret Drewal demonstrates how the *abiku* can wreak havoc among the living: "An *abiku* is a child whose soul is considered 'irresponsible' because it never completes a full life cycle. The child dies young and its spirit lingers nearby, continually plaguing the mother with rebirths and sudden deaths. Once identified, diviners perform special rituals of verbal abuse to mercilessly shame such children into remaining in the world" (59). Knowledge about these spirit children almost inevitably affects readers' interpretations of

Beloved; in fact, Morrison's novel seems to recapitulate Gelede iconography. As Carole Boyce Davies has noted, the *abiku* are "marked so that they can be identified when they return," just as there are "marks of the saw on Beloved's neck" (3). The only significant difference from Drewal's version is that the "verbal abuse" in the Clearing does not keep the child alive, perhaps because the world around it is so destructive to the young. Yet the novel is consistent with Lawal's description of the tradition—that the *abiku* must leave the earth after a short while, or their "spirit doubles will harass them" (261). This would indicate that the ghost's appearance was always intended to be temporary.[3]

Ultimately, the past in Morrison's book literally sucks life from the present. The ghost threatens the household at 124 Bluestone Road, which has managed to fashion a life apart from, but dependent on the community. Not only does the ghost's irruption disrupt Sethe's home life, but it also puts her job at the restaurant in jeopardy. Hence, the need to exorcize the succubus.

As I shall discuss later, this exorcism occurs as the two kinds of women come together, maintaining their distinctions but joining in a common purpose. This collaboration functions as redress of the original breach. Furthermore, the exorcism of the ghost repeats the Bottom's need to scapegoat Sula, for, like Sula, Beloved refers back to a past too painful to confront, a history that is "unspeakable," even as it seeps into and colors the present. Beloved, too, cannot be reintegrated, and in the end, she is "in pieces" (212). She must be forgotten, because her initiation is into a cruelty that the others wish to leave behind. As in Morrison's earlier novels, however, forgetfulness is not entirely possible. The unresolved social drama of the narrative is reflected in Morrison's style, which remains fragmented, multivocal, and elliptical, a record of the breach created by a resurgence of the past or (re)memory.

The perils of denying or being cut off from African traditions are re-emphasized in *Jazz*, a work about spiritual and actual orphanhood, about individuals uprooted from their cultural forebears. The one allusion to conjure is, in fact, a lie among whites: "Whitefolk said he [a skilled hunter] was a witch doctor but they said that so they wouldn't have to say he was smart" (125). The African-American community in the novel denies the possibility of magic or conjure. Not only are the characters cut off from their African roots, but they are isolated from their past in rural America, from what Morrison refers to as "village" culture (LeClair 25).

Joe and Violet Trace have come up to New York from the South; Dorcas Manfred and her aunt have come from elsewhere as well, and Dorcas has lost both parents. Her friend Felice is virtually an orphan as well, as her parents work for a white family during the week and come home only on weekends. It is no wonder then that Violet finds herself drying up, loveless, and that Joe and Dorcas seek an illicit affair to compensate for the essential lack of passion or energy in their lives.

The death of Dorcas forces a crisis, and Violet must confront the waning of her marriage. In keeping with Morrison's other works, the crisis in this novel is linked to Africanisms. Violet's life is marked by two eruptions of African culture: she keeps birds, and she makes a living setting other women's hair. But her birds are not guardians in her time of need; in fact, she sets them free to "freeze or fly" (3), after Joe kills Dorcas. These creatures lack the power of night birds in Gelede. But among the Mende, domestic birds are "the first sign of human habitation"(Boone 208), and, significantly, Violet's action indicates that her apartment is not a home, even as it draws attention to the fact that these Africans cannot fly. Moreover, Violet slowly loses or relinquishes her hairdressing business, which has taken her into others' homes and into the community (though other hairdressers have always resented her). The recuperation of the marriage is accompanied by Violet's reconnection to these influences. She buys more birds and nurtures them with music, even as her love for Joe returns and flourishes.

In the end, the narrator says, "Something is missing there. Something rogue. Something else you have to figure in before you can figure it out" (228). She alludes to the "rogue" trickster, a symbol of the African cultures that keep resurfacing like a background design in Toni Morrison's work. This "something" gives depth and meaning to the whole, for you cannot "figure it out" (expose it, understand it, or even put it to rest) until you acknowledge this influence or "figure" it in.

The failure of the men of Ruby to "figure in" difference leads to their inability to "figure it out" in Morrison's 1997 novel *Paradise*. Like *Sula*, this work focuses on a black community and the disastrous effects of its rigidity and calcification on a household of women linked to the ancestor. Indeed, Ruby is at once a later version of the all-black town of Eatonville in Zora Neale Hurston's *Their Eyes Were Watching God* and the prosperous community in Gloria Naylor's *Linden Hills*. In all three cases, black male leaders have become enforcers of the white middle-class values they equate with success, such as propriety, the acquisition of wealth, and the suppression of sexuality. They buttress themselves and their righteousness by defining a certain kind of Africanized femininity as dangerously other.

In her nonfiction work *Playing in the Dark*, Morrison contends that in white American literature, "an Africanist character is used to limn out and enforce the invention and implications of whiteness" (52), and that whiteness is defined as human in contrast to a savage and bestial blackness: "It was this Africanism, deployed as rawness and savagery, that provided the staging ground and arena for the elaboration of the quintessential American identity" (44). In *Paradise*, Morrison goes one step further, showing a similar process at work in terms of gender. For instance, if one were to insert "female" after "Africanist" and replace "person" with "woman" in the following quotation from *Playing in the Dark*, it would become an expression of the central conflict in *Paradise:* "we need to analyze the manipulation of the Africanist narrative (that is, the story of a black person, the experience of being bound and/or rejected) as a means of meditation—both safe and risky—on one's own humanity" (53).

The efforts of the male "fathers" of the community to restrain women lead them to exclude those who fall short of their standards by suggesting that they are somehow inhuman and unnatural. These women function as the *aje* of the town. The existence of uncontrolled femininity, like the appearance of blackness in white texts, allows men to "reinforce class privilege and power; . . . it serves as a marker and vehicle for illegal sexuality, fear of madness, expulsion, self-loathing" (*Playing in the Dark* 52). And indeed, all of the latter are qualities of the women's refuge, the Convent. In an ironic reversal of novels by white authors, perhaps one of the greatest threats posed by the Convent is its sheltering of a white woman, a rebuke to the black town that prides itself on its racial purity and deprecates the one family with white blood (paradoxically named the Bests). The importance of this detail is best signaled by the fact that it appears in the first sentence of the novel, "They shoot the white girl first," signifying that just as whites cannot erase blackness by segregating themselves, the people of Ruby cannot ignore race simply by isolating themselves. Their emphasis on skin color is an acquired trait that distances them from their African heritage just as surely as if they were white. When the young people try to impose "some African-type thing full of new words, new color combinations and new haircuts," one of the older women realizes that all she "knew about Africa was the seventy-five cents she gave to the missionary society collection" (104).[4]

The men of Ruby have installed in place of an African heritage a complicated and variable account of the "Old Fathers" and the founding of the town. It is a narrative that begins with the end of slavery and nine families being "cast away in Fairly, Oklahoma" (188). The "Disallowing came from fair-skinned colored men" (195) and led to the founding of Haven by the families, called "eight-rock" by the town historian after their dark color and hardness, like "a deep deep level in the coal mines" (193). During the drought and Depression, Haven suffered, and by the end of World War II, fifteen families had moved on across Arapaho and Creek country to found a new town, Ruby, named after the first and only person ever known to die there. In Ruby, one of their first acts was to reconstruct the town's Oven, marked by the mysterious text, "Be the Furrow of His Brow." This story, including the rise of the Morgan family (apparently named after one of the country's foremost capitalists), has become fixed in family Bibles and is performed annually with significant variations by the schoolchildren as if it were at once the story of the exile of the Jews and the Nativity.

Like many histories, it has become exclusive: "The town's official story, elaborated from pulpits, in Sunday school classes and ceremonial speeches, had a sturdy public life. Any footnotes, crevices or questions to be put took keen imagination and the persistence of a mind uncomfortable with oral histories" (188). Recounted in church and other ceremonies, the telling of history has become a ritual of instruction. It has the weight of the Word and cannot be questioned. Yet Pat Best, the town historian, who is disrespected because of her pale skin, acknowledges that "where proof was not available she interpreted—freely" (188). Ironically, this woman on the fringes of the leading families has become the enforcer of the town's boundaries through her role as gatekeeper of history.

Prosperous and ruled by propriety, the town has become as hard as the gem it is named after, as metallic and cold as Medallion in *Sula*, as moribund as the woman it is also named after. Reverend Misner, an outsider and newcomer, realizes that "they think they have outfoxed the white-man when in fact they imitate him" (306), his choice of the predatory fox for his metaphor appropriate. The families' history of exile and migration has come to replace the griot's knowledge of an African heritage; the children learn "Negro history" within the United States (209), and Pat Best argues with the new reverend in town that they do not need to know about Africa: "it just doesn't mean anything" (209).

Set in marginal relation to the town is the household at the Convent, which has its own history. The building was always a liminal place. Built by an embezzler, it was designed for wild parties and decorated with erotica, "nipple-tipped doorknobs. Layabouts half-naked in old-timey clothes, drinking and fondling each other in prints stacked in closets. A Venus or two among several pieces of nude statuary beneath the cellar stairs. . . . brass male genitalia that had been ripped from sinks and tubs . . . the testicles designed to release water from the penis" (72). Significantly, the house has retained only representations of the erotic: stony sculptures, metal accoutrements, prints—all in fragments or hidden in the cellar—suggesting that genuine love was absent. After the place closed down, it was turned into its apparent opposite, a school where nuns educated and acculturated Arapaho girls as well as Consolata, or Connie. With its emphasis on conversion and baptism, the Convent functioned as a novitiate. Finally, after the girls left, the house has served as a *communitas,* a refuge for women who were "lost" or "needed a rest" (11), women who arrived as hungry as Beloved and as needy as Sethe carrying Denver. Some of them, like Mavis, who accidentally killed two of her children, embody the doubleness of caring maternity and maleficence found in the *aje.* A few of the town wives visit occasionally to buy eggs and vegetables, get abortions, or collect herbs for tonics, and one man stays there while drying out, but otherwise, the townsfolk view the place with suspicion.

As much as the town is depicted as rigid and deracinated, the Convent is presented as a place where boundaries are fluid. The Convent's Christian name seems ironic, since references to herbal healing, mysteries, and Africanisms abound. The frequent baths of the women at the Convent suggest the cleansing nature of the place. While the Morgans are dying out, the Convent is a place of abundance and fertility, its table always bounteous, its chickens fecund, and milk sitting on the table waiting to be drunk. Its bounty resembles the positive aspect of the Gelede *aje.* The garden breaks many of the unwritten rules of Western agriculture, but prospers nevertheless, with "flowers mixed in or with or parallel to rows of vegetables. . . . staked plants grew in a circle, not a line, in high mounds of soil. Chickens clucked out of sight. A part of the garden . . . gone to weed became, on closer inspection, a patch of melons. An empire of corn beyond" (41). In contrast, the women from town must supplement their groceries with produce from the Convent, while the men have to hunt for meat.

The Convent, whose very name echoes the word *coven,* is located in a liminal space between Ruby and another town. Like Sande initiates, the women are cut off from news of the outer world. Resembling at once the plague of robins in *Sula* and the predatory night birds of the Gelede *aje,* buzzards flying over town are a bad omen, but the Convent and the town women who are willing to visit there are associated with the domesticity of the chicken. On the day of the wedding that confirms the breach between town and Convent, Soane Morgan, one of the women who visits the Convent, fears a vision of bloody chicken feathers in her sink (155).

At the Convent, though, magic appears as natural as birthing. Consolata, or Connie, who leads after the original Mother Superior's death, is much more than the drunkard she might appear. She revives one of the Morgan sons after a car accident and keeps "stepping in" (247) to prolong the life of Mary Magna, her power resembling the mysterious qualities of the African *aje.* Mavis is visited by an incubus (171). Dovey Morgan, one of the women in town who has access to otherness, frequents an empty foreclosed home acquired by her husband and is visited by a "Friend" there, a protective apparition. Near the end of the book, the Convent women begin "loud dreaming" that resembles the power of the *aje:* "How the stories rose in that place. Half-tales and the never-dreamed escaped from their lips to soar high above guttering candles, shifting dust from crates and bottles. And it was never important to know who said the dream or whether it had meaning" (264). Alcohol becomes Consolata's lifeblood in a strange communion as the women mark their forms and dreams in chalk on the floor, giving their spirit selves visual manifestations. The chalky medium also suggests the fragility and impermanence of their creations. Judylyn Ryan indicates that chalk is valued by the Yoruba (like the Mende) for its cleansing properties and "power to transform the negative energy within an entity into a positive potential" (qtd. in Tally 210). In this way, the women's shapes, sketched on the cellar floor, become a means toward transformation and unity.

The leaders of Ruby, though unaware of the exact nature of the strangeness of the Convent, are increasingly disturbed by its disorder, which they see as the cause for troubles arising in town. The breach hardens after the women from the Convent attend a town wedding "looking like go-go girls: pink shorts, skimpy tops, see-through skirts; painted eyes, no lipstick; obviously no underwear, no stockings. Jezebel's storehouse raided" (156–57). But the women's greatest sin in the men's eyes is that they have fun, dancing wildly until they are asked to leave, and then fighting on the way home. On a day celebrating the patriarchal institution of marriage, the women are obviously content without men. Their appearance is a vivid rebuke to the institution, for one of the Convent women, Gigi, had an affair with the groom and almost broke up the match (Consolata had a brief affair many years past with Deek Morgan as well, and Deek has never forgiven her for having this powerful secret to hold over him). The Convent women have become the repositories of all the energy that has been suppressed in the women in town, who for the most part have suffered metaphorical clitoridectomies. The "eight-rock" men are frightened by their inability to control these women who now embody the negative aspects of witchcraft.

Ironically, the women's dance through town resembles the reentry of African initiates into the community, with the bride, a kind of initiate, the one dressed in white. It seems entirely appropriate, then, to consider that whiteness is associated with death in many West African communities, for in Ruby, marriage brings an end to women's expressions of individuality. The weird assortment of women from the Convent functions as a collection of *Gonde* figures, at once ridiculous and grotesque, forbidden and necessary for the town's self-definition.

As in *Sula* and *Beloved*, the breach cannot be resolved without scapegoats. Everything that goes wrong in town is cited as proof of the wickedness and perversion of the Convent women: "Outrages that had been accumulating all along took shape as evidence. A mother was knocked down the stairs by her cold-eyed daughter. Four damaged infants were born in one family. Daughters refused to get out of bed. Brides disappeared on their honeymoons. Two brothers shot each other on New Year's Day. Trips to Demby [another town] for VD shots common. . . . The one thing that connected all these catastrophes was in the Convent" (11). Significantly, most of these crises are blamed on women's lack of respect or uncontrollable sexuality, qualities that are also attributed to the inhabitants of the Convent.

After a secret meeting at the Oven, a group of the town's male leaders attacks the Convent, killing most of the women. But the brutal, unsuspected attack fails to bring Ruby back together. First, Soane and Dovey, sisters and wives of the Morgan twins, acknowledge their differences when Soane realizes that her silence has rendered her complicit in the killings, while Dovey cannot admit to an opinion other than her husband's: "Whores, though, and strange, too. . . . That's what Steward says, and if he believes it" she must, too (288). Other women, including Lone DuPres, the town midwife, object as well (not surprisingly, Lone was adopted into the town and is not truly a member of one of the "eight-rock" families). The outlaw women's bodies and car disappear, conveniently releasing the murderers from fear of the law, but increasing the mystery surrounding the Convent. Indeed, while self-righteous versions of the event are created by the participants, some of whom seem to prosper and are "uncontrite" (299), others lose business or continue to pull rank. A child dies, the second mortality in the history of the town. The Morgan brothers, like their wives, are divided by difference, Steward being "unapologetic" (299), while Deek "Had looked in his brother's face and did not like himself any more" (300).

The expulsion thus confirms divisions within the town; no rapprochement is possible. Billie Delia, one of the few rebels in Ruby, has spent some time at the Convent and is "perhaps the only one in town who was not puzzled by where the women were or concerned about how they disappeared. She had another question: When will they return?" (308). She faces up to the fact that Ruby is "a prison calling itself a town . . . A backward noplace ruled by men whose power to control was out of control" (308). Even though the narrator insists on the identity of the town —which is located geographically for readers in the second sentence of the book and whose history forms a major part of the narrative—having lost its nuns, it is a "noplace," an imitation of whiteness (306), scared of women who are "nones" in various senses of the word.

And the women do return, not to the town but to those who had hurt them before their exile and refuge at the Convent. These ghosts are less violent and rapacious than Beloved, even though they disturb parents, siblings, and children, who catch visions of the past without being able to make contact or amends. The lost women of the Convent gain power over these others, causing guilt and discomfort. They are fragments of what has not been "figured in," trickster figures, associated with liminality and the pain of a lost heritage. What had previously been mostly a stylistic quality of the text with its multivocal narrative and unstable histories has become a part of its imagery.

Significantly, the novel closes with a dream of Consolata's, which is set by the shore: "In ocean hush a woman black as firewood is singing" to a younger woman. The face of the woman, Piedade, "framed in cerulean blue" (318), recalls the stereotypical portraits of the Virgin Mary or Pietà, even though this figure holds a younger woman, not a son, suggesting a female succession. Moreover, the women recline on sand covered with the trash, the detritus of their lives, bottle caps (reminiscent of Consolata's drinking), and a broken sandal (recalling one of the other women's lost huaraches). Their very isolation is emphasized by the fact that "a small dead radio plays the quiet surf" (318), indicating the uselessness of the American Dream with its colorless, anonymous technology. Song replaces the silence of women throughout the rest of the novel, and the women experience "the unambivalent bliss of going home to be at home" (318). No longer exiles on this shore that might face Africa, the women look up to see a boat containing the "lost and saved" who have been, without Consolata, "disconsolate" (318).

Even as this scene is underscored by Christian references, it is significant in terms of Yoruba iconography, where "the movement of the sea is a reverberation of the drumming, dancing, and feasting going on in the rambling palace" of the Great Mother goddess, Osun, at the bottom (Lawal 74). This Great Mother in her watery element receives spirit visitors and the dead, like the woman with Consolata, matriarch of the Convent.

In the end, though, this vision is ambiguous, for the landing people are "shouldering the endless work they were created to do down here in paradise" (318). The obvious paradox indicates that these people are analogous to slaves being brought to the "New" World. The dream of a dead woman becomes the ultimate liminal place, where "words evoke memories neither one has ever had" (318), perhaps of Africa. The other side of the ocean is evoked by the ship, but it cannot be seen or accessed by the dreamer.

Morrison's most recent text ultimately ends even more pessimistically than her previous works about liminality and the loss of heritage. Yet *Paradise* is marked by a type of Africanism less apparent in Morrison's earlier fictions, one that adds significant layers of meaning to any reading of the text. Specifically, the book contains numerous twins—the Morgan brothers, Mavis's dead infants, and, in its story of origins, two founding fathers, Zacharias or Coffee ("a misspelling of Kofi," 192) and

Tea. Additionally, Soane and Dovey function as twins, and Soane's sons are virtually indistinguishable as well, both of them dying at war.[5] Twins are important figures in West African mythology, especially among the Yoruba. Babatunde Lawal cites twins as originary figures in the Gelede society, which probably came into being before the eighteenth century (70), when the Yoruba stopped practicing "twin infanticide" (69). He argues that the society arose out of a conflict between twins over succession to the throne (47–48), not unlike the quarrel between Kofi and Tea. Where the trickster Esu-Elegbara is Janus-faced or double, twins have two separate bodies and are spiritual doubles on earth (unlike *abiku*, where only one of the spirit doubles inhabits an earthly body). Twins are perceived as special beings, meriting respect and the "protection" of Esu (260), while their unity renders them powerful against witchcraft (261). The Morgan twins lead the attack on the Convent, while Mavis's youngsters haunt and torment her. On the other hand, when they are divided, as the Morgan twins are at the end of the novel, these spirit doubles seem especially vulnerable to witchcraft (261). Alienation between twins indicates a separation between the body and its spirit double, much like the emptiness shadowing the material prosperity of Ruby. And Mavis's dead twins are like the Yoruba children who must go back to their spiritual doubles (51) after a short sojourn on earth. These references remind us that the work, like Morrison's other novels, is ultimately about heritage and the recurrence of histories that have been lost or ignored.

Reviewing Morrison's first seven novels, it becomes clear that they can be read as litanies on the continuing importance of African culture (or the lack thereof) in shaping the lives of African-American women. Consistently, Morrison alludes to conjure, female enclosures, and other elements of West African iconography. At the same time, Morrison's novels narrate social dramas of initiation and liminality, offering *communitas* or female communities in contradistinction to larger, more ordered towns or cities, where many females strive to conform to white mores, even when these efforts crush their souls and families. Through these women, Morrison reveals and emphasizes the harmful consequences of being cut off from an African notion of female solidarity or community. In contrast, other women are linked to Africanism and ancestry, transformation and conjure, for good or bad. These powerful women may be destroyed in the conflict between African and European cultures. Indeed, although many critics have noted that the community of women is one of Morrison's most prominent subjects, an Africanist reading helps us to understand the complexity of women as well as to distinguish among them. Women's power, alternately shunned and revered, is depicted as an essential part of a system of social control, as well as of a plot based on liminality that cannot contain the "rogue." By enacting and reenacting this narrative in a ritual manner, Morrison's novels illustrate what she has stated in articles and interviews about the deleterious effects of cutting one's self off from the ancestor.

4

Mother as Colony, Colony as Mother

Jamaica Kincaid and Cultural Dislocation

In Naylor's *Mama Day*, the island of Willow Springs is other to the American mainland, a gendered space representing Africa. In Morrison's work, otherness resides in liminality and contingency. For Jamaica Kincaid, as for Naylor and Morrison, otherness is gendered, but Kincaid perceives this difference as unstable. Partly defined in opposition to European colonization, otherness in Kincaid's novels includes remnants of African and indigenous traditions in addition to elements of a hybrid island culture. Her narratives invoke a kind of cultural claustrophobia, arising from the crowding and jarring of various traditions within the islands as well as from the literally confined spaces of Antigua and Dominica.

Given her insistence on the distinctive nature of Caribbean islands, the effects of European colonization, and the intrusiveness of contemporary technological and tourist economies, Kincaid's work is very much about geography. Recent theorists on geography and region have made cogent cases for viewing geography like any other structure of knowledge; that is, they argue that geography as it is traditionally understood is primarily a construction of white European men that values certain elements while rendering others invisible. The glorification of the great explorers who "discovered" uncharted territories suggests that only places that have been seen and named by white men exist, and the language of exploration, beginning with its assumption that unmapped lands are virgin, has put into play a series of metaphors that gender the land as female to be possessed and known by men. For example, a nineteenth-century cartographer might feature ports and trading sites as important cities in Africa, while marking as less important cultural and social centers of local life. Claims to the objectivity and professionalism of physical geography correspond to similar nineteenth-century trends in other disciplines, such as medicine. Contemporary maps have a limited usefulness as well. Those purchased by many Europeans and Americans tell how to find a tourist site but not how to locate the nearest school. Despite the gendering of land as female, maps tend to emphasize physical features that mark political boundaries and important resources for industry rather than those that more directly affect the daily lives of women.

Contemporary theorists on geography and region, however, posit a different view of the discipline, arguing that there are many possible geographies or perspectives on geography. Francesco Loriggio, for instance, claims that "Along with the horizontal dimension that maps consign us, there is a vertical dimension to consider" and suggests the importance of "Viewing geography as a two- or three-tiered field, as a combination or dialectic of what there is and what people believe or imagine there is" (6). These additional layers may incorporate a temporal dimension, so that "historical identity is inseparable from geography" (Rody 173). Opening up the field in this way allows us to see, first, that much of what passes for geography is interpretation and, second, that "space is . . . the dimension of power and resistance" (4). Feminist geographer Gillian Rose concurs, "asking for a geography that acknowledges that the grounds of its knowledge are unstable, shifting, uncertain and above all, contested" (160).

These views of geography provide rich material for a reading of Kincaid's works and the manner in which they create topographies within topographies, charting places that might go unrecognized otherwise. Loriggio's concept of a "third tier" or dimension finds its expression not only in the three traditions superimposed on one landscape, but also in other aspects of Kincaid's texts. Moreover, Loriggio carries his theories on region into a discussion of plot, offering a view of narration based on topology as well as chronology (22). He reminds readers that plot is about movement and boundaries, transgression and domination, concepts that are everywhere evident in a review of Kincaid's works, even in her nonfiction book *My Garden*. By creating alternative geographies of her heroine's worlds, Kincaid is able to make a "paradoxical" space of resistance against and within dominant ideologies and oppressive colonial histories: "in order to acknowledge both the power of hegemonic discourses and to insist on the possibility of resistance. . . . This geography describes . . . subjectivity as that of both prisoner and exile; it allows the subject of feminism to occupy both the centre and the margin, the inside and the outside" (Rose 155). Because this geography remains contingent on and defined by larger forces, it is only temporarily "emancipatory" (Rose 160). Thus, whereas Naylor's Mama Day feels at home in her other place, and Morrison's individuals occupy territories along borders and liminal spaces, Kincaid's characters inhabit a place defined as a negative or oppositional territory, socially unrecognized, politically invisible, yet powerful in its very absence from public discourse.

Caroline Rody, too, uses geographic and directional terms to describe plot elements in Kincaid's work, as well as in that of other authors. She posits that African-American and Caribbean women's novels offer two kinds of female bonds. Vertical relationships are matrilineal and transcend history, while horizontal relationships are based on simultaneity and may cross racial barriers, as when the wife of Xuela's first employer seems to befriend her, when the white woman helps Sethe give birth, or when Dessa Rose joins Rufel. Novels with a horizontal plot, she says, "substitute" friendship for the irrecoverable "mother-of-history" (192). Although Rody is ultimately optimistic about a trans-racial female community, I do not believe that Kincaid's novels embrace such a possibility.

Like Naylor and Morrison, Kincaid explores the spaces of cultural difference through the roles of mothers and other strong female characters. Specifically, women's bodies and their lives are analogous to various aspects of the islands and their histories. Men take and abandon multiple wives and mistresses as imperialists possess nations. Mothers and mother figures suppress their African and indigenous heritages, only to internalize European cultural norms, which is why Caroline Rody refers to them as "mothers-of-forgetting" (110). Not only do these norms devalue the women themselves, but they cause further damage as mothers attempt to pass them on to their children. It is not surprising, then, that maternal figures in Jamaica Kincaid's novels lack the benevolence of Mama Day or the ferocious protectiveness of Sethe or Eva Peace. Indeed, they evoke mixed emotions in their daughters, especially as the latter approach adolescence and initiation into the codes and rituals that define femininity. The struggle between mother and daughter becomes an expression of the strains between colonial powers and the lands they have dominated. As Moira Ferguson remarks, the painfully contradictory

emotions between daughters and mothers are one version of "the relationship between the powerful and powerless" ("A Lot of Memory" 176).

Much criticism of Kincaid's fiction replicates this dominance as well,
interpreting her novels in a Eurocentric context and neglecting influences of African and indigenous models of mothering. A preponderance
of criticism discusses the mother-daughter bond in Kincaid's works with
reference to Nancy Chodorow's *Reproduction of Mothering*, a book at
once written in opposition to and highly influenced by Freudian and
Lacanian psychology. Chodorow's study, which is renowned for its analysis of girls' differentiation from their mothers, is alluded to in criticism of
Kincaid's writing by such authors as Diane Simmons (25–26), Eleanor Ty
(120), H. Adlai Murdoch (328), James Nagel (240–41), and Nancy Chick
(92). Kincaid's novels fit Chodorow's theory, but its use is problematic
given the complicated transnational and multicultural nature of
Kincaid's work. Quite simply, Kincaid's work inhabits an alternate geography. The subtitle of Chodorow's work—"Psychoanalysis and the Sociology of Gender"—indicates that the book is culture-bound, dependent
on social trends and psychological theories. One of Chodorow's central
tenets is that motherhood is socially constructed. Yet Chodorow contradicts herself repeatedly, exhibiting a tendency to universalize and erase
differences among women in favor of a Western hegemonic viewpoint.
Examples may be found from the opening of her book ("In our society, as
in most societies" 3) to her conclusion ("the issues I discuss are relevant
in all societies" 216).

These contradictions in Chodorow's approach limit its usefulness as a
perspective from which to study Kincaid's novels; indeed, to understand
the full complexity of Kincaid's fiction, it is imperative to acknowledge
cultural differences and to realize that maternal figures embody a great
deal more than Western oppression or an African heritage. Much of the
narrative tension in Kincaid's novels stems specifically from the conflicts
between Western notions of motherhood, African views of maternity,
and remnants of indigenous traditions, as they come together in the roles
created by contemporary Caribbean women. Diane Simmons recognizes
the ambivalence surrounding mothers in Kincaid's texts, but instead of
arguing that the ambivalence comes solely from the mother's internal-
ization of European values, she suggests that "the mother presents the
daughter with an unmistakable model of African-based female power,

that of the obeah woman" (32). Generally considered a hybrid form of conjure, obeah's power derives in part from African traditions. Michael Porobunu, a Nigerian familiar with traditional practices, has commented at length on the resemblances between West African medicine and obeah (Mistron 108–16). He cites the wide variety of materials used for poisons in obeah as well as the importance of chickens and other objects in West African practices (114), and concludes that "The West Indian religious beliefs are like the African beliefs. It is a direct transplantation from Africa to the Caribbean. Some plants were also brought over from Africa with the slaves, and other plants in the Caribbean were similar because of the similar climate. . . . And there may have been a disproportionate number of Obeah practitioners sent to the New World, because they were often punished in Africa by being sent into slavery, especially when they are [sic] considered a threat to the rulers of the society" (114–15). Ironically, then, men and women who were considered a "threat" within African cultures were sold abroad, where they could propagate their beliefs and turn their powerful practices to resistance against white slaveholders. In a discussion of slave resistance, Mistron draws on texts that suggest that women were involved though not necessarily named in the organization of rebellion in the 1700s, and that their rites included an initiation ceremony in which women were smeared with dust from the graves of their dead (45). This ceremony is reminiscent of Sande initiations, where the young women are smeared with river dirt. Furthermore, Mistron's evidence shows that one of the women rebels named Queen acted as an Akan mother-ruler (45).

As in Naylor's *Mama Day*, when Kincaid alludes to practices based on African traditions, they are gendered as female and exist alongside or in a parallel space to Western medicine, which is professionalized by men. When Annie John sickens, she takes medicines ordered from Ma Jolie, the local healing woman, as well as those prescribed by Dr. Stephens, who is British trained. Ultimately, her grandmother's particularly potent brews heal her. Women's ability to use herbs, roots, and other objects in this way gives them power in a society that is both colonial and patriarchal. Like the slave women studied by Deborah Gray White, Lucy learns from her mother how to induce an abortion (69–70), allowing her to exert some control over her own body.

Not only do many of Kincaid's maternal figures share the *Sowei*'s abilities with conjure and medicine, but magical powers are associated with spirits and animal transformations. The title story in the collection *At the Bottom of the River* begins with a man "crossing and recrossing the threshold" (66) like Legba (Esu-Elegbara), god of crossroads, transformation, and multiplicity. The man soon realizes the futility of his acts, and the story shifts to a vision of death, followed by a creation tale regarding "a small creature, and it lived as both male and female inside a mound that it made on the ground" (70). The animal, living in a small "mound," is doubly gendered like Esu-Elegbara and reminiscent of the termite hill in Alice Walker's *Possessing the Secret of Joy*, another work about transformation and (re)creation.

Aside from the above example, transformation is almost inevitably linked to female movement in Kincaid's work. Women's power to transform themselves or others enables them to open up a space confined by restrictive ideologies and traditions. In the first story from *At the Bottom of the River*, the *jablesse* spirit appears as a beautiful, evanescent woman (9). In a later story in the book, a mother transforms herself into a reptilian form, able to travel on land or water, powerful as serpents and birds in Sande. Elsewhere in the text, a woman beckons children from the water. When a boy jumps in to find her, she keeps receding into the distance, until he swims too far and drowns (a similar episode appears in *Autobiography of My Mother* 36–37). This account recapitulates the Sande traditions of female initiates rising from the water and male interlopers in women's spaces being destroyed. From a Yoruba perspective, the women in the water may also be seen as incarnations of the goddess Osun, though Osun is not ordinarily a force of destruction of men.

As these examples suggest, many of the powerful female figures in Kincaid's work who are charged with transformations and spells are not biological mothers, but grandmothers or characters who protect the main character. At the end of *Annie John*, for instance, the heroine is cured of her illness by her grandmother Ma Chess, who works formidable conjure. In *Lucy*, the heroine learns from her female employer, Mariah, who gives her an African necklace ("It was the most beautiful thing anyone had ever given me" 143) and a book in which to write her story. Diane Simmons uses Patricia Hills Collins's terminology in referring to such women as "othermothers" and argues that in each work, "Kincaid's young protagonist, nearly destroyed by her struggles with the relationship with her mother, turns to a substitute mother figure" (27). But, like biological parents, substitute mothers are occasionally malicious instead of kindly. Obeah among women may take maleficent forms as well. Often, the concubines and wives of men strive to obliterate rivals and their children. Thus in *Lucy*, "the woman with whom my father had had a child . . . tried to kill my mother and me through obeah" (150). In *The Autobiography of My Mother*, Xuela, the heroine, is given a poisonous necklace by her jealous stepmother. Ma Eunice in *The Autobiography of My Mother* functions as a *Gonde* figure but is cruel, and the teachers in this book as well as in *Annie John* enforce the dominant culture. In *The Autobiography of My Mother*, Xuela notes ironically that her instructor "was of the African people . . . and she found in this a source of humiliation and self-loathing, and she wore despair like an article of clothing, like a mantle, or a staff on which she leaned constantly, a birthright which she would pass on to us" (15).

Xuela's teacher carries her self-hatred as a staff of office in a female sodality that is oppressed and alienated. She is a kind of parody of the *Sowei*, even as the stepmother, another strong female in the text, connives at killing the heroine only to see misfortune fall on her own children. In a sense, the othermother's awkward relation to an African or Carib culture is reflected in her distance from the heroine as well as in her lack of status in a community of women. In fact, no such community seems to exist—instead of pulling together as they do in *Mama Day*, the females in Kincaid's novels turn outward to pleasing men, conforming to colonial cultural norms (which might be the same as satisfying the men), and policing difference among themselves. In doing so, they relinquish the liberatory space of transformation and change, returning to the imprisonment of a Eurocentric male-oriented society.

Kincaid's concern with alienation and difference is expressed in the style and imagery of her writing as well as in its themes. The space of narrative itself becomes an iteration of the confining quality of her characters' worlds. Her works to date are replete with increasingly oppressive resemblances and revisions, incantatory lists of objects, as well as repeated allusions to canonical works. For instance, *Annie John, The Autobiography of My Mother, My Brother*, and *Lucy* incorporate autobiographical elements, such as Kincaid's problematic relationship with her mother or her father's many mistresses. The inclusion of actual events allows Kincaid to work and rework her own past, seeking to come to terms with a present that is deeply influenced by European traditions as well as with an absent past that is inflected with Africanisms. One feels at times as if one is reading the same story over and over with only minimal differences. Some of the changes are shifts in perspective; for instance, in *At the Bottom of the River*, the daughter tells her mother about throwing stones at a monkey until it casts them back (44). In *The Autobiography of My Mother*, the daughter tells her father about this experience (50). The oneiric quality of some of these accounts echoes the second kind of repetition described in J. Hillis Miller's *Fiction and Repetition*, a repetition that is at once same and different. Miller bases his theory on Benjamin's analysis of a type of relationship "that reflects only vaguely the deeper resemblance of the dream world in which everything that happens appears not identical but in similar guise, opaquely similar" (8). Miller suggests that this form of repetition acts as a "subversive ghost of the first" that exists "in the gap of difference"(9), analogous to Loriggio's extra tier of geography. In this case, the fact that Xuela has no mother is emphasized by the difference in the repetition. In *Annie John* (70) and *Lucy* (54), the mother is involved in the stone throwing, suggesting the daughter's relative powerlessness against the trickster monkey. The almost obsessive quality of this reworking is evident when one notices that the account appears in three of the four cases at roughly the same place in the book, between pages 44 and 54. These constant repetitions signal eruptions of an African past that has not been completely assimilated. As such, the monkeys, along with other repeated elements, give the work a rough, almost fractured, texture. Similar eruptions of the African past in novels about slavery will be discussed in the second part of this book.

Kincaid repeats certain points until they become cadences in a rhythm; in *My Brother*, she refers to her stepfather as her brother's "real father, a father not really mine" (141) or "their father, our mother's husband" (171), continually distancing him and reiterating the absence of her own father. As language is repeated, it gains an opacity that slows readers and forces them to consider the meanings of words, in a manner similar to that evoked by Gertrude Stein's repetitions. Moreover, lists are ever present, as noted by Diane Simmons (47–50), especially in "Girl," the first, one-sentence story in *At the Bottom of the River*. Caroline Rody points out that negatives are repeated as well, so that a "tone and a grammar of negation rules," especially in *The Autobiography of My Mother*, where "'not' becomes the most vital word in Xuela's mother-tongue" (128). Lists and negations force readers to be aware of similarity and difference simultaneously. One assumes that all items in a list are grouped for a particular reason, even if they appear dissimilar, and negatives remind readers of both what is present and what is absent.

Another level of repetition occurs in ironic allusions to canonical texts, particularly *Paradise Lost* and *Jane Eyre*, which, though taught to children on the islands, do not fit their experiences. Kincaid herself has mentioned the importance of Milton's influence in an interview (Cudjoe 223), and it is also evident in the many references to Paradise in her works (for example, in the title story of *At the Bottom of the River*, where she refers to "a world not yet divided . . . as it revealed itself to me—how new" 78). In *Lucy*, the heroine's realization that she has been named after Lucifer draws attention to another point: for the most part, Kincaid reads Milton from the point of view of the rebel outcast, rendering difference in terms of race, gender, and colonial status. Allusions to Charlotte Brontë are also evident throughout Kincaid's works, beginning with *Annie John* and the chapter titled "Somewhere, Belgium." Although many critics have discussed the influence of *Jane Eyre* (including Moira Ferguson, *Jamaica Kincaid* 62, and Diane Simmons 57–72, which is also about Milton), the startling connections between *Lucy* and Brontë's *Villette* have received short shrift. Kincaid's novel revises—and in some ways reverses—the nineteenth-century work about a young woman named Lucy who goes abroad without ties to forge a life as a teacher. Whereas in Brontë's semi-autobiographical novel the heroine goes to Belgium instead of to the United States, both Lucys love men named Paul. It is as though Kincaid's characters are trapped in worn plots from other cultures that determine their understanding of their own worlds. Ultimately, fiction itself becomes a "small place," which the narrator attempts to expand or excavate through irony and inversion. It is therefore significant that the conclusions of *Lucy* and *The Autobiography of My Mother* record their own beginnings, turning the text inward on itself.

Annie John, Kincaid's first novel, illustrates how narrative repetition contributes to the development of the theme of claustrophobia through the use of such small places as the space under the porch, a classroom, and the heroine's bedroom, as well as the larger small place of the island itself. These places function like the gaps in Miller's second kind of repetition. The first enclosures in the novella are coffins and burial plots, for the story focuses on the heroine's mingled fear of and fascination with death. The use of the coffin in this episode sets the tone for enclosures later in the book, and they are associated with African and Carib traditions that erupt into the present in obeah and other seemingly inexplicable occur-rences. Coffins and the cemetery may be closed, but they are not confin-ing: "We were afraid of the dead because we never could tell when they might show up again" (4). Spirits of the past may arise in dreams or "they would show up. . . . Then they might follow you home" (4). The girls talk among tombstones at school, implying that their own selves are doomed to be buried under the load of an Anglicized culture. So the liv-ing, the seemingly unconfined, find themselves shadowed and haunted, and, in particular, Annie associates her mother with the dead for whom she cares. Significantly, Annie's feelings for her mother are conflicted precisely because the relations between mother and daughter are another iteration of the permeability of the boundary between past and present. Later, as Annie must separate from her mother, she is ambivalent because she grieves the loss of their closeness, even as she despises what her mother represents.

The second chapter of the text, "The Circling Hand," begins to explore the shifting relations between mother and daughter. As the chapter opens, we see the two bathing together, often with herbs recommended by the obeah woman (14), and we learn of the mother's insistence on protecting her daughter from possible harm wrought by the father's mis-tresses (17). This closeness is contrasted with the father's occupation of building houses for others, an expression of the colonial experience. It is reemphasized as the two clean the mother's trunk, lovingly going through Annie's discarded clothes. As the contained space of the trunk is unpacked, Annie's memories merge with her mother's, "as she held each thing in her hand she would tell me a story about myself. Sometimes I knew the story first hand, for I could remember the incident quite well; sometimes what she told me had happened when I was too young to know anything; and sometimes it happened before I was born. Which-ever way, I knew exactly what she would say, for I had heard it so many times before" (21). At this point, Annie is her mother's construction.

Adolescence is initiated by the mother's insistence that Annie stop wearing clothes just like hers when the daughter turns twelve. At the same time, Annie enters a new school, where she is further acculturated into European customs, studying Latin and French (29). The earlier ac-count of closeness while bathing is replaced by Annie's fear of being abandoned while swimming at Rat Island with her mother. Although Annie finds herself confined in a new school and pubescent body, she is most isolated when she discovers her parents engaging in intercourse. This discovery heightens Annie's alienation from her mother. Annie feels confined in her own body because it is apart from and smaller than her mother's, but also because it takes her into other confined spaces of the adult, colonized world.

In a reversal of the madwoman in the attic motif, Annie's private place becomes the space under the house. There, she creates an interstitial world, hiding her stolen books, a sign perhaps of her ability to appropriate texts. It is also the place where she and the devilish Red Girl play with marbles that resemble "miniature globes" (55), enacting plays of power that in fact they do not possess. Marbles are forbidden, a boys' game, yet when her mother discovers the girls' hiding place, Annie never reveals their whereabouts, saving a small space of resistance for herself. In digging under the house, she literally undermines the society that is founded on African and indigenous traditions but controlled by patriarchal European cultures.

The personal space under the house is contrasted to the oppressive place of the classroom where the drama of "Columbus in Chains" is enacted. In the same way that Annie undermines the house, she subverts the account of conquest and colonialism, focusing on an episode in which the explorer is captive. She is sentenced to copy the first two books of Milton's *Paradise Lost* as punishment, as if by transcribing sentences from one of the quintessential texts of the Western canon she were inscribing it on her very soul. But Annie retains a different sense of this work about transgression and boundaries than her teachers and classmates do, because she perceives the irony that for some natives of Antigua, England as well as the island can be home (76).

Ultimately, it is as if her mother and the island become one—and to leave the prison in which she feels like she is in exile, Annie must go into an exile that feels like prison, putting distance between herself and the other. But Annie cannot leave until she has one more physical confinement—her long illness and ensuing spiritual rebirth, the long biblical rain that carries much away, and the restoration through the African medicine of her grandmother Chess. Significantly, during her illness, Annie destroys the photographs of her family, literally rubbing out the images that determine the confining past.

Annie's trunk, the place that held first her mother's memory and then her own past, becomes the one item that will accompany her into another world. While the time of the day of her departure is marked, as it is every day, by the Anglican church bell (134), Annie dons underwear that has been vetted by an obeah woman, even her last motions marked by the opposing cultures on the island. This chapter is titled "The Jetty," focusing on the stretch connecting land and sea, fixity and motion, road and ship. As the ship pulls away, Annie feels as if a vessel is being emptied (148), suggesting that the pressure she experiences in small places has been relieved.

Yet this choice—like so many of those faced by women in the novel—is a false one. The heroine is headed back to England, where she will train to become a nurse (the story of Florence Nightingale and her fledgling training program is a quintessential example of Victorian class control through education). While she may be leaving the smaller space of Antigua, Annie is traveling to another island nation where she will be marginal and perhaps invisible. Worse, England is the "mother" land in many ways—both as a colonial power and as the country whose culture her mother has adopted. Both exile and prison, Britain exemplifies the "paradoxical space" of Rose's geographical theory.

Annie John thus offers a useful example of Kincaid's working and re-working of the relationship between Africanisms and European culture. For the most part, women like Annie's mother literally embody the cultural contradictions. Even as they represent a world where women work obeah and root medicine, they also become enforcers of an alien tradition. The small spaces with which they are associated represent the way opposing worldviews trap them. And yet there seems to be no real larger space, either. *Lucy*, for instance, is a story of a woman like Annie John who leaves a homeland that is associated with maternal oppression. But Lucy trades her island existence for a series of small rooms she inhabits as an au pair and later as a worker in a series of meaningless occupations. For her, too, exile and prison resemble each other. At the end of the novel, Lucy acquires a notebook and is set to become the narrator of her own life, a sign that many critics consider to be positive (see for instance, Ferguson, "*Lucy* and the Mark of the Colonizer" 255). However, as Kristen Mahlis indicates, the notebook itself is an enclosed space. Women are trapped in patriarchal plots: "Lucy's story is written on a page that looks blank but isn't . . . [it is] inflected by cultural dislocation and maternal betrayal: she is aware that she has been 'written on,' i.e., that she has absorbed the cultural narratives of the colonizer" (181). The space that offers only the alternatives of prison or exile (or both at once) is inscribed in words as well as on maps.

Kincaid's next novel, *The Autobiography of My Mother*, deals with similarly intertwined themes of maternity, self-invention, and cultural alienation. Xuela, the heroine, resembles the protagonists of many fairy tales and nineteenth-century Victorian novels—her mother dies as she is born (3). Her father remains distant and authoritarian, first sending her to board with his laundress, then placing her in school, and finally bringing her into his new family, where his wife is responsible for Xuela. Yet because Xuela's own mother is dead from the beginning, the narrative plays itself out differently: "this fact of my mother dying at the moment I was born became a central motif of my life" (225). Instead of embodying half of a dichotomy such as mother/father, she becomes an absent but important third term, always unavailable and unreachable.

Late in her life, Xuela asserts, "This account of my life has been an account of my mother's life as much as it has been an account of mine, and even so, again it is an account of the life of the children I did not have, as it is their account of me. In me is the voice I never heard, the face I never saw, the being I came from" (227). To create the impression that the mother's life is being constructed as the narrative moves forward, each chapter begins with a partial picture of a woman. For the first chapter, just a corner of her head is visible, while the remainder of the page is blank. With each following section, the picture is filled in a little more. By the last chapter, the page is filled by a three-quarter-length portrait of the woman, presumably Xuela's mother.

Oddly, readers never learn much about Xuela's mother beyond her heritage. The account is not literally an autobiography of her mother (for one thing, the title is a contradiction in terms). The book does not give voice to the dead woman. Nor can the dead woman act in any way as a leader of a community of women; in fact, with the exception of the schoolroom, there is little communal sense of any kind in this work. People are fractured by their efforts to survive in an island home where they are treated as interlopers, culturally inferior and physically ugly.

In fact, what seems most important about Xuela's mother is her Carib blood. While many of the critics already mentioned suggest that Kincaid's texts obsessively work and rework the pre-oedipal relationship between mother and daughter, in this case, the mother is metaphorical— she represents the distinctive island culture that has passed, Xuela's lost heritage. In writing a fictive autobiography in the tradition of James Weldon Johnson's *Autobiography of an Ex-Colored Man*, Kincaid gives us a heroine who attempts to recreate herself in a manner that negotiates the schism between European and African heritages. Being Carib introduces a third variable or term in an equation that never works, because "they were extinct, a few hundred of them still living. . . . They were like living fossils, they belonged in a museum, on a shelf, enclosed in a glass case . . . my mother's people, were balanced precariously on the ledge of eternity, waiting to be swallowed up in a great yawn of nothingness" (197–98). Significantly, the Caribs are seen as existing only on display in confined spaces, where they are to be viewed as curiosities by powerful others, or as on a precipice before "nothingness," blankness.

The inaccessibility of Xuela's mother's world is perhaps best summarized by a recurrent dream vision in which she sees her mother descending a ladder enrobed in a white garment that exposes only her ankles: "she came down and down, but no more of her was ever revealed" (18). The maternal figure is always above the child, who must remain grounded, literally and figuratively. The mother is doomed always to descend, but never to touch the earth. Her daughter will never see her face. The nature of her white apparel—bridal costume, nightclothes, African funerary garment, ghostly garb, or other clothing—is similarly never revealed.

At the same time, this mysterious passage subverts the biblical story of Jacob's ladder. When Jacob falls asleep on a pile of rocks, he dreams of angels ascending and descending a ladder, and ultimately God grants him the land on which he sleeps, even as He pronounces, "thy seed shall be as the dust of the earth, and thou shalt spread abroad to the west, and to the east, and to the north, and to the south: and in thee and thy seed shall all the families of the earth be blessed" (Genesis 28:14). Like the tribes of Israel, Xuela finds herself homeless in her own world, descendant of one race that is extinct and of another whose people are dispersed. In a coma after a self-induced abortion, Xuela imagines flying over her mother's homeland: "And that is how I claimed my birthright, East and West, Above and Below, Water and Land: In a dream. I walked through my inheritance, an island of villages and rivers and mountains and people who began and ended with murder and theft and not very much love. I claimed it in a dream" (88–89). Kincaid signifies on the biblical account with the ironies that her heroine can visit her heritage only in a dream and will never have children. Although Xuela's stones do not turn into the phallic pillars of the Bible, she does find herself eager to see her father "and be in his presence constantly" after the dream (18). Kincaid replaces the dream angels with a maternal figure, and places the authoritarian father figure squarely on earth. Even more importantly, she makes her father a policeman, enforcer of colonial rule, inside of whom "the Scotsman and the African people met" (185).[1]

Kincaid comments ironically on Christian tradition elsewhere in the text, just as she refers to *Paradise Lost* in *Annie John*. Early in her life, Xuela breaks a plate belonging to Ma Eunice, the laundrywoman who cares for her. She finds herself unable to apologize for the destruction of this treasured possession, its surface painted with a flowered field: "underneath it was written in gold letters the one word HEAVEN. Of course it was not a picture of heaven at all; it was a picture of the English countryside idealized, but I did not know that" (9). If heaven is a stereotyped picture of pastoral England, then Xuela will never have access to it, and it is no wonder that she cannot apologize to her surrogate mother for breaking the plate. In fact, her ability to shatter the artifact reflects the fragility and triteness of the object, reduced to little more than decoration. This inversion of traditional views resembles Toni Morrison's *Paradise*, where the town is anything but heavenly, and *Sula* where the Bottom is above the white community.

The multiple dimensions of Xuela's otherness are apparent once more in her first school. Xuela feels alien because she is the only girl in her class as well as the sole person of Carib descent. Her dead mother comes to represent the dying people, while the only decoration in the simple, sparsely furnished schoolroom marks it as an oppressive place—a map bearing the words "THE BRITISH EMPIRE" (14). Required to speak English in this space of cultural induction, Xuela remains an outsider as well as a subject, and she is constantly reminded by her teacher that she is "possessed" (16), like Satan (and Lucy, whose name comes from Lucifer).

Xuela is even further outcast when her father remarries, and, significantly, he comes to collect her looking like a prison warden (22). Xuela joins his household, occupying a simple room of her own, blissfully solitary, away from the living quarters of the others. This separation is a physical manifestation of her ambiguous position as a daughter who does not "belong" in the home, "not to be trusted, . . . like a thief in the house" (52). She also creates for herself a female enclosure, "a small place in the

everlastingly thick grove of trees" behind the building until her stepmother discovers her refuge and sends a magical creature to keep Xuela
away (34).

. While she incarnates the evil stepmother of European children's fairy
tales, Xuela's stepmother is the chief practitioner of obeah in the book
and the representative of African culture combined with French traditions. In a scene somewhat reminiscent of the poisoning of the dog at the
end of Morrison's *The Bluest Eye*, the stepmother gives the girl a necklace that is seductively beautiful. Xuela refuses the gift and puts it on her
stepmother's dog instead, and "within twenty-four hours he went mad
and died" (34–35). The older woman is suspicious of her stepdaughter's
development; after Xuela enters puberty she comments that she will
"have to guard herself" against the younger woman. The stepmother
thus turns her powers to hate, but it is hate born out of the fragility of her
own position and fear that she will be supplanted in a world in which she
has little authority.

The motherless Xuela has no access to obeah because it is linked to the
past from which she is cut off, but another woman who works herbs and
roots is Madame LaBatte, the wife of a friend of Xuela's father. Madame
LaBatte used a spell to make her husband marry her, and when Xuela is
sent to live with the LaBattes, she finds herself in an uncertain position
yet again. Her room is adjacent to the kitchen, which is apart from the
main house (67). Again, she finds solace in her solitude, even as her friendship with Madame LaBatte develops as they find kinship in their loneli-
ness. Unfortunately, Madame LaBatte attempts to free herself by turning
Xuela into a second, younger version of her youth, dressed in her own
clothes as a "gift to her husband" (68). Again, medicine is used by a
mother figure to control a younger woman. It is a sign that the practitioner does not recognize the boundaries between herself and others. In
fact, Xuela does have an affair with Monsieur LaBatte, not on the dirt
floor of her little room, but in the chamber where he counts his money,
for she is little more than a possession to him. Significantly, he first comes
to fetch her from a "a small shaded area behind the house, where some
flowers were planted, though this place could not be called a garden, for
not much care was applied to it" (69)—another version of an African
female enclosure disguised as the Garden of Eden. Madame LaBatte continues to enact a maternal role similar to that of an African female leader,
bathing Xuela, braiding her hair, and telling her monitory tales, even

though she is sending Xuela to be taken advantage of by a representative of colonial power. This behavior is yet another sign of the way sisterhood has been suppressed in Kincaid's universe.

This life ends when Xuela becomes pregnant and goes to a practitioner of root medicine for an abortion that almost kills her. Recumbent on a bed "of rags in a house that had only the bare earth for a floor" (90), Xuela's world contracts to her painful body. Once again, she is exiled from society and the community as she knows it, for her cell-like house lies by a road that is unfinished and presumably unmapped. In contrast, her father's face resembles a "globe" (91), since he represents colonial authority. Physically healed, Xuela works on the road project, sifting sand like the time that passes while she pursues this occupation, stalled by a road that cannot yet be traveled. She wears the clothes of a dead man, cuts off her hair, and stops speaking because there is only emptiness within her. In a sense she is nothing, existing in a slip of space between two places. She voids herself of all connections and associations, even gender, believing that only then can she know herself. Ultimately, in a kind of ritual cleansing, she sets fire to her clothes and then bathes thoroughly (104).

While this simple existence allows Xuela to transcend the definitions that have constricted her, it is artificial and cannot last. Xuela finds herself hired by Philip, another friend of her father's, a white man whom she marries after his wife dies. It is as if she is a possession to be passed around without volition in a geography that is mapped by powerful men. The relationship begins when she moves into her quarters, which had formerly been inhabited by a nurse, appropriately, since Xuela ministers to Philip's physical and emotional needs without ever loving him. She is aware, too, that the room was intended for a person of higher social rank (150). There is no question that Philip is after conquest—he represents the British world that is fading, even as he reads incessantly about ruins and exercises power over the plants in his garden, many of which end up crushed between the pages of his books.[2] Even nature must be destroyed by the victors, but Philip and his wife are the end of the line: "all the bad deeds had already been committed; he was an heir . . . [his] were hands that could lose a world" (146).

This situation comes to represent Xuela's uneasy relationship within the dominant island culture, serving those who reflect British culture, even her body a site of domination, though she protects a small space of resistance within her mind. Eventually, this space expands as she begins

an affair with a stevedore named Roland. In contrast to Philip, Roland
suggests open space: "His mouth was like an island in the sea that was his
face" (163). It is not because he can travel, or because he works only on
docked ships. Rather, like Xuela, he is "an event in somebody else's history" (167) and longs for "something beyond . . . one room with walls
made of mud and roof of cane leaves, beyond the small plot of land"
(177). But ultimately, Roland comes to signify the third term in a triad
that hinges on Philip and Xuela's father, which in turn reflects the trian-
gular slave trade. His seductive island mouth "was dangerous and could
swallow things whole" (178).

Men in the novel thus come to represent different layers of geography
on the island: the histories and topologies of the European conqueror and
the oppressed African. Her father comes from the second group but aspires to the first, a man who must constantly "invent" himself (53), living "a copied life" (54). Xuela can never really love any one of them, and
this defines her isolation as much as her lack of a mother who is identified with the third, indigenous strand of island culture. In fact, despite the
seeming paradox in the title, the text is ultimately revealed to be an autobiography of her mother, for Xuela has to mother herself, attempt to create a self in a world where stronger forces succeed in controlling her.

Yet the end of the book contains certain ambiguities. Xuela, who
claims that she lives for the present (205) and that her text does not constitute a history (228), has just completed a narrative that is intensely
about the past even if it is not history as it is traditionally constructed.
The closing truism about the inevitability of mortality is impersonal in
its triteness. The account remains locked in the contradictions that have
defined its heroine's life: the detached tone and superficial clichés mask a
being that is not one thing or another. Xuela's attempts at defining herself involve alternately the crowding of conflicting identities and erasure,
being nothing. No future can arise out of these paradoxes, as is evident
from Xuela's "refusal of motherhood as a radical political act" (Rody 129)
as well as by the inability of other women in the novel to generate:
Xuela's mother dies in childhood, Madame LaBatte is sterile, and Xuela's
stepmother loses her children.

For Kincaid, then, the nostalgia for a West African women's sodality is
no more evident than a wish to assimilate into European cultures. Living
mother figures are primarily women who have internalized alien values;
their closeness becomes as claustrophobic as the small spaces the heroine

inhabits on the island. And the dead mother remains inaccessible, a third term, a gap, an extinct genealogy. The heroines who choose differently from Xuela's passivity must leave the imprisoning island for Europe or America, and even then, they find that many of the old oppressions follow them. In the next chapter, I will explore what happens when characters in Alice Walker's novels attempt a return to Africa.

5

Alice Walker and the Ethics of Possession

Traditions linking blacks in Africa and America are an important force in Alice Walker's fiction. In *Possessing the Secret of Joy,* Walker focuses on one tradition in particular—female excision followed by infibulation. Her depiction of the devastating and far-ranging effects of this ritual complicates our study of Africanisms in novels by black American women, because it reveals how African influences may be a continuing, visible force in the lives of contemporary women, as well as a powerful legacy. At the same time, Walker's method of using Africanisms differs significantly from what we have seen in works by Naylor, Morrison, and Kincaid. Walker's approach appears more direct and deliberate, since she sets important parts of her novels in Africa itself. Instead of dealing with transmission through obeah, voodoo, Gullah, family rites, and folklore, Walker increasingly tells stories about African women and African Americans who travel to Africa. Thus, in discussions of Walker's texts, the term *Africanism* takes on another meaning. In earlier chapters, the term referred primarily to continuations of African traditions in the United States; here, the term primarily alludes to an African-American's perspective on or interpretation of African culture *in situ.* The difference in the two uses of the term raises critical questions about Africanism and authenticity, which will be discussed in this and later chapters.

To date, both kinds of Africanisms are most evident in Walker's trio of novels, *The Color Purple, The Temple of My Familiar*, and *Possessing the Secret of Joy.* Yet Walker's earlier uses of Africanisms are significant, too, because they more closely resemble those found in texts by Kincaid, Naylor, and Morrison. In the collection *In Love & Trouble*, African influences are most apparent in the "rootwork" in "The Revenge of Hannah Kemhuff" and "Strong Horse Tea." These stories reveal the presence of

African elements in the folklore of Southern American blacks, so that the term "rootwork" becomes an allusion not only to herbal medicine but also to characters' abilities to "work" with their African legacy. In "The Diary of an African Nun," Walker begins to take the second approach to Africanisms. She addresses the harmful effects of the intrusion of Anglo-European culture on the African continent, a study that continues in *The Color Purple* and *The Temple of My Familiar*, as well as in *Possessing the Secret of Joy*.

In the title essay of *In Search of Our Mothers' Gardens*, Walker focuses on America, tracing her lineage through her mother and grandmother. According to Houston Baker, this essay is germinal because it illustrates the way an image grounded in African-American culture may recover a lost past: "By phenomenologically recovering her mother's vernacular *garden* and presenting it as a literate poetic image . . . Walker opens the field of Afro-American women's consciousness in its founding radiance and claims for herself an enduring spiritual legacy" (*Workings of the Spirit* 52). Although Walker's essay primarily concerns the life of the black woman in America, the "great-great-grandmother who died under some ignorant and depraved white overseer's lash" (233), she also emphasizes that her creativity springs from another continent, or at least from her vision of that continent: "perhaps in Africa over two hundred years ago, there was just such a mother" (243), who gave her daughter spirit.

Walker's trilogy of novels, *The Color Purple*, *The Temple of My Familiar*, and *Possessing the Secret of Joy*, resembles Naylor's sequence of books; both authors use later texts to add to the stories of characters in earlier works, thus deepening the meaning of the initial books. Yet while Naylor's characters, with the exception of Mariam in *Bailey's Cafe*, live in America and are influenced by an African past prior to the diaspora, Walker uses a synchronous approach, exploring what happens when characters who continue to live by rural African values are transplanted into American culture and vice versa.

Walker rarely distinguishes between rural and urban life in Africa, even though many traditional African practices, such as female excision and infibulation, are increasingly being abandoned in major cities (Bean 325). Thus, many would argue that Walker's works contain a "latent Eurocentrism" (Kieti 157), perpetuating the colonialist vision of the subcontinent as primitive. For instance, in "Homesick and Eurocentric? Alice

Walker's Africa," Nwikali Kieti enumerates the ways in which Walker's depiction of women in the subcontinent differs from the lived experiences of African women. Not surprisingly, African-American characters' responses to Africa reflect Walker's attitudes as well. In *The Color Purple*, several major characters are missionaries among the Olinka, introducing them to Christianity and Western notions of civilization. During their years in Africa, the missionaries question the values of the Olinka community, revealing the problematic nature of their own rhetorical position: "Here we have two African-Americans who have accepted a religion, foreign to their ancestry, that was once used as a justification for slavery; in turn, they are asking Africans to replace their beliefs with this same religion" (Buckman 91). The missionaries initiate the destruction of village life, and they are followed by the arrival of white men who construct a road that further disrupts the community, much like the appearance of colonials in Kincaid's Caribbean.

In *The Temple of My Familiar*, too, Africa appears as the site of contemporary political struggles, but it is also a revered ancestral homeland in Lissie's descriptions of her earlier incarnations. For Lissie, Africa is the site of a series of dream memories, a prelapsarian world disrupted by an awareness of racial difference, a desire for territory, and the coming of white men. Many of her tales function as parables or myths, as she instructs the young African American, Suwelo, in the ways of the world. As Lissie explains, "to me all daily stories are in fact ancient, and ancient ones current" (172).

For Suwelo's wife, Fanny Nzhinga (the granddaughter of Celie, the heroine of *The Color Purple*), Africa is home to her father's people. She comes to terms with herself in part through conversations with her father and half sister concerning the struggles of Africans. In these discussions, Fanny makes constant comparisons between the status of blacks in Africa and the United States. In addition, she focuses particularly on the lives of women, noting that "nothing is harder for the men in power than to contemplate what the African woman knows" (352).

A third vision of Africa is embedded in the text in the character of M'Sukta, the African woman living in a London museum. M'Sukta stands for the disappearance of traditional African communities, for she has no one to return to, being "the last of her people" (225). M'Sukta thus represents the way traditional Africa has become an object for Western scrutiny, a curiosity safely caged, timeless and placeless.

In short, *The Temple of My Familiar* offers a triple vision of Africa: as a mythic place where timeless truths may be found in the images and symbols of folk tale, as a living continent, where actual events are inscribed in the history of the people, and as a dead land, its people extinct after years of colonial depredations. These varying visions of Africa are analogous to the shifting roles of the mother's garden (and the continent is metonymically related both to that richly Edenic green space and to the forest enclosures of African women's societies). Yet, ironically, within the space of the text, all of the Africas are fictive representations inflected by Walker's complicated, contradictory, and controversial views of the continent. Critics' opinions range, for instance, from seeing Walker as slightly addled in the head by her contact with California (Lauret 10) to describing her grandiosely as an idealist who "invites us into her magic temple for the ritual act of transforming appliqués and racio-cultural intensives of her art into a quest for the metaphysical basis for reality" (Dieke 137).

In *Possessing the Secret of Joy*, the controversies regarding Walker's work gain further intensity with the focus of the plot. Walker concentrates on the lives of individuals, in particular Tashi, who marries Celie's son Adam. Tashi spends most of her adult life in the United States and Africa dealing with the pain caused by excision and infibulation. The suffering created by the ordeal is akin to possession; at times, she is frenzied and commits acts of violence against herself. In overcoming the suffering, she must confront not only the part men have played in the continuation of the ritual, but also the role of women. Thus, whereas maternal figures in *The Temple of My Familiar* are primarily sources of wisdom and endurance, in her more recent novel Walker questions whether patriarchal traditions have distorted the role of mothers. Rather than merely establishing a transmission of African values in the Americas over several hundred years, Walker focuses primarily on twentieth-century connections.

Walker's increasingly explicit use of Africanisms contrasts Naylor's and Morrison's works, where the transmission seems indirect, even at times coincidental. Her valuing of the survival of traditional African ceremonies differs from Naylor's and Morrison's as well. For the latter two, African influences are primarily positive, while in Kincaid's works they are problematic. But in Walker's universe, African culture can be as sexist and cruel as American culture. This is in part because African culture is seen through an American lens; for instance, not every African woman who has experienced excision has suffered as much as Tashi does. Walker's refiguration of the role of the matriarch revises others' impressions as well. While Naylor's Mama Day and Morrison's Pilate, Eva Peace, and Baby Suggs retain mystical power in their association with an African ancestry, the ritual circumciser M'Lissa in *Possessing the Secret of Joy* appears purely malevolent. A key part of Walker's intent is to illustrate the multiple layers of oppression in the lives of black women. In this way, Walker suggests a continuous relationship in the experiences and suffering of women on the two continents, instead of treating the African presence as other (as Naylor does) or of focusing on individuals negotiating between cultures (as Morrison does).

In depicting the lives of women in Africa, Walker confronts readers with the failures of societies they might idealize as authentic and uncorrupted in contrast to American civilization. Having deconstructed these images of the subcontinent, she forces readers to examine similarities between their lives and cultures many of them would consider barbaric. Her work constitutes a contemporary revision of Countee Cullen's poem "Heritage," with its refrain "What is Africa to me?" (24).

In "Heritage," Cullen anticipates the predicament of Walker and other African Americans who may be "three centuries removed / From the scenes his [or her] fathers loved." Imag(in)ing, let alone representing, a culture so distant in time and space is a difficult venture. The opening of the poem reflects Cullen's problems in picturing; although the images offer a critique of European conceptions of "savage" Africans, they replace the stereotype with an equally extreme vision of nobility. Furthermore, Cullen does nothing to alter the common definition of the black woman in terms of her sexuality and fecundity:

> Copper sun or scarlet sea,
> Jungle star or jungle track,
> Strong bronzed men, or regal black
> Women from whose loins I sprang (24)

Cullen's retreat into fantasies of Africa anticipates the dilemma apparent in Walker's work: replacing a distorted view of a distant life and culture with one's own impressions is inevitably a task fraught with contradictions and ethical constraints.

These difficulties are especially apparent in *Possessing the Secret of Joy*, where the narrative of Walker's novel centers on the effects of the ritual surgery on the heroine, Tashi, as well as on those around her. But Walker's interest is not limited to the characters themselves; she uses them to convey information about female genital mutilation in African countries (as well as in the United States) and to trace complicity in its continuation. Specifically, the multivocal narrative seeks to answer these questions: how could this still happen? What does it mean for women in Africa? in America?

The most obvious answer to the first question is that excision is traditional in the fictional Olinka culture, and that Tashi feels pressure to conform to the rules of her community. But Walker's representation of Africa is more complex than that. At the time that Tashi has her surgery, the Olinka community is in disarray because of the intrusions of white society and its values. One could, in fact, say that just as M'Sukta is the last of her village, no community exists for Tashi to be initiated into. Although many of the female elders have been circumcised, as the townspeople convert to Christianity, excision has been discouraged. This sudden disruption of social life recalls the interruption of African culture with the introduction of the slave trade.

In contrast to the Europeanized communities, the man referred to as the Leader and the rebels advocate excision (121–22). Just as Jomo Kenyatta's support for the ritual contributed to its perpetuation in East Africa (Wallerstein 166–67), the Leader's influence has kept female circumcision alive among the Olinka: "Our Leader, our Jesus Christ, said we must keep all our old ways and that no Olinka man—in this he echoed the great liberator Kenyatta—would even think of marrying a woman who was not circumcised" (122). The Leader, like Kenyatta, endorses circumcision because the ritual precedes European colonization and is therefore perceived as authentic to the culture; in this way, the claim to authenticity supports the patriarchy.

Ultimately, then, one irony of the novel is that the revolutionaries, the vanguard of resistance against Western oppression, are reactionary when it comes to their treatment of women. According to M'Lissa, most of the women abandoned the rebel camp after they realized, "it was the camp itself that needed liberation. When the women came they were expected to cook and clean—and be screwed" (243). Ideology has become a mask for perpetuating male dominance and female sexual submission. The parallel between these soldiers and some black nationalists in the United States, though implicit, is obvious.

This portrait of revolutionaries raises questions about the definitions of resistance and liberation. Walker suggests that since Kenyatta and the people's leader sanction the continued suffering of women, they are not truly liberators. She signifies on the way those in power manipulate language, in this case, so that the term *liberation* appears to exist for only one sex, as the "freedom fighters" inscribe their possessiveness on the bodies of women. In this way, Walker shows that resistance consists not only of combating Western hegemonic ideologies, but also of struggling against restrictions imposed in the name of tradition.

Similarly, in *Gyn/Ecology,* Daly asserts that African female genital mutilation is a particularly virulent atrocity that has been protected by patriarchal taboos, because "leaders cooperate in the conspiracy of silence" (155). Daly considers two tasks essential: convincing readers of the role of the state in rendering such crimes against women "normal, ritualized, repeated," and demonstrating that the "rituals in the so-called underdeveloped regions of the planet are deeply connected with atrocities perpetrated against women in 'advanced' societies" (155). Audre Lorde has criticized Daly for "distort[ing] our commonality as well as our difference" in suggesting that the experiences of Western women are "identical" with the oppressions of women in other parts of the world (70), and Walker's comparisons, too, have drawn fire from a variety of critics, including Inderpal Grewal and Caren Kaplan.

Within *Possessing the Secret of Joy,* the ethical issues are even more complex. Tashi explains to Olivia, her sister-in-law, why she insists on the surgery, even though it killed her sister. In Olinka culture, "expressions of concern" such as Olivia's are "interpreted as outside interference from colonial and neo-colonial states" (Dorkenoo and Elworthy 20). What Tashi finds most "valuable" (*The Color Purple* 212) about the rite is that it marks her as different from Westerners, even African Americans. The ritual is important because it is one of the few remaining traces of the distinctive culture of the Olinka. Participating in customs such as facial scarification and circumcision—no matter how painful—is therefore a form of resistance for Tashi. In contrast, Olivia stands in for the author, whose criticism of female excision has been described as "cultural condescension" by Margaret Kent Bass (2).

Ironically, later in her life, when Tashi lives in the United States, this sign of difference becomes haunting and oppressive, so that when she gives birth, her body becomes a "sideshow" (61), more grotesque even than M'Sukta in the London museum. The doctors and nurses examine her like "some creature from beyond their imaginings" (60). While Americans' "imaginings" have transformed Africa into an exotic distant place, the body of a "real" African appears monstrous to them. Tashi has thus become an instrument for the reintroduction of Africa into the Americas.

In contrast, when Mariam, an Ethiopian Jewish woman who has been infibulated, gives birth in Naylor's *Bailey's Cafe*, the event is joyful. Eve, who owns the house where Mariam boards, has filled the birthing room with light (224). Although Mariam is bleeding and in pain, Eve is prepared to help her and minimize her suffering. The community gathered around the birth bursts into song for an hour before anyone wonders about the baby's sex (226). What makes Naylor's approach so different? The event is narrated by Bailey, one of the bystanders, while Mariam, the mother, is not empowered to speak (even the earlier account of her story is told indirectly through Bailey's wife, who hears it from Eve, who interjects the voice of Mariam's mother). The infibulated woman's mother's role differs as well; like Dura, Tashi's mother, Mariam's mother causes her to be infibulated, but Mariam's mother also helps smuggle her daughter out of the country when she becomes pregnant and claims that no man has touched her. Thus, the event in Naylor's work is seen as something of a miracle: "maybe it's meant for this baby to bring in a whole new era" (160). Eve goes out of her way to recreate Mariam's African environment, for the birth to bring Africa into the United States. Even though her decor is a pastiche of African stereotypes, it is created with respect, and the baby is circumcised in the Jewish tradition. The presence of the neighborhood community instead of Walker's impersonal assortment of doctors is also significant, because Naylor's characters do not pass judgment on the birth and declare it foreign or other. Ultimately, Naylor's treatment of a birth following female excision and infibulation is more positive than Walker's, in keeping with her general treatment of Africa and Africanisms. Naylor's baby grows up to be George in *Mama Day*, a man who refutes his African roots but does not betray his wife Cocoa/Ophelia.

Like Kincaid, Walker finds that husbands and male lovers often deserve blame for the suffering of women. Adam, Tashi's American husband, is initially shocked by the operation and helps to nurse her. As time passes, however, he regards his wife with disappointment, sorrow, and disgust. Her grief does not prevent him from engaging in an extended extramarital affair with a relative of Carl Jung's. This relationship mirrors the triangles in *The Color Purple* (consisting of Shug, Celie, and Albert) and *The Temple of My Familiar* (the first involving Suwelo, Fanny, and Carlotta, and the second including Zédé, Ayurveda, and Carlotta). Aside from the triangle in *The Temple of My Familiar* of Mr. Hal, Uncle Rafe, and Lissie—an exception in every way herself—all of these groupings include a man and two women. As such, they replicate the structure in traditional African families, with the wives frequently coming to terms with each other, even though the structure is inherently unequal.

In *Possessing the Secret of Joy*, the triangle benefits Adam and reveals another effect of Tashi's genital mutilation. Tashi acknowledges that she has experienced sexual pleasure once or twice since her surgery, but only during anal intercourse. This position is distasteful to Tashi, making her feel like "something other than myself." M'Lissa responds, "You had been made into a woman," equating "something else" (otherness? animality?) with femaleness, and establishing femaleness as an artificial rather than a natural category. More ominously, M'Lissa adds that this confirms Adam's sense of manhood (246). This insight is congruent with research on the surgical procedure, which suggests that one of its major functions is to strengthen men's sense of control (Dorkenoo and Elworthy 12–14) and sexual gratification (Wallerstein 183–84).

Not only do men pressure Tashi to undergo the procedure, but the Olinka women are complicit in her fate as well. Tashi's mother is so frightened of her elders that she assists during the operation on her older daughter, Dura, a known hemophiliac. M'Lissa herself performs the operation on countless girls, even though she has been crippled by the surgery (her dragging foot an echo of Eva Peace's amputated leg, another price of admission into black womanhood). M'Lissa persists because she has received national fame and prestige, and also because she has become virtually anaesthetized to girls' suffering.

In an inversion of other works, where the matriarch of the town is a midwife and healer, M'Lissa delivers babies and cures the ill. Although she calls her ritual procedure "healing," she is wounding her countrywomen (63). Once again, language contributes to the secrecy that has shrouded the procedure, facilitating its continuation. This silence differs from the secrecy surrounding Mama Day's cures, which render

women fertile and prolong their lives. In her maleficence, M'Lissa resembles some of the mothers and threatening older women in Kincaid's
works.

Significantly, even the chicken takes on a nearly opposite function in
this novel. While Naylor depicts chickens as beneficent and protective of
women, the mutilated Tashi views herself as "a chicken bound for market" (45). Tashi also associates the bird with M'Lissa's voracious cruelty.
One of the circumciser's hens ("not a cock") lunges after her sister's excised clitoris, and "in one quick movement of beak and neck, gobbled it
down" (75).

In her study of the ritual of excision, Walker tries to universalize the
problem, though she mostly succeeds in placing it in an American context. She indicates that excision is not merely an African tradition, introducing a white American woman whose mother arranged for her to be
circumcised as a child (185–90). This subplot enables Walker to offer a
brief history of the operation in the United States, where it was touted as
a cure for female hypersexuality. She includes an account of how doctors
learned the procedure by studying slave women's bodies (188), revealing
another way in which female genital mutilation has been used for social
control. This account also echoes descriptions in other novels discussed in
the second part of this book, where the violence committed on the body
of a woman is equivalent to her silencing.

Jung's niece, Lisette, who has the affair with Adam and bears his child,
also complicates the narrative. Lisette is, in many ways, a sympathetic
character, carrying on an extended affair with a man she will never
marry, writing his wife, trying to understand her. Yet her effort at sisterhood is questionable, for she continues the affair, even though she knows
that Adam's visits provoke Tashi's bouts of depression and madness (49).
Eventually, Lisette dies of stomach cancer, her internal malignancy an
expression of the contradictions in her ideology. Walker thus signifies on
educated white women and their supposedly good intentions toward
their African sisters. Ironically, the comparison does not extend to Walker
herself and the fact that as a writer, she has benefitted in some ways from
publicizing the suffering of African women.

In the novel, perhaps the greatest culprits are the Olinka people as a
group, many of whom rally around the Leader and his revolutionaries,
supporting the elevation of M'Lissa to the rank of a national monument.
The people's court condemns Tashi to death for killing M'Lissa. In this

way, Walker offers a dual critique—of those who blindly follow male authority as well as of those who glorify tradition for its own sake. Not only does she describe Tashi's miseries, but she portrays young women who acquire AIDS after being encouraged or forced to undergo excision (251–52), a concern also expressed in a report prepared by Efua Dorkenoo and Scilla Elworthy for the Minority Rights Group International (9). Ironically, a procedure that is described as "cleansing" or "healing" women has instead become a mechanism for spreading a deadly virus among them. If the people are collaborators in Tashi's sufferings, the structures they create, governmental and otherwise, are equally responsible for the perpetuation of the ritual. In this way, Walker makes it impossible to glorify an abstract ideal of community, as one might after reading *Mama Day*. As in Kincaid's novels, the community has been corrupted and broken by the conflicts of colonialism and postcolonialism.

While Walker is critical of social structures, she suggests that certain characters ameliorate the conditions of individuals like Tashi by establishing a bond through suffering. The first such character, Carl Jung, plays an ambiguous role in the novel. Referred to as Mzee, or the Old Man, Jung makes a brief appearance as Tashi's avuncular analyst. The portrait of Jung is generally sympathetic, for he learns from Tashi's pain: "I am finding myself in them [Adam and Tashi]. A self I have often felt was only halfway at home on the European continent. . . . An ancient self that thirsts for knowledge of the experiences of its ancient kin. Needs this knowledge, and the feelings that come with it, to be whole. A self that is horrified at what was done to Evelyn, but recognizes it as something that is also done to me" (86). As Jung idealizes the "ancient self" and "knowledge" of the Africans, he strives to find evidence for his theories of universal archetypes, to prove that violence was "also done to me." All of the sentences after the first one are incomplete; the European "I" drops out. In the process, Jung emphasizes otherness, relegating the "ancient" to the status of the less civilized, to be desired, "needed," even "thirsted" after, a distant mother who remains appealing even though (or because) her sexuality has been excised. His desire to keep (M)other Africa at a safe distance, as fascinating as she may be, is apparent when he calls Tashi by her European name, Evelyn, which implies both the sexual and maternal.

Like the so-called liberators who cannot free women because they remain oppressors themselves, Jung cannot exorcize Tashi's demons because he is rooted in the white patriarchy. In *Gyn/Ecology*, Mary Daly explains why such paternal or professorial males must inevitably remain suspect: "'Father' is precisely the one who cannot exorcize, for he is allied with and identified with The Possessor. . . . However possessed males may be within patriarchy, it is *their* order; it is they who feed on women's stolen energy" (2). Indeed, Jung benefits personally and professionally from analyzing Tashi. He may be called Mzee or the Old Man, but he is not a traditional African elder. Instead, he resembles Bwana, a white man prospering from the colonial enterprise—in this case, the conquest of the "dark" mind.

Where Jung's work is most useful to Tashi is in modeling a reconstruction of the past through psychotherapy; as the novel proceeds, Tashi circles and recircles events in her life, gaining new understanding. Psychoanalysis imposes a narrative form on discrete experiences and dream images, rendering it a kind of literary genre with its own tropes and conventions. This genre is particularly appropriate to Walker's oeuvre, because it combines memory, language, sexuality, and violence. Yet psychoanalysis does not lend itself as well to understanding similar qualities in Naylor's and Morrison's work since it is based on a Eurocentric, paternalistic understanding of identity and grounded in archetypes derived from a Western framework. What is similar about the three authors' narratives is the fact that, as various characters contribute sections of the texts, their novels begin to resemble an extended version of call and response, their spoken qualities suitable to the orality of the culture they portray.

If Europeans such as Jung and Lisette are suspect, Walker indicates that the next generations may redeem them. Her portrayals of the young people who must inherit their elders' cultures involves less tension than the question of succession in *Mama Day* and less pain than the appearance of the ghost in *Beloved.* Instead of founding a new race, Adam and Tashi-Evelyn give birth to a developmentally disabled boy, appropriately named Benjamin. While Benjamin plays a minor role in the narrative, Adam and Lisette's son Pierre becomes a major force in Tashi's recovery. Initially, Tashi feels hostile toward Pierre. The first time she meets him, Tashi throws stones at him (145). When viewed in a context that includes the pebble-like palm nuts in Ifa divination, the rocks carried by Pilate in *Song of Solomon* (142), and Carlotta's stones in *The Temple of My Familiar,* these stones may be perceived as metonyms for Tashi's African heritage, which she is literally throwing in the face of an anthropologist. But Pierre, whose name means *stone* in French, is undaunted. He suggests that there is a chain of suffering, a "connection between mutilation and enslavement that is at the root of the domination of women" (139). His ability to perceive "connections," or to do "rootwork," enables him to interpret the imagery in Tashi's dreams, helping her come to terms with her suffering.

Pierre initially appears to be another anthropologist mocked by African-American women writers, such as the one in *Mama Day*, who does not know how to ask or listen (10). But in his study of Tashi's problem, he returns Tashi's past to her and gives her an awareness of the folklore behind the termite dream that has disturbed her for years. In the end, his approach resembles Zora Neale Hurston's brand of insider anthropology, which Walker has repeatedly admired (see *In Search of Our Mothers' Gardens* 83–92). Indeed, Pierre's equation of mutilation with the "domination" of other women renders him a spokesman for Walker, who reiterates throughout *Warrior Marks* that female excision serves as a symbol for the universal "sexual blinding" of women.

Moreover, Pierre is a "blended person. . . . In him 'black' has disappeared; so has 'white'" (174). As an individual who is bisexual and biracial, Pierre is capable of understanding Tashi's multiplicity, her three names (Tashi, Evelyn, and Mrs. Johnson) expressing her various existences. Through their son, Lisette and Adam give Tashi some relief despite their contributions to her suffering. Named after Saint Peter in the European tradition that he shares, Pierre holds the key to reducing Tashi's suffering, if not to heaven.

Another character in the novel who establishes a community in suffering is the American therapist, Raye. I disagree with Kadiatu Kanneh's assertion that in contrast to Walker's negative depiction of Africa, "affection, strength and salvation live within Europe and the United States" (113). Raye introduces Tashi to Amy, an American woman who has experienced the same mutilation. Amy's mother calls the excision a tonsillectomy, and the girl is silenced by the genital surgery as she might have been shortly after a tonsillectomy. With the use of a euphemism, the source of Amy's depression remains unnamed and unknowable prior to extensive therapy, which, like Tashi's, involves reconstructing the past.

Raye provides continuity in another way as well. She elects painful dental surgery, or "gum mutilation" (133). Even though Raye undergoes the procedure with the assistance of anesthesia, Tashi recognizes the importance of the gesture: "she was intuitively practicing an ageless magic, the foundation of which was the ritualization, or the acting out, of empathy" (134). In an inversion of Freudian symbolism, where the loss of teeth is equivalent to castration, oral surgery is made to correspond to female circumcision and infibulation. Here again, Walker prepares for the problematic equivalence of genital excision with her own blindness in *Warrior Marks,* which will be discussed later.

Nevertheless, such gestures of sorority enable Tashi to acknowledge the pervasiveness of suffering: "an American looks like a wounded person whose wound is hidden from others, and sometimes from herself. An American looks like me" (213). Walker extends this analogy in *Warrior Marks:* "in the 'enlightened' West, it is as if genital mutilation has been spread over the entire body, as women (primarily) rush to change their breasts, their noses, their weight and shape" (9–10).

Tashi finds support in Africa as well. Mbati, who is first seen serving M'Lissa, breaks away from the orthodoxy, and, by the time Tashi is executed, leads the opposition. With help from Tashi's family and closest friends, she unfurls a banner bearing the inscription, "RESISTANCE IS THE SECRET OF JOY!" In redefining the title saying, Mbati succeeds in reappropriating a patronizing expression (281).

But the novel's ending is somewhat ambiguous. Throughout Walker's earlier works, women who struggle, such as Fanny's mother in *Temple of My Familiar* or Sophia in *The Color Purple,* are punished for their assertion. Their gestures of opposition are muted. Yet at the end of *Possessing the Secret of Joy,* a group of women rise against the patriarchy, (re)asserting a community of their own. As Tashi is taken to be executed, these women line the way, holding up their babies and exposing their intact genitals in a "protest and celebration" that the men do not notice (280). Clearly, the effectiveness of such a gesture is questionable. One could argue that the women subvert patriarchy by flaunting the taboo against speaking of, let alone showing, girls' genitals; nevertheless, for the most part, the African women in this novel are passive and sustain themselves in serving others. While for Walker this is an accurate representation of the lives of women in Africa, in Naylor's and Morrison's works, African influences are more empowering, and critics of Walker's texts have pointed out that women are increasingly finding ways of exerting power within traditional African societies.

Even the significance of Tashi's fate is uncertain. At the beginning of the novel, Jung patronizingly asserts that black women's analysis fails to heal spiritual wounds because "they can never bring themselves to blame their mothers" (19). If that is the case, Tashi begins her cure in acknowledging the complicity of her mother and M'Lissa; she completes her healing when she murders M'Lissa. Yet Tashi is executed for the murder, which implies that blaming mother figures who carry out the wishes of male leaders is insufficient. Thus Walker joins Morrison in questioning the presumption pervading feminist models such as Chodorow's that mothers are responsible for the reproduction of oppressive cultural norms.

At best, the last generation in the novel—Mbati and Pierre in particular—do more than alleviate the pain of their elders. They learn from the pain and break away from the destructive aspects of the past. In doing so, they inscribe a new story across the sufferings of their parents, one that acknowledges the presence of Africa in their lives, not as a distant heritage, a symbol or metonym, but as a vital force, affecting their thoughts and actions on a daily basis. For them, the answer to the question "What is Africa to me?" (or what is authentically African) is lengthy and complex, for it must include not only the continent that has been pillaged since the beginning of the slave trade, but also the societies that have been built and rebuilt since then, and the constant communication between the continents. In refusing to be possessed by the demons of the past, they have come into a spiritual life that transcends continental boundaries and renders them the most liberatory gift of all, self-possession. The novels discussed in the second part of this book further explore the points of contact between the two worlds as well as the themes of possession and self-possession, both in their spiritual and physical manifestations.

Part II

6

The Violation of Voice

Revising the Slave Narrative

The novels discussed in the first part of this book present tension and conflict between African and American cultures, especially as manifested in organized Christianity. In her novels on Brewster Place, Naylor exposes the sanctimony of Reverend Moreland Woods; the preachers in Morrison's *Paradise* are alternately inflexible and lost; the missionaries in Alice Walker's *The Color Purple* disparage and attempt to eradicate African beliefs. Jamaica Kincaid depicts Christianity as an incoherent mélange of beliefs or the tool of corrupt colonials and their minions. These representations of institutionalized Christianity are not necessarily evidence that the authors have abandoned the religion, and reference to their biographies reveals the importance of Christian beliefs in many of the authors' lives.

Christianity is problematic in these texts because it often comes to represent white culture. In a similar manner, the authors of antebellum slave narratives had to wrestle with the contradictions between their desire to expose religious hypocrisy and their need for the acceptance of predominantly white audiences. This conflict is so prominent in their works that James Olney has labeled the exposure of slave owners' religious hypocrisy a generic feature of the slave narrative (153). The major difference between the picture of Christianity in the original slave narratives and in the contemporary works I have analyzed is that the former address white Christians, whereas the latter question Christianity among African Americans as well.

These concerns are particularly prominent in the contemporary novel about slavery, a form of fiction that offers readers the perspectives of nineteenth-century African Americans through the eyes of their twentieth-century descendants. Examples by women include Toni Morrison's *Beloved*, Sherley Anne Williams's *Dessa Rose*, J. California Cooper's *Family*, and Margaret Walker's *Jubilee*. This genre's significance is also apparent in the surge of critical studies of the phenomenon, such as those by Deborah McDowell, Stefanie Sievers, and Elizabeth Beaulieu.

The new genre of fiction raises the question: why are so many contemporary African-American women writing novels that appear to be slave narratives? These novels are set in part or in their entirety in pre–Civil War America; moreover, they follow conventions of slave narratives, including acts of rape or other forms of physical violence committed against the heroine. Certainly, the antebellum period has a hold on writers' imaginations, and it is also critically important as a time in which European conventions inserted themselves into African culture. This circumstance is encoded in many novels, including *Beloved* and *Jubilee*, in acts of rape or violence against women. The results are narrative discontinuities that indicate attempts to suppress voice. As one of the characters in Alice Walker's *Temple of My Familiar* comments, "if you tear out the tongue of another, you have a tongue in your hand the rest of your life. You are responsible, therefore, for all that person might have said" (310). Not only do these novels show the deleterious effects of violence, but they also emphasize the importance of authority in testifying to the cruelty of slavery and keeping its memory alive.

More importantly, in linking issues concerning voice, violence, and genre, these texts contribute to the dialogue on the role of gender in African-American cultural production. Black women writers turn repeatedly to writing about slavery because the topic allows them to focus on themes of power, identity, family, and authenticity. These themes gain rich inflections before a variety of audiences as they find expression in their play across the gendered human body that is the heroine's, as well as across the body of language that is the text. Finally, the contemporary version of the slave narrative reflects the political concerns of recent times as well; according to Elizabeth Beaulieu, "The fictionalized slave narrative of the late twentieth century is the inevitable literary outgrowth of both the civil rights movement and the feminist movement" (4). Framed by these two social efforts, the novel of slavery also reflects the varying relations between African-American women and black and white communities.

A brief study of *Incidents in the Life of a Slave Girl* by Harriet Jacobs suggests that similar concerns were present from the form's inception. At the same time, *Incidents in the Life of a Slave Girl* provides a useful basis for a comparison with more recent works to reveal how contemporary authors have reshaped the genre. As Hazel Carby and others have suggested, Jacobs's narrative is a highly mediated, self-conscious cultural production (*Reconstructing Womanhood* 48–49). The book's white editor, abolitionist Lydia Maria Child, "pruned excrescences" (Jacobs 3) and suggested changes to improve the book's continuity (Jacobs 244). The text is virtually devoid of the kinds of Africanisms apparent in the novels discussed in part one; Jacobs's avoidance of references to black traditions or folk elements is necessitated by the cultural devaluing of Africa as primitive as well as by forces governing Jacobs's literary self-representation.

Jacobs made accommodations to the primarily white, female reading public, including her adoption of the vocabulary and framework of sensational novels such as those written by Lydia Maria Child. The story of the villainous master pursuing the innocent slave also conforms to the conventions of the genre. In the descriptions of attempted seductions, Jacobs (as her pseudonymous persona, Linda Brent) emerges as a curiously asexual being. Although she speaks repeatedly of Dr. Flint's advances, she does so in an unphysical way, stressing the foulness of his words (27) and referring to the advances primarily as a manifestation of his power. In deference to nineteenth-century sexual mores as well as literary conventions, Jacobs's body is virtually erased from the text.

For all the delicacy of the allusions to sexuality, the text contains numerous passages describing punishments inflicted on slaves. As in her accounts of sexual harassment, Jacobs maintains a dry, almost emotionless tone. Often she describes violent acts themselves rather than their effects, again erasing slave bodies. For instance, after two men steal ham and liquor, "they were summoned by their master. No words were used, but a club felled them to the ground. A rough box was their coffin, and their interment was a dog's burial. Nothing was said" (46–47). In "Sketches of Neighboring Slaveholders," most punishments are inflicted on men. Violence against women is restricted primarily to rape, alluded to only indirectly when Jacobs notes that the victims have become mothers.

Many of the passages about punishments and violence were added at the instigation of Lydia Maria Child, rendering them another sign of white intervention in the work's publication. Child suggested, "write what you can recollect of the outrages committed on the colored people, in Nat Turner's time. You say the reader would not believe what you saw 'inflicted on men, women, and children without the slightest ground of suspicion against them.' What *were* those inflictions? Were any tortured to make them confess? And how? Were any killed? Please write down some of the most striking particulars, and let me have them to insert" (qtd. in Jacobs 244).

Obviously, descriptions of violence against male and female slaves aided the abolitionist cause. Yet the urgency of Child's request merits further attention. Scenes of torture and murder might enhance the sensational tenor of the proposed work, but they also threatened to undermine the delicacy with which Jacobs wished to approach her audience. Perhaps Jacobs perceived an element of voyeurism in the desire for graphic visions of torture, a voyeurism that might reinforce power imbalances as comfortable whites read about the sufferings of black others. Certainly, such concerns would explain Jacobs's only partial compliance with Child's request.

Jacobs's difficulty with graphic physical descriptions of rape and female punishment in particular stems not only from generic concerns but also from the demands of two related nineteenth-century discourses: the rhetoric of slavery on the one hand and the rhetoric of femininity on the other. Both discourses are tremendously powerful when used to name and recognize (or, alternatively, to ignore and repudiate) social circumstances affecting black women. For instance, within the world of slavery, there is no vocabulary to talk about rape and violence against slaves as such. Dr. Flint's advances are not perceived as criminal by the white community, and the lack of negative language to describe his behavior perpetuates a violence of its own. While Flint describes resistance as "waywardness" (Jacobs 60) and "ingratitude" (Jacobs 61), the white community perceives rape as "sexual compliance" (Carby, *Reconstructing Womanhood* 22) and promiscuity. Similarly, rhetoric obscures the role of the rapist, "the white slave master was not regarded as being responsible for his actions toward his black female slaves. It was the female slave who was held responsible for being a potential, and direct, threat to the conjugal sanctity of the white mistress" (*Reconstructing Womanhood* 27). Such misnaming distorts the facts and perpetrates a secondary violation.

The substitution of compliance and agency for rape and powerlessness in discussions of slavery effectively excludes many black women from the ideology of true womanhood. Deborah Gray White has noted that other forms of violence and physical display have been construed as evidence of black women's moral laxity as well. For instance, because of the public association of "nudity with lascivity," the "exposure of the slave woman's body" at an auction might lead "to an unconscious equating of black women with promiscuity" (White 32). And "the exposure of women's bodies during whippings had similar consequences. . . . Without doubt, some whippings of female slaves were sexually suggestive" (White 33). Jacobs's reticence indicates an awareness of such equations. In avoiding prolonged descriptions of violence, she resists the negative stereotyping of slave women.

Although Jacobs is in many ways restricted by her social position as well as by the conventions of the genre, it is an exaggeration to claim, as Cynthia Hamilton does, that when dealing with violence, "the traditional slave narrative" employs a "limited, partisan, and voyeuristic perspective" (438). Hamilton's view of the slave autobiography seems oblivious to the history and details of the texts, for she argues that "all narratives pander to the abolitionist polemics of victimization" and that when slaves attempt to escape "the intepretative framework" they fail to "gain back some measure of control" (433). Manuscripts such as Jacobs's reveal instead an alert intelligence capable of juggling competing discourses and astonishing agency not only in escaping slavery but also in writing the narrative.

Jacobs's careful and ultimately subversive manipulations of stereotypes as well as her only partial compliance to editorial intervention render the text a multivocal work rather than an unmediated expression of her own voice. As Houston Baker suggests in *The Journey Back*, "the voice of a self transformed by an autobiographical act" becomes "a sharer in the general [read white] public discourse about slavery. . . . much of the lived (as opposed to the represented) slave experience is lost in the transformation" (43). Thus, if the powerful institution of slavery threatens the female body with violence and sexual violation, the demands of the text and nineteenth-century audiences present a different form of violence, one that is inherent in rhetoric and "en-gendered in representation" (de Lauretis 240). As Teresa de Lauretis notes, "From . . . an order of language which speaks violence—names certain behaviors and events as violent, but not others, and constructs objects and subjects of violence, and hence violence as a social fact—it is easy to slide into the reverse notion of a language which, itself, produces violence" (240).

More recent works about slavery by African-American women attempt to redress the double violations of rhetoric and representation. They signify on the conventions of nineteenth-century sentimental novels as well as on the slave narratives that manipulate those conventions. Margaret Walker's *Jubilee* is an important example of such a novel, and it prepares for more contemporary works by Morrison, Williams, and Cooper. Because of its pivotal position in the tradition of African-American women's writing, as well as its subtle reappropriation of a genre, it will form the focus of the remainder of this discussion. Significantly, Africanisms reemerge in this text published in the midst of the struggle for civil rights and African Americans' increasing assertions of the value of their own culture (1966).

Like Jacobs, who insists on her own piety to win the audience's approval, Walker presents Vyry, her heroine, as a devoted Christian. Several critics have commented on Christian humanism as an essential theme of the text (see, for instance, Gwin 147–48), and Walker herself asserted that she was unable to "write a book that is not influenced by Christian theology and by Christian faith" (Bonetti 122). Yet Walker's novel is more complicated than it initially appears. While Eugenia Collier argues that in Walker's poetry the "vision of the African past is fairly dim and romantic" (520), Hazel Carby claims that "Walker's social commitment to realism tempers her approach to her [African-American] folk material. She carefully documented folk sayings, beliefs, songs, and folkways for inclusion in her text, but she deliberately avoids a romantic evocation of an undifferentiated rural folk" ("Ideologies of Black Folk" 133). Eleanor Traylor and B. Dilla Buckner go one step further, finding allusions to Yoruba cosmology in Walker's oeuvre. Traylor, for instance, compares Randall Ware, the blacksmith, to the Yoruba Ogun, described by Wole Soyinka as "master craftsman and artist, farmer and warrior, essence of destruction and creativity" (qtd. in Traylor 516). Buckner, on the other hand, focuses more on the translation of African rituals into voodoo and conjure (142).

Walker exposes and resists the violence imposed by white literary conventions and social mores through her use of African and African-American folk elements. Many of these African elements manifest themselves as ruptures in the otherwise realistic surface of the narrative. For instance, Walker interrupts an early chapter for a reminiscence by the slave master Dutton, who is also Vyry's father. This memory, which is irrelevant to the plot, concerns a "coon" hunting expedition. Suddenly, Dutton and his father face an uncanny apparition, "a very large and glittering rooster. He appeared to be all of two feet high. . . . But his eyes were fantastic. They looked like the eyes of a human being. He was wide-eyed and unblinking, and stared back at them unruffled, calm, and steadily" (28). The hunters confront the judgmental eyes of this unnaturally large rooster, a creature that has symbolic and ceremonial significance in many African societies. And although the slaves accompanying the hunters immediately agree that it is neither a possum, coon, chicken, or rooster, the white hunters cannot acknowledge this eruption of the supernatural. Dutton's father calls off his hunt; similarly, his son retreats from the memory to contemplate the land. But the rooster remains in the text, as well as in Dutton's memory, as a mark of the culture Southern whites would destroy (an equally intrepid rooster stands out in *Beloved*, but this one seems to be flaunting its freedom while Paul D is wearing a bit, reminding him of the depth of his degradation as a slave 70–71).

Other Africanisms in the text involve rituals and knowledge from which whites are excluded. Eleanor Traylor notes that the death scene at the novel's opening resembles Yoruba mythology and asserts that "the 'ghost' of some antecedent world, its wholeness shattered, resides within the world of *Jubilee*" (514–15). Vyry's mother is compared with an "African queen from the Congo" (7). Later, Vyry's anticipation of her baptism illustrates how remnants of African life are embedded within plantation culture, for her immersion in water invokes not only Christian tradition but also Sande initiations. Voodoo, influenced by African beliefs, surfaces when Grimes, the overseer, loses a daughter. Shortly thereafter, he finds a fetish under his steps: "the face, which had been buried in the soft clay, had been painted chalk white and marked to resemble his little girl as much as if her picture had been painted." Even though his employers tell him to ignore the doll, Grimes is dejected, because "I reckon I can't fight this kind of stuff" (56). Nevertheless, he responds by treating the slaves even more cruelly than before.

James Spears has compiled an extensive list of "superstitions and folk medical remedies" in *Jubilee*, almost all of which involve women as the subjects of beliefs. As examples, he notes that female healers concoct medicines and that "young girls should not let their feet straddle rows in field crops" (17). In the same vein, when Vyry enters puberty, Aunt Sally explains, "us colored folks knows what we knows now fore us come here from Affiky and that wisdom be your business with your womanhood: bout not letting your foots touch ground barefooted when your womanhood is on you" (45). This admonition genders Africanisms, rendering the female body a site of resistance to white culture. At the same time, Aunt Sally functions as an African "othermother" (Beaulieu 17), comparable to a secret society leader.

While the discontinuities consist of brief appearances of an endangered but still powerful African voice, a second kind of rupture may be found in the text as well. In contrast to Jacobs, Walker provides explicit descriptions of violence and sexual violations (which are frequently juxtaposed with the slave owners' expressions of Christian charity), and looks away only *after* she has rendered them in detail. In doing so, she finds names and words for the events that occur daily on the plantation, revealing how much violence is part of the Southern definition of black womanhood. At the same time, she manages to recreate scenes of tremendous pain without rendering them titillating or sexually suggestive.

The first part of the novel records the heroine's education at the Big House through a series of violent acts. The violence, which escalates as the narrative progresses, is primarily directed at young slave women. Significantly, the three male victims in this section are elderly men who are unable to participate in the field labor that defines manhood on the Dutton plantation (and the most virile African-American male in this section, Randall Ware, is a free man). For the women, pain is often inflicted by the mistress or overseer in a moment of rage or jealousy. Initially, Vyry is slapped (25), a chamber pot is emptied on her (26), she is hung by her wrists in a closet until she loses consciousness (26), and she witnesses her half sister's branding, her own body "tightening like a drum" (95). Later, two women are hung for murder, the gallows rope cutting into their necks (103), and Vyry herself is whipped viciously (145). As a result of these incidents, the black female body becomes prominent and highly visible in the text as the site of much of the action. Moreover, scarred, branded, or destroyed, it remains marked by the violence of Southern culture, a record or text of the slave's life.

Each of these episodes or clusters of episodes is followed by a break in the narrative or a change in direction. This shift is often marked by physical space, extra blank lines within the chapter, the closing of a chapter, or the end of a section of the book. For instance, after Vyry loses consciousness in the closet, Walker jumps two weeks to discuss the master's progress in local elections (and this is the section that is interrupted by the appearance of the rooster). After Lucy is branded, Walker jumps to the preparations for the wedding of Vyry's other half sister, Lillian, the master's daughter. And after Vyry herself is whipped for an attempted escape, the first part of the novel ends and Walker shifts to the death of Master Dutton.

In *Liberating Narratives*, Stefanie Sievers is critical of this aspect of the narrative. She claims that each "rupture" indicates Walker's cooptation by a white viewpoint that restricts her ability to present, let alone solve, "the psychological and/or emotional disturbances" of the characters (40): "Walker deals with her own contested status by creating a narrative voice whose attitude to the fictional characters approximates that of the [white/male-oriented] mainstream audience" (41). Yet from another perspective, the link between breaks in the surface of the female body and interruptions in the flow of the narrative is as deliberate as it is effective. When Walker shifts from violent actions to events among the Duttons, she indicates the casualness with which whites pass from the pain they inflict on others to events within their own lives. Within the discourse of slavery, the cruel slave mistress can perceive herself a good Christian, but Walker's depiction of her callous hypocrisy exposes what Southern rhetoric obscures. Furthermore, by shifting directions suddenly, Walker draws attention to the way conventions of narrative continuity flatten individual events. The violence in her work is emphasized and rendered even more horrifying by the abrupt contrasts.

The breaks and visible gaps themselves are markers of silence, of pain that is unspoken because it is inexpressible—and not because "the dynamics behind *Jubilee* . . . have a particular stake in winning white sympathy and approval" (Sievers 53). It is as if whenever European culture intrudes on the black female body, its prejudices do as well, and the narrator can no longer gaze at it or speak of it. Blackness, which has been so prominent, becomes virtually invisible.

Indeed, Vyry's self is damaged and dominated. But her voice does not disappear altogether—it remains present in the spirituals she sings incessantly, whose content alludes to events in her life. If there is "always a slender undercurrent of a nameless fear" for Vyry, she can "unburden herself as Aunt Sally had by lifting her voice in song. . . . She was surprised to discover how much she enjoyed singing and what a relief she felt when she sang" (125). Singing, Vyry feels connected to Aunt Sally and the past, and she can express her condition not only through the words of the spirituals, which reveal a yearning after freedom, but also in dance and music, which are derived from African rituals (Traylor 522). Thus popular culture becomes a repository for the African voice when it is threatened by European culture.

The exploration of the relationship between voice and violence shifts in the second section of the novel. This part of the text reverses the first; while the opening traces the imposition of Southern white culture on black bodies, this section tracks the disintegration of plantation culture through a series of violent events involving whites. References to medicine and folk beliefs diminish with the shift in focus. The slave owner falls off his horse, and his eventual death contributes to the decline of the plantation. His son and son-in-law are killed in the Civil War. During Sherman's march through Georgia, his wife suffers a stroke, which, significantly, deprives her of the power of speech and proves fatal. A final violent event involves Lillian, Dutton's daughter and Vyry's white half sister. A Union soldier attacks and rapes Lillian, hitting her in the head so that she never recovers her sanity.

These depictions of violence involving whites are a departure from the conventions of the slave novel, one which redresses some of the imbalances in representation. Whereas Jacobs emphasizes the way white women are protected and shielded, Walker does not privilege slave mistresses or their daughters. The attack on Lillian is ironic because in a similar situation, Vyry is rescued.

Walker also overturns the stereotype of the vengeful black found in white popular culture. In *Jubilee* the violence against whites is either accidental or inflicted by other whites. The attack on Lillian by a white man comments implicitly on the myth of black male violence reinforced so strongly by the film *Birth of a Nation*.

Moreover, the assault is a crucial element in Walker's exploration of the relationship between naming and violence. While slave punishment and abuse are graphically depicted in earlier sections of the novel, the rape of Lillian is never named, and readers must infer its occurrence from Walker's observation that Lillian's dress is torn. Lillian is speechless, unable to describe the events, and the doctor comments, "the honor of this house is dead this morning" (243). Then the scene shifts to a conversation between Vyry and Innis Brown, but not before the doctor speaks to Vyry "like he talking to Big Missy" (243).

This reversal is a radical move on Walker's part. Instead of showing the sexual violation of the enslaved heroine, she shows a white woman who is physically attacked and victimized by the nineteenth-century rhetoric of femininity as well. Lillian's madness is presented as a helpless retreat from difficult circumstances, its unspoken cause another discontinuity in the text, one which Walker never renders explicit. Vyry's black half sister, Lucy, has been branded and marked for life with an R for runaway. What is intended as a badge of shame is transformed by Lucy into a mark of defiance, an accusation. But the body of Lillian, Lucy's white counterpart, is not inscribed with an R for rape. Because the source of her pain is never acknowledged, she cannot respond to it or overcome it.

With the silencing of Lillian, the Duttons all but drop out of the action, as Vyry's family travels about the South seeking a modest living and freedom from persecution. Like many of the wise women and conjurers in African societies, Vyry becomes a midwife. Her choice of occupation as a black woman birthing mostly white children is another expression of the complicated and problematic interrelationships of white and black cultural (re)production, which are further explored in the following chapters. Furthermore, the text remains punctuated by Vyry's singing, which expresses her emotions—joy, fear, sadness.

In the last section of the novel, Walker turns her focus specifically to violence against black men. Vyry's first husband, Randall Ware, is nearly killed by Klan members, who force him to sell his successful mill. Her son Jim is beaten by her second husband, who resents Jim's laziness. News of this beating precipitates Ware's search for his family. As a result of these and other events, both Jim and Randall become emblems of anger. The rhetoric of the white South has turned more strongly against black men now that there is no economic benefit to be gained from rape and black reproduction, but the men are not silenced.

Indeed, Ware is especially vocal in asking Vyry to choose between her husbands. Her decision to stay with Brown offers a critique of the two-suitor convention of the courtship novel and revises the nineteenth-century slave narrative as well. In American and British courtship novels, the heroine loses or rejects one suitor, only to marry someone who is more admirable and socially acceptable. The heroine's choice establishes her identity and concludes the novel. In Jacobs's narrative, the ex-slave comments self-consciously on how her story differs from romances: "Reader, my story ends in freedom; not in the usual way, with marriage" (201). Walker offers a third alternative. Vyry has no control over her separation from her first lover, and that match is not sanctioned by white society. She does choose a second lover after she is freed; her very ability to make such a choice becomes an expression of her liberation and desire to participate in the creation of new black communities.

In revising these plot elements, Walker is also able to signify on conventions pertaining to both white and African-American literature. This manipulation of conventions recurs in more recent works about slavery, including *Beloved* and *Dessa Rose*. But more importantly, Vyry's choice is significant within Walker's study of the relationship of voice and violence. In announcing her decision to remain with her second husband, Vyry begins a prolonged diatribe, her most extended speech in the novel, about her experience and her feelings toward whites. She seeks to defend herself against Randall Ware's charges that she has compromised the race by serving as a midwife to white women. In the midst of this speech, she bares her back so both men can see the scars for the first time. It is scarcely credible that Innis Brown, by whom Vyry has had several children, would be unaware of the scars; it seems rather that at this point Walker is referring to psychic scars as well as physical ones. The marks record Vyry's history, which in turn exemplifies the experiences of African-American female slaves. Caroline Rody's comment that the tree-like scars on Sethe's back in *Beloved* represent a "family tree" (33) is apposite here as well. Walker turns violence to rhetorical use in telling the story of her foremother.

The baring of Vyry's back and her accompanying verbal self-assertion are linked by more than coincidence. If earlier acts of violence against

Vyry are accompanied by the imposition of white culture on the African body and by narrative discontinuity, from this point on the narrative flows smoothly to its conclusion.

This episode signals a different kind of continuity as well. For the first time, Vyry's body is bared by choice. Although serious scars remain, her wounds have healed and, concomitantly, she has been able to form a family. And it is because of this that she chooses Brown, for "here was the first time I had ever seed a colored family what looked like they was a loving wholeness together, a family what slavery hadn't never broke nor killed. I just couldn't leave there" (408). Rather than compromising the race, Vyry chooses to continue it.

Again, Sievers offers a critique of Vyry's behavior, noting that the heroine looks down on some blacks, especially "low class folks" who "doesn't do nothing but drink and give they money to them bad womens" (*Jubilee* 306). To Sievers, such remarks prove that Vyry "keeps herself and her family apart from the black community" (53); however, instead of being a sign of "the omission of a communal context" (53), Vyry's comments censure blacks who adopt some of the worst behaviors among *whites*. Throughout, she is willing to help others—black and white—who have less than she does. Her decision to stay with Innis Brown, who has sought to create a home in a stable black community, is evidence of her commitment to her people, even as it reflects Walker's position at a time when the role of the black community, feminism, and civil rights were critical topics of public discourse.

The final emphasis on community and continuity is associated with the reemergence of a distinctively African-American voice. Earlier narrative discontinuities, which are linked to ruptures in the African-American female body, are markers of the imposition of Southern white culture. But at the end of her novel, Walker is able to demonstrate that the African voice is not lost. Its existence is evident in the closing scene, which might be out of an African compound as well as an American farm, as Vyry tends her chickens, calling them home, to her home, to roost.

7

Ghostwriting

Authenticity and Appropriation in *Family* and *Beloved*

Since the publication of *Jubilee,* a number of novels by African-American women have incorporated first-person accounts of slavery and thus resemble slave autobiographies. Many of these novels also feature ghosts or the kinds of surreal events found in Margaret Walker's novel. For instance, in the first part of *Jubilee,* the eruptions of the magical signify the continuing presence of an African heritage, even after it has been suppressed. In Toni Morrison's *Beloved* and J. California Cooper's *Family* the supernatural exists as well, as ghosts rise after slave women murder their children to protect them from bondage and suffering. In Morrison's novel, Sethe, the mother, stabs her daughter, who later resurfaces as the ghost, Beloved. Various characters tell parts of the story, and some sections are narrated by Beloved. Once again, the mother's wounds represent the ruptures wrought on her body by slavery, but now they also extend to children's bodies. In *Family,* the children survive the attempted infanticide, but their mother dies. The dead woman narrates the story from beyond the grave.

On one level, these works and others like them might be categorized as ghost stories or ghostwritings, since for at least part of the time, a spirit speaks to the audience. This genre might also be considered ghostwriting in the sense that one woman, a contemporary author, tells the story of another (and her family), giving it shape and significance. *Beloved* is based on the life of a slave named Margaret Garner; works such as *Family* reflect the experiences of countless women, instead of offering an account of a historical individual. Finally, these texts may be considered ghostwriting because, in addition to revisiting the themes and rhetorical devices of slave autobiographies, they construct critiques of white texts about slavery, most notably, Margaret Mitchell's *Gone with the Wind*. Not only do *Jubilee* and *Family* allude to Mitchell's novel, but controversy over Margaret Randall's parodic revision of *Gone with the Wind*, *The Wind Done Gone*, is a reminder of the continuing inequities in cultural transactions involving people of African descent in the United States. While no one sued white authors such as Mitchell and Lydia Maria Child for appropriating stories of blacks, the Margaret Mitchell estate attempted to stop publication of Randall's book, claiming it plagiarized the earlier bestseller. As Toni Morrison pointed out in her deposition for the case, the accusations of piracy risked silencing yet another African American: "To crush the rights of an African-American writer seems to me not only reckless, but arrogant and pathetic. . . . Who controls how history is imagined? Who gets to say what slavery was like for the slaves?" (Reardon).

A brief exploration of the notion of ghostwriting yields valuable insights into this genre of novel, and particularly into the themes and narrative techniques that characterize it. Ghostwriting implicitly involves mediation in the act of composition. The mediator, or ghostwriter, is present to give form and expression to a story that might not otherwise be coherent. Because the ghostwriter helps make a book more readable and often more marketable, he or she participates in the marketing and publication of the work, a cultural product. Moreover, whereas a defining characteristic of nineteenth-century slave narratives is the marker "written by himself" (for instance, in the *Narrative of Frederick Douglass*), ghostwriting is identified by the tag "as told to," a phrase that, significantly, renders manifest the transition from oral to written text. In fact, when contemporary African Americans ghostwrite accounts of slavery, they emphasize the roots of their stories in oral narratives and folklore. As Philip Page comments of *Beloved*, "circularity is part of that oral tradition. . . . the circling, spiraling, and digressive narrative pattern of *Beloved* has parallels in African folk narratives, which tend to be built on repetition" (35).

The content of a ghostwritten work is primarily autobiographical; like most autobiographies, it is by definition teleological. Even though a work such as *Beloved* may appear circular and retain qualities of oral narratives, it is a written text. All the events in the account are included for a specific purpose. In the process of accounting for things as they are, the ghostwriter accents, minimizes, or even omits certain events. Ghostwritten books are most notorious for their treatment of subjects' personal lives; a busy, traveling movie star may be depicted as the ideal parent, celebrities drop years from their ages, and lovers are painted as being infinitely glamorous or utterly abominable. While similar shadings of the truth may be found in any autobiography, the ghostwritten text is inflected by the presence of a mediator who may be responsible for additions or omissions.

Even as the descriptions of the subject's personal relationships render family an important theme in any discussion of ghostwriting, the inevitable presence of mediation evokes questions about authenticity and voice. Another form of mediation occurs when critics such as myself offer interpretations, further complicating the situation. Is the text an authentic expression of the subject? Whose voice is narrating? To whom do we refer when we speak of the "author" (and what does "author" mean in this context)? What are the power relations involving speaker, writer, and critic? What does it mean when Arnold Rampersad, a prominent literary critic and professor, ghostwrites Arthur Ashe's autobiography? How does Alex Haley's involvement in the *Autobiography of Malcolm X* affect our view of the Muslim minister and activist, especially in light of the questions about the authenticity and originality of Haley's *Roots*?

Beloved, Family, and similar recent texts, as well as nineteenth-century slave narratives, challenge the power relations found in celebrity autobiographies "told to" professional writers. Until recently, in most such works by African Americans, the subject is not a powerful individual paying another for a tale of notoriety or adventure. Instead, the situation is virtually reversed. In nineteenth-century narratives, abolitionists and white editors frequently stand in as ghostwriters, adapting the stories of slaves and ex-slaves to the demands of a primarily white audience. Although the white ghostwriter wields considerable power in the production of the text, the black author may find subtle and subversive strategies of resistance. For instance, when editing Harriet Jacobs's *Incidents in the Life of a Slave Girl,* Lydia Maria Child urged the author to include more sensational and titillating details of violence (qtd. in Jacobs 244). Jacobs objected on the grounds that such accounts would reinforce stereotypes of blacks' excessive sexuality (some of these concerns are evident in the gaps and disjunctions in *Jubilee;* however, for Jacobs they are more immediate and pressing, because she is closer to slavery). As shown in the previous chapter, she resisted by providing almost clinically terse and factual descriptions of violence, focusing more on the slaveholders' cruelty than on gruesome descriptions of the violated bodies of slaves. In addition to emphasizing the atrocities perpetrated on black bodies, Jacobs's technique reveals how those bodies are literally overlooked in the focus on the actions of whites.

Contemporary African-American authors of books about slavery attempt to reappropriate the genre by inserting themselves in the storytelling process and referring more obviously to the continuing presence of an African heritage. In writing stories of those who have been silenced, these writers question "the logic that equates black with blank" (Pérez-Torres 94). Such writers as Toni Morrison have considerable fame and prestige, again rendering the power relationship opposite of that found in a more typical ghostwriting situation. Nevertheless, these women offer viewpoints that might not have been included in earlier works. In telling and retelling stories of slavery, they "de-authorize the original figures in power . . . by methods that authorize the teller and the thematically disenfranchised through the foregrounding of their perspectives" (Sale 45). Specifically, they create narrative space for the persistence of Africanisms. Moreover, whereas Jacobs must construct complicated explanations and justifications for her behavior as a mother, Morrison powerfully conveys the slave's perspective, indicating that "to love a child enough to take its life redefines motherhood" (Woidat 187). Despite the dissimilarities then, the term *ghostwriting* provides an illuminating (if imperfect) analogy, one that implicitly links the themes of authenticity, voice, and family.

All three of these themes come into play in an analysis of *Beloved* and *Family*. In using ghosts, Morrison and Cooper imply the continuing presence of the past in the families of their characters, as the dead rise and participate in the experiences of the living. The authors suggest, as well, the importance of literary traditions in their texts, as they revise original slave narratives. Third, and more important, Cooper and Morrison render manifest an essential circumstance of contemporary fiction about slavery: that in a sense, it is always ghostwriting, a ritual of constructing the lives of suppressed others and then speaking for them, of unburying their African roots and exposing them to the light. Like Beloved, each of these characters "inhabits both West African and American cultural spaces; she is at once found and then lost, visible and then invisible, tangibly alive and then a part of language, emblematic of both African survival and

American loss" (Handley 679). By making the interloper an articulated if ghostly presence, the authors can refer to Africa in a manner that is sufficiently complex to expose the problematic intricacies of mediation, the ways in which "Rituals of speaking are politically constituted by power relations of domination, exploitation, and subordination" (Alcoff 15). Fourth, these novelists draw attention to what is lost in the transition from oral to written narrative—specifically, to the "voice of the unwritten self," which, as Houston Baker has indicated in *The Journey Back*, once "subjected to the linguistic codes, literary conventions, and audience expectations of a literate population is perhaps never again the authentic voice of black American slavery" (43).

The problem of locating an "authentic," "unwritten self" gains expression in the climactic scene in *Beloved*, the exorcism of the ghost from the Clearing. Commonly, critics read the episode as a victory for the reunited community of women, which, in claiming its voice, banishes the ghost of slavery's past. Barbara Mathieson, for instance, comments that "the women of the Cincinnati outskirts are also able, as a group, to unite their power and reclaim a member fallen from fellowship. Though alienated from Sethe since her baby's death, the community responds decisively to her personal need" (16–17). Similarly, Jacky Martin notes that "Sethe is finally reintegrated within the Cincinnati community. The outrage caused by her excessive suffering finally provokes the compassion of the people around her" (88–89). And Terry Otten remarks that the "reassertion of community is necessary. . . . Only the help of the community that ostracized them can save Sethe and Denver" (93). In some ways, this mode of reading is compelling, but ultimately it does not satisfy, because it does not consistently account for the effects of mediation or for what is lost when the ghost is exorcised.

Despite the disparate narrative voices in *Beloved*, this type of reading tantalizes with the promise of so many texts regarding slavery, suggesting that there might be a single, authentic voice to be recovered by a unified, homogeneous community of black women. If the women could speak together, one might find an unmediated moment in which the voice of slavery was unaffected by the demands of history, editors, or readers, "a moment of plenitude that would restore us to the real, rich 'thing' itself before discourse touched it" (Spillers, "Changing the Letter" 29). Yet Dwight McBride cautions against "the overly popular catch-all phrases or calls to unity like 'Blacks' and 'the Black community' . . . Such terms function as totalizing descriptors or appellations. They serve to make us think . . . that 'the Black community' is knowable, totalizable, locatable" (139).

In fact, Morrison consistently disappoints such expectations of cohesion and harmony. She suggests that for all its significance, the exorcism does not result from the expression of an "unmediated" or "pure" African-American female voice. Indeed, the women who converge in the Clearing earlier deserted Baby Suggs for serving too many pies, and they bear a variety of fetishes, "what they believed would work. Stuffed in apron pockets, strung around their necks, lying in the space between their breasts. Others brought Christian faith—as shield and sword. Most brought a little of both" (257). Many more stay home. The women do not come with a single set of beliefs. Nor do they propose unselfishly to join another in a communal gesture; their Christian faith operates not only as weapon (sword), but also as shield or self-protection. As I have indicated in an earlier chapter, the scene in the Clearing also encodes the banishment of the *abiku* or spirit child. The "key, the code, the sound that broke the back of words" (261), is a hybrid, mingling African medicine, African-American folk beliefs, and European religion.

Furthermore, the performance in the Clearing, itself a liminal space between the woods and the household, is overseen by the white Mr. Bodwin, who owns the house and once "buried things there. Precious things he wanted to protect" (259). If the ghost represents an Africanized version of the past, the site is also occupied by a different history, that of the white Mr. Bodwin and his family. Therefore, to read the episode simply as a reassertion of black women's identity misses the full complexity of Morrison's intent. As Morrison herself has suggested throughout *Playing in the Dark*, African-American and European-American histories are inextricable, because the African-American "character is used to limn out and enforce the invention and implications of whiteness" (52). Similarly, in "Changing the Letter: The Yokes, the Jokes of Discourse, or, Mrs. Stowe, Mr. Reed," Hortense Spillers argues that any attempt to reconstruct an unmediated expression of slavery must be frustrated by "the dizzying motions of a symbolic enterprise," as "it becomes increasingly clear that the cultural synthesis we call 'slavery' was never homogeneous in its practices and conception, nor unitary in the faces it has yielded" (29).

The very act of representation, or the "symbolic enterprise" (a term

that, significantly, recalls the commodification of culture), can only reflect the multiple and disparate voices of blacks in the diaspora, even as
they merge with or are absorbed by the dominant white discourse. Indeed, reading back through *Beloved*, it quickly becomes evident that
Morrison is deeply involved in exploring and exposing the dangers of the
"symbolic enterprise." She constructs a vision of the relationships between blacks and whites, and then carefully deconstructs it so that we
may see the power imbalances embedded in that relationship. Specifically, whites appropriate blacks as means of cultural, economic, and
sexual reproduction (all of which are inextricable), so that, in essence,
African Americans become the subjects of a ghostwritten or "stage-man-
aged" (Morrison, *Playing in the Dark* 27) version of their own culture,
down to their very families. Sethe makes the ink for the schoolmaster's
writing and serves as subject for his text; Baby Suggs's children are sold
away from her; the nephews of the schoolteacher suck Sethe's milk as if
she were their mother. Morrison complicates the picture when the indi-
gent young white woman, Amy, assists Sethe in birthing Denver, contradicting the stereotype of black women assisting as midwives at the birth
of white babies, while retaining a class dimension.

Every time Morrison offers a picture of relations among blacks and
whites, she shifts the perspective, disrupting any attempt at understanding the "symbolic enterprise." For instance, as Michelle Pagni Stewart
indicates, "contrary to Moynihan's man who runs away, Paul D runs *to*
Sethe," while the childless white family at Sweet Home is as dysfunc-
tional as the household at 124 Bluestone Road (99). Often, Morrison unsettles by switching narrators and offering a new version of part of the
story, one that ascribes a different meaning to an event or circumstance,
such as the scar on Sethe's back. But the dangers of settling on a single
perspective are also evident when one realizes that the white Bodwins,
who help slaves escape and provide a home for them, display a grotesque
representation of blackness by their back door, "a blackboy's mouth full
of money. His head was thrown back farther than a head could go, his
hands were shoved in his pockets. Bulging like moons, two eyes were all
the face he had above the gaping red mouth. His hair was a cluster of
raised, widely spaced dots made of nail heads. And he was on his knees.
His mouth, wide as a cup, held the coins needed to pay for a delivery or
some other small service, but could just as well have held buttons, pins or

crab-apple jelly. Painted across the pedestal he knelt on were the words 'At Yo Service'" (255).

This quotidian object, a small work that might pass for something between kitsch and folk art, radically alters our view of the Bodwins from benevolent abolitionists to patronizing individuals who set blacks in their place at the back door. Critics have interpreted this figure variously. For Rafael Pérez-Torres, the "image at once suggests commercial exchange . . . , servitude (the kneeling figure), and the grotesquely twisted neck of a lynching victim" (97). Marianne DeKoven points out that for all their assistance and risk-taking, the Bodwins "do not see or treat African Americans as equal to whites" (115). To her, the statuette has other significances: "Beyond exploitation, dehumanization, degradation, reification, and theft of labor, this remarkable figure suggests the tortures both of slavery and postwar violence against African Americans . . . . The nails driven into the head suggest at once a generalized violence and also the more drastic sort of bodily imprisonment" (116). My own interpretation is that the artifact reinforces the stereotypes that blacks cannot handle money (after all, the coins all but choke the boy) and must be kept on their knees to service whites with items of small value. Finally, the nail heads that form the statue's hair parody the nails decorating Kongo carved figures, even as they recall the crucifixion. Viewed through their back door as it were, the white family embodies the problematic role of abolitionists as mediators in black cultural production. As helpful as they appear, the Bodwins exhibit a representation of African-American culture that is highly derogatory.

Moreover, as Linden Peach has pointed out, "the impotence of many of the white liberals to deliver the promise of emancipation is illustrated in the way in which Edward Bodwin constructs a text of his own past as an abolitionist" (99). When the Bodwins come to the Clearing, then, they no longer seem so beneficent, and we must question their motives. Are they merely present to gaze with fascination on a spectacle of otherness? Have they come to reclaim their land? In some ways, Sethe's initial misreading is accurate; the scene does repeat the ominous approach of the schoolteacher.

Thus contradicting our initial impression of the Bodwins, Morrison inserts herself as mediator in the production of the text, exposing the complex motivations of the abolitionists. She reappropriates the story of slavery, so that even as the women banish the ghost of Beloved, she exorcises the specter of white intervention.

While questions of authenticity remain unresolved by the critical readings of *Beloved* cited above, another aspect common to interpretations of the novel is equally problematic. Specifically, critics often and rightly assert that Morrison gives voice to those who have been silenced or rendered invisible (see, for example, Karla Holloway's "*Beloved:* A Spiritual" 516–17 and Horvitz 157), and imply that Sethe in particular has lost her voice. Similar theories are found in analyses of other texts as well, including Deborah McDowell's "Negotiating between Tenses: Witnessing Slavery after Freedom—*Dessa Rose*" and Abena P. B. Busia's "Words Whispered over Voids: A Context for Black Women's Rebellious Voices in the Novel of the African Diaspora." But if voice is lost, where does it go? In *Beloved,* what are the connections among the wall of sound, women's voices, and the disappearance of the succubus?

A close reading of *Beloved* suggests that prior to the exorcism, Sethe finds expression in the ghost's many, contradictory impulses (and this constitutes a more literal form of ghostwriting in the text). According to Stephanie Demetrakopolous, "Sethe's guilt has recreated Beloved" (56), and the spirit acts out her mother's emotions. The ghost succeeds in frightening away the sons who remind Sethe of the infanticide, acts out her lust for Paul D, and, with her voracious appetite, ultimately relieves the guilt Sethe has felt for years. Significantly, the ghost takes form when Sethe reconnects with Paul D, and, in beginning a new love, is likely to forget the past; Beloved performs Sethe's rage, her grief, and most of all, her fear of forgetting.

As a ghost, Beloved has no material existence. She has risen from a word—not intended as a name—on a gravestone ("Everybody knew what she was called, but nobody anywhere knew her name" 274). Thus, sound that can "break the back of words" is the most appropriate weapon against Beloved, forcing her back into Sethe, her memory, and her identity. When Sethe is returned to herself, it is not the child, but Sethe who is her own "best thing" (273).

Finally, in interpreting the novel's conclusion as a kind of victory for the community, it is tempting to ignore or deny the fact that the infanticide is repeated. Terry Otten, for instance, reads the conclusion as "the recovery of order and wholeness" for Sethe and the community (93). Yet Morrison indicates the deceptive nature of that wholeness, for it is dependent on a definition of community which excludes the past and its dead: "In the place where long grass opens, the girl who waited to be loved and cry shame erupts into her separate parts, to make it easy for the chewing laughter to swallow her all away" (274). Beloved relinquishes her ravenous hunger to the appetites of the living, whose "chewing" is at once reminiscent of the symbolic sacrifice of communion and of the cannibalistic urges of a group determined to survive. Indeed, in contrast to Otten, critics such as Marianne Hirsch emphasize the "costs of familial reconstruction" (198), because Sethe must once again lose her child.

The inhabitants of Bluestone Road and the vicinity have reconstructed a version of history that excludes the violent story of the child: "They forgot her like a bad dream. After they made up their tales, shaped and decorated them" (274), because "it was not a story to pass on" (275). The conclusion reminds us that any narrative, especially concerning family, is itself a fiction and that alternative fictions are equally possible (in fact, the story is passed on and Beloved's name is the last word in the book). In choosing or "passing on" one fiction or version of biography, one risks erasing others, such as the story of the *abiku*, perpetuating what Teresa de Lauretis labels the violence of rhetorical representation (240).

By reading counter to several interpretations of *Beloved*, I have hoped to indicate that the contemporary narrative about slavery by African-American women is a mixed genre, asserting multivocality rather than an essentialist identity. On the most obvious level, the story is told in various voices, including those of Sethe, Denver, and Beloved. But it is also multivocal in revealing the complicated layers of mediation in the act of narration. Morrison inserts four manifestations of ghostwriting in her text: first, as whites appropriate the African American as "surrogate and enabler" (Morrison, *Playing in the Dark* 51) in the creation of a racially inflected culture; second, as the contemporary African-American author reappropriates the story of slavery and speaks for her ancestors; third, as communities and individuals "pass on" limited versions of history; and fourth, as ghostly African presences within the fiction inscribe or voice alternative plots.

Instead of supporting the view that slavery silenced black women with its violence and oppression, this genre reveals how voices find alternative channels, ones that might be destructive, but are powerful nonetheless. The latter point is critical, for it enables authors to assert their continuity with an African past and traditions. It allows a rendition in fiction of the point scholars have increasingly emphasized: that African cultures were not silenced or erased by the slave trade, but rather that Africans in America found strategies of resistance and expression. Finally, in stressing that any narrative presents only one of many possible fictions, Morrison also exposes the inadequacy of stereotypical notions of the "nuclear family," which read Sethe merely as a child murderer by decontextualizing the complex circumstances surrounding her past. As Gloria T. Randle has argued, the truth is that "Sethe is conspicuous not because she kills her child, but because of the ferocity of her mother-love" (291).

J. California Cooper's *Family* provides another example of the fusion of genres and traditions in a novel about family. Cooper's long dedication, which includes a multitude of "special others" ranging from Dostoevski to Muhammad Ali, from Richard Pryor to Beethoven, and from Cleopatra to her cat, immediately indicates the novel's hybrid nature. Cooper's novel most obviously combines four strains: it refers to African stories and traditions, it revises nineteenth-century slave narratives, it "signifies" on white novels about slavery, and it alludes to other contemporary novels by African-American women, most noticeably those by Toni Morrison. Because the latter two strains or influences are themselves informed by nineteenth-century slave narratives as well as by each other, the heritage of Cooper's work is as rich and complicated as that of her characters.

Situated at the intersection of these genres and traditions, *Family* constitutes a kind of meta-discourse on voice, authenticity, and race. Its primary modes, disruption and revision, are identified by Mae Gwendolyn Henderson as "a model for reading black and female literary expression" (131).

Family opens with a pronounced divergence from the realistic mode of nineteenth-century slave narratives. Instead of beginning with the standard account of the slave's birth and parentage, Cooper recounts a parable about the earth mother, her child, and the sun. The earth mother asks, "And when does a tree bear fruit that is not its own?" Her child responds, "never," and the sun explains, "everyone knows that. That's what makes a family!" This parable, which sets the story in a mythic realm of universal beings, is deconstructed by the remainder of the narrative, which demonstrates that a woman can make a family out of children who are not her own. Thus from its very inception, Cooper's novel asks us to question the nature of myth. And the beginning of the first chapter raises questions about textuality and orality as it echoes Houston Baker's remarks about the difference between oral and printed narratives. As Cooper indicates, "[history] lived, not written, is such a thing not to understand always, but to marvel over" (1).

The opening of the main plot submerges us in history as it takes us to Africa. The narrator traces her lineage back before the slave trade, noting that her blood is Egyptian, Greek, African, and Italian. This immediately unsettles any notion of an "authentic," original African self. In fact, when Cooper indicates African influences in her characters' lives, they are present as a single level in a multilayered, densely textured work. The characters know how to use different herbs as medicine, as we learn when one of the white characters asks for an abortifacient. The speaker as well as her daughter Always, who is in many ways the main character, are repeatedly associated with chickens and seek refuge in old chicken houses. Although one could read this circumstance simply as an indicator of the women's low status, a more Africanist interpretation seems possible, given the prominence of poultry in many African societies and their particular associations with women and domesticity, as described in chapter 2.

These references to Africa constitute only one strand of Cooper's text. In many ways, Cooper's work does follow the traditions of slave autobiographies, with the narrator describing her childhood, her master's advances, her mistress's hatred and jealousy, and her attempt to kill herself and her children rather than to have them live in slavery. As in the narratives studied by James Olney, Cooper's story incorporates an account of a brave male slave who withstands incredible torture because he has learned to read (153). Later, the speaker describes the struggles of her family after the Civil War, as well as their continuing relationships toward their enslavers.

A final generic feature of the novel is that the characters, like the protagonists of many autobiographies and novels about slaves, are light enough to pass as a result of generations of women having been raped by their masters. In fact, as the story proceeds, it becomes clear that the white family and black family are inextricably interwoven, to the extent that it is impossible to separate the two, or even to make distinctions between the races. The relationships among characters are so complicated that readers may become confused, but this confusion ultimately serves

Cooper's purpose. By mingling black and white until they are indistinguishable, Cooper challenges essentialist definitions of race, even as she exposes and undermines a determining feature of the slave system—that there can indeed be any logical differentiation between the white family and the black family. She reveals the arbitrariness of white constructs of race and of ghostwritten versions of an Africanist culture.

In mingling the two families, Cooper draws audaciously on not only nineteenth-century African-American autobiographies and novels about slavery, but also white texts. In doing so, she engages in a process that resembles the second form of ghostwriting in *Beloved*—a reappropriation or revision of white fictions about race. This process is most apparent in the central episode of the novel. In this scene, a slave woman exchanges her child for the baby of her mistress, her son's half brother. The "white" baby is raised as a slave who works hard and looks after his half sibling, who is spoiled and terribly corrupt. The story thus emphasizes how racially typed behaviors are cultural products.

The plot element of babies exchanged at birth has a history in popular nineteenth-century novels, especially in Lydia Maria Child's *Romance of the Republic.* Cooper seems to allude consciously to Child's text, so marked are the similarities. While Child's heroines are named after flowers, Cooper's are named after fruits. In Child's novel, as in Cooper's, the babies are switched at birth, and the black child raised as white is spoiled and corrupted. Significantly, in Child's version, the "white" boy is ultimately redeemed, and he forgives his mother, though he is conveniently killed in the Civil War. The child who has been raised as black is never told of his heritage, and he is packed off to Europe by his black relatives, so his presence and resemblance to whites raise no opportunities for exposure or embarrassment.

Child's story reappears prominently elsewhere, including in *Pudd'n-head Wilson* by Mark Twain. I have not been able to trace this plot feature to earlier novels by blacks, only by whites. And it is a highly threatening story for some whites, implying as it does the arbitrary nature of racial distinctions as well as the corruptive nature of slavery. Both Child and Cooper send the white child raised as black off to Europe to be educated in the ways of white society, implying that culture rather than essentialist definitions underlie conceptions of race. Twain, too, indicates that the new heir (the white child raised in slavery) faces deficiencies in education, and that his "manners" rather than his essence reflect "the negro quarter" (225). In doubting essentialist definitions of race, these authors simultaneously question the notion of racial authenticity.

What is perhaps most significant is Cooper's treatment of the corrupted son. Doak, Junior, once he is told of his racial heritage, cannot forgive Always, his slave mother. He focuses his energies on dismantling the estate she has amassed and joins the Klan. Initially, it appears that Always is punished for her reconstruction of family that exposes the cruelty and randomness of white figurations of race. Ultimately, however, Cooper makes it clear that those very conceptions of race, instilled in Doak, are responsible for the violence and corruption.

Cooper further complicates the notion of family when Always's white half sister, Loretta, has a child by Always's son Sephus (who is Loretta's half nephew and stepson). Loretta then gives this child, Apple, to Always to raise as her own. While this might be read as a reification of the Mammy stereotype, Always's refusal to remain subservient contradicts this possibility.

A final white influence in this novel is *Gone with the Wind*, which Cooper rewrites in Always's dedication to the land and desire for wealth. Cooper wrenches the land away from whites temporarily when Always names cows and fields after the children who were sold to purchase them. In doing so, the landscape is inscribed with blackness; slave labor becomes a visible and linguistic marker, whereas Mitchell tends to erase it in her emphasis on Scarlett's single-minded pursuit of land. Cooper even goes so far as to revise the famous scene in which Scarlett mutters an oath as she crumbles the earth of Tara in her fingers. In Cooper's version of the scene, Always "reached down to the rich black earth and took up a handful. She stared at it, rollin it round in her hands" (201). Addressing God, she asks "do freedom mean I got to leave my home?" (201), and later, "She raised the dirt to the sky, tears flowin. 'It mine, it be mine, it be me, Lord'" (202).

Cooper's bold refashioning of one of the quintessential white representations of Southern plantation life is melded with her equally fascinating adaptations of elements from novels by her contemporaries. Most obviously, Cooper refers to Morrison's *Sula* and *Beloved*. Always's children are named after fruits, and the story of her Plum alludes consciously to the story of Plum in *Sula*. Morrison's Plum is saved from death when his mother reaches into his cramped bowels with her last teaspoon of lard to loosen them; he later turns out to be a ne'er-do-well, whose death his mother Eva hastens. Plum's story exemplifies at once the lengths to which a black mother will go to save her child's life and the limits of her sacrifices.

Cooper's Plum is a little slave girl being raised by her sister, Always. Her mother is dead, and her brother has escaped. When Always is sold, Plum stows away on the bottom of the wagon carrying Always. She is literally ground to pieces by the motion of the wheels and axles. Plum dies wordlessly, for she is afraid to scream or otherwise announce her presence. Plum's death is accompanied by her sister's rape in the woods. Afterwards, Always is unable to bury Plum promptly because her new owner insists that she cook his dinner first. In her appropriation of Morrison's story, Cooper reinscribes it with gender and makes whites' role in the literal tearing apart of black youth visible. While in Morrison's text a racist economic system is implicitly behind Eva Peace's inability to care for her child and Plum's giving up of volition, Cooper renders such white intervention visible.

Even more, Cooper comments on *Beloved*. The speaker tries to kill herself and her children in a scene that resembles Sethe's infanticide, but succeeds only in destroying herself. As a result, most of the novel is told by a ghost. The fear of slavery thus robs the children of a mother, further fracturing the African family in America.

By making the ghostly mediator of the narrator an articulated presence in the novel, Cooper can point to the problematic intricacies of mediation. For instance, the narrator takes a nap and misses sixty years of the characters' stories, indicating and parodying the way authors of historical narratives include or highlight only events that interest them. Furthermore, by making the ghost storyteller a black woman, Cooper confirms her reappropriation of white versions of slavery and highlights the status of black women as invisible presences, virtual ghosts, in white culture. Finally, Cooper's narrator, like those in *Beloved* and Sherley Anne Williams's *Dessa Rose*, insists that the story is being told, even as we hold the book in our hands. This contradiction forces us to consider the difference between the oral and written narrative—and, most of all, what lies (in every sense of the word) in between.

Despite the boldness of Cooper's narrative and formal experiments, the ending of the novel remains ambiguous and ultimately unsatisfying. The family is scattered, many of its members passing for white: "All my family, my blood, is mixed up now. They don't even all know each other.

I just hope they don't never hate or fight each other, not knowin who they are" (231). Family is so spread out that it is unrecognizable; it has extended itself so far that its distinctive identity is lost. Not surprisingly, Africanisms have virtually disappeared from the text by this point.

Moreover, Doak's dismantling of his black mother's estate contradicts the facility of the closing words: "all these people livin are brothers and sisters and cousins. All these beautiful different colors! We! . . . We the human Family. God said so! FAMILY" (231). Cooper's allusion to the biblical act of creation as a linguistic gesture emphasizes that her claim of unity, too, is verbal. She reminds us as well that the "God" and "human Family" to which Doak refers are the inventions of white Christians, and that historically the latter was often construed to exclude people with African blood. The statement also reminds us of the slippage between "unwritten" and textual experience. In "history lived, not written," sons may still hate their mothers, and children may deny their African heritage. The unsuccessful assertion of oneness indicates a longing, almost a nostalgia, for unity that may never be achieved, similar to the desire for community evident in so many readings of *Beloved*. Even as Cooper deconstructs the myth of family, the ideal lingers, another ghost haunting the space of narrative.

The conclusion of Cooper's novel expresses the interwoven dilemmas of authenticity, relationship, and appropriation present in her work and Morrison's. *Jubilee* concludes with a picture of a united African-American family with a strong, loving mother and an allusion to a traditional African compound. Morrison and Cooper construct critiques of prescriptive, mythic definitions of black motherhood. In addition, they contradict any notion of the family and community as easily delineated entities to be inscribed as other in political, economic, and cultural discourses around us. By exposing white appropriations of African-American history and then revising them, these women disrupt and complicate popular narratives, gaining authority as the ghostwriters of their stories. That this task is never fully accomplished is, ironically, an achievement in itself, for to force narrative into a clear and unambiguous closure is, as both authors indicate, to reduce the diversity of the African-American experience to a univocal, and hence unsatisfying, version of history, one that excludes Africa.

8

"We Wasn't Nothing"

Leadership and Vision in *Dessa Rose*

Dessa Rose, by Sherley Anne Williams, combines many of the features of the contemporary novels discussed in the previous two chapters. The book recounts the stories of a woman slave who escapes and rebels against whites, a former slave who has an affair with a white woman, and a group of ex-slaves who make money by repeatedly selling themselves back into slavery and escaping. All three strands of the narrative record acts of resistance and empowerment by African Americans; these accounts gain complexity as they are told from multiple and often conflicting viewpoints. The multivocal nature of the novel that begins with the narrative of a white man raises issues of authenticity and appropriation similar to those found in *Beloved.* The disfiguring beating of the heroine after the death of her husband serves as an initiation into violence, while scars turn her body into a text, as in *Jubilee.* In this way, Williams's book echoes the intertextual qualities of other contemporary fiction about slavery. *Dessa Rose* signifies on *Jane Eyre* with its inclusion of a story about a manor that has no attic or second floor. Like Grace Poole, its red-haired white inhabitant is considered mad, and she looks after a hidden, darker-skinned woman who slides in and out of delirium. Moreover, *Dessa Rose* refers not only to original slave narratives and historical documents, but also to white persons' accounts of slavery: in this case, Margaret Mitchell's *Gone with the Wind* and William Styron's *The Confessions of Nat Turner.* In fact, Williams deliberately set out to write a critique of Styron's novel when she began *Dessa Rose.* Williams also undercuts *Roots* by Alex Haley (who in turn was charged but not convicted of plagiarizing *Jubilee*). The long title of the book about slave revolts written by the white character Adam Nehemiah is abbreviated to *Roots.* Finally, the white character's name inverts that of Nehemiah Adams, author of a novel titled *Sable Thunder*, which, significantly, argued that "a system which makes Uncle Toms out of African savages is not an unmixed evil" (qtd. in Diedrich, "Mastering American Destiny" 254).

In an essay titled "Some Implications of Womanist Theory," Williams also indicates an awareness of the African roots of literature by authors such as herself: "I am an Afro-Americanist and enough of an Africanist to know something of the enormous differences between African literatures and Afro-American literature, and something, too, of the remarkable parallels and similarities between them" (68). *Dessa Rose* exemplifies these distinctions, because it contains Africanisms even as it emphasizes the unique experiences of African Americans. Moreover, the novel illustrates the importance of race in expressing a continuity between what is African and African-American. At first glance, the book appears to contain only superficial Africanisms; it seems to depict a time when slavery has suppressed almost all of the characters' history. When the heroine's husband Kaine lies dying, she calls on Legba for help, but the invocation seems almost random, given that she calls on "all the names I know bout, thought bout" (12). Additionally, the text is generally unmarked by the elements of supernatural found in *Beloved, Family,* and *Mama Day,* and it lacks most of the direct references to Africa found in *Jubilee.* The few exceptions include references to the use of roots to prevent conception (42), cause abortions (42), and silence others (11), as well as mentions of chickens and their closeness to the black characters (200). The text also contains repeated mentions of intimacy among women when they are braiding and arranging each other's hair (see, for instance, 84, 257–58), and the former slave Nathan tells his white lover Ruth marvelous stories about "animals that talked, trees that had spirits, people who refused to die, and tales that he swore were 'true to life'" (157). When Dessa escapes, Nehemiah argues that her flight was not the result of "spirits or 'haints'" (69), contradicting other European-Americans who suspect magic has been at work.

In fact, the book is deeply marked by Africanisms. Even though Kaine's name recalls Cain of the Old Testament, he gets his banjo and music from an African. The instrument is an important link to his heritage: "if he have it, home be his and the banjo be his. Cept he ain't got no home, so he just onliest have the banjo" (33). The banjo becomes a bridge to Africa and freedom in much the same way as Tea Cake's guitar functions in Hurston's *Their Eyes Were Watching God*. One of the first indications that whites do not know how to "read" blacks in Williams's novel is that neither the slave master nor the writer Nehemiah can comprehend the importance of the banjo to Kaine; Dessa has to explain to Nehemiah that "when Masa break it, it seem like he break Kaine" (34).[1] He silences Kaine figuratively with the destruction of the musical instrument and silences him literally when he kills the black man. The white mistress and Nehemiah can understand these events only in terms of sexual rivalry, a motif that is repeated among the blacks as well when Dessa objects to Nathan's affair with Ruth.

The first part of the novel also includes African-inspired call and response among the slaves in songs that hold together the community and encode resistance (Sievers 55). Thus, orality (in the form of Dessa's interruptions of Nehemiah's discourse as well as song) serves to reappropriate language by disrupting its apparent meaning. The spirituals invoke common Christian images, but references to the flight of a dove (31) have significance in African and African-American cultures as well. These birds might just as well be allusions to the story of the Flying African or the *aje*'s night flight. Moreover, pigeons, which are related to doves, are notable in Gelede iconography because they represent "good luck" (Lawal 240). Later, the call and response preceding Dessa's escape from captivity refers to going home to heaven (64), code not only for physical freedom but also for the liberty to return to an Afrocentric culture. Thus, the song is doubly masked.

This chapter will extend the discussion of the way in which contemporary novels about slavery record contact and conflicts between European-American and African cultures by considering Williams's novel from three perspectives. While much scholarship regarding this work has focused on the importance of orality and literacy, an approach that brings Africanism into consideration must emphasize sight as well, particularly in scenes in which bodies are exposed or in which characters are out of their minds in one way or another. Therefore, I will first take a closer look at the motif of loss of consciousness, which is also apparent in *Jubilee*. Second, I will reveal how the novel constructs a matrix of imagery pertaining to race and visibility. Third, I will consider the novel from an Africanist perspective, demonstrating how the prior two readings are supported by and in turn illuminate this final angle of reading. For example, the novel seeks to disrupt the commodification of humans as capital in the exchange of slaves, and this unsettling is attained through reference to the market place in Gelede. An Africanist reading will also involve a return to the emphasis on black women as leaders and, specifically, attention to how Dessa *rises*. As Elizabeth Beaulieu has indicated, her full name, Dessa Rose, indicates her growth (52). During the course of the novel, she emerges as a female leader as strong as those in Gelede and Sande. Dessa bonds with Harker, who proposes the false slave sales; similarly, in Yoruba myth, the trickster Esu is linked to the *aje* and said by some to endow her with maleficent powers (Lawal 31).

Yet Dessa seems powerless at the novel's opening. In an ironic inversion of Yoruba custom, she wears shackles and chains instead of anklets. Her situation is underscored by relentless thoughts of her own degradation. She grimly realizes that a white woman would have passed out if she had had to watch her husband brutally beaten. While a white woman would faint at "any little thang," Dessa can only "guess" how it would feel to lose consciousness in that way (9). Like Sojourner Truth in her renowned address and Vyry tending the Duttons, Dessa draws attention to her race and gender by distinguishing between her treatment and the privileges accorded to white women. Dessa's statement shows a canny understanding of the ways in which white women could turn the cult of true womanhood with its emphasis on women's fragility into a strategic means of exerting power over others. As a result, envy and scorn tinge her remarks. No such means of resistance are open to her at this point.

For white women, lack of consciousness presents a means to ignore the truth. The blacks at the Glen consider Ruth "touched" and "strange in the head" because she denies that her husband has abandoned her, and she fails to obey all the strictures regulating relations between blacks and whites (121). Indeed, prior to Dessa's arrival, Ruth has frequently retreated into depression, and she has ignored or refused to see many of the realities surrounding her. Only when she grows closer to Dessa and Nathan does Ruth begin to acknowledge her own complicity, especially in violence against slaves: "she had accepted this as long as she didn't hear the screams. Rufel bit her lip. Could she be that blind again?" (161). In her ruminations, Ruth equates lack of awareness with blindness.

Dessa defines fainting as being "out of the world." For her, it offers an opportunity to flee with the mind from the oppressions of everyday life in a culture dominated by European-American men. She experiences a prolonged episode of obliviousness after she arrives at the Glen, during which she dreams of her youth with her family. When Dessa first wakes in Ruth's bed, she is confused and frightened by the light and whiteness of the room, as well as by Ruth's pale face. Quickly, she falls back into unconsciousness. Nicole King distinguishes Dessa's condition from Rufel's by suggesting that the latter is in a "semi-sane state," while Dessa "is awakening from a state of semi-consciousness and delirium "(361). Yet Dessa's state differs from that experienced by the white woman because it offers an escape into memories of a black community. In fact, for a while Dessa believes that the dreams are her reality and that her existence in the white woman's bed is the dream. As she begins to heal, Dessa discovers she can use her condition to her own benefit by feigning unconsciousness. In fact she is watching those around her, "cautious in her waking" (119). This reverses the power relations of the first part of the text when she is the object of Nehemiah's attention. While Nehemiah's prejudices keep him from truly seeing or understanding Dessa, "she knew she could understand what the white woman said if she would let herself" (119). Her use of consciousness as a tool of resistance becomes apparent when she realizes that "if she understood the white woman, she would have to" respond in some way (119). Dessa has learned a strategy to protect a small place for herself, a place where she can feel part of a family of African descent.

In the final scene of the novel, the reversal in the use of unconsciousness or madness is completed when Nehemiah's behavior is categorized as mad—and indeed, he ultimately seems completely out of control. Dessa is well aware that Nehemiah's unkempt appearance will work against him, as will the improbability of his story (even though it is true). Just as Nehemiah's prejudices have rendered him incapable of truly seeing Dessa, so the code of femininity blinds the sheriff to Ruth's trickery. The descent into madness by a white person when his power is usurped is prepared for by Wilson's delusions after his coffle has been attacked (15). The women's victory is not complete, however; walking together after dark, they cannot "hug each other" (256) or make visible their closeness.

Following the allusions to madness or unconsciousness, readers may trace Dessa's increasing power as the novel progresses, as well as the way that her own unconsciousness reconnects her to her heritage. These references are also linked to a network of images pertaining to race and color, which are evident in the numerous evocations of whiteness in the text. These, too, reflect Dessa's shifting role in the narrative.

Throughout the text, black and white identities are contingent. Dessa's indignities make Nehemiah feel superior, while according to Nicole King, "Dessa's identity as a slave is dependent upon Rufel's identity as a slave owner" (364). The narrative also records Ruth's growing realization that she depends on the runaways who manage her estate to maintain her fiction of being a white woman of rank and property.

More specifically, whiteness resides primarily in several sites: the pages of the text, Nehemiah's notebook, Ruth's bed, and Ruth's skin and milk. Whiteness is a quality of paper, fresh fabric, and (linguistically, if not actually) European-American flesh, from which those of African descent are denied access for much of the narrative. Although whiteness is not the same as blankness, the two are often linked in the novel, and both carry negative and positive value. As mentioned previously, in African iconography, white is the color of initiation and death. Blankness may refer to potential and to emptiness, like the spiritual vacuity in Nehemiah's eyes (189). In European-American cultures, blankness is linked to whiteness and purity as well. As Harker points out when he teaches the others some French, in that language "'blank' was white" (201).

Dessa refers to whiteness in the opening remarks quoted above, which are transcribed into Nehemiah's "hastily scratched notes" and then onto the paper of his journal "as though he remembered them word for word" (10). The white page of the journal, then, is a mediated document two removes from the speaker. The ink inscribes the story of a woman of African descent, anticipating the schoolteacher's notebook in *Beloved*. Nehemiah himself is in a predatory position, aiming to profit from his book financially and socially. When he hears about a root that prevents conception, he imagines how he might benefit from that, too. Yet there is another text as well, the scarring on Dessa's thighs and genitals that "bespoke a history of misconduct" (13). Inscribed on flesh like the narratives borne by Vyry and Sethe, these marks reflect the imposition of white culture, and Mae Gwendolyn Henderson asserts that such scars "attempt to deprive the slave woman of her femininity and render the surface of her skin a parchment upon which meaning is etched by the whip (pen) of white patriarchal society" (127). Yet the text of white violence fails to erase the women's femininity, for the scars can be read only in metaphors and similes derived from European-American domesticity. Vyry's scars resemble a "tuck in a dress" (145) and a "washboard" (406) while Dessa's are "corduroyed" (245) and take the form of "some kind of garment" or a "mutilated cat face" (166).[2] These descriptions reveal not only the limits of the characters' experiences but also the inadequacy of language to conceptualize the pain and suffering marked by the scars as well as the European-American context in which they were inflicted.

The black body also marks the whiteness of Ruth's bed. Dessa focuses almost obsessively on the contrast between her flesh and Ruth's. She is initially surprised to find herself supine in the stranger's bed, but this does not fully account for the fact that the word *white* recurs eight times in one paragraph. The tint is rendered palpable and oppressive through repetition: "Dessa watched the white woman. She knew she had lain like this before, body rigid, heart hammering against her ribs, watching the white woman through half-closed lids. The white woman stood at the door. This, too, had happened before . . . maybe [ellipsis in original]. A white woman moving quietly around her bed—*bed*? . . . She was in a bed, a white woman *white* stared at her from the shadows of some room—She would be still. The white woman moved. Her heart thudded in her chest. The white woman passed beyond her line of vision" (83). This passage renders whiteness visible and other, rather than normative. Part of Dessa's growing power is that she can draw attention to and name whiteness, whereas the emphasis in Nehemiah's narrative was on her darkness, signifying an African heritage. In another reversal, Ruth's nursing and naming of Dessa's baby echo the baby exchanges in Cooper's *Family*. It is no wonder, then, that Dessa resents having her child nursed by Ruth. To her, this is just another intrusion of whiteness on black bodies. She particularly objects to it because Ruth has so clearly limited herself to a superficial knowledge of slavery, her life resembling one of the caricatures she is so quick to draw.

Two scenes of exposure and racial difference in the bedroom—the first when Rufel sees Dessa's scars for the first time, and the second when Dessa interrupts Rufel's sexual encounter with Nathan—revise the voyeurism in Nehemiah's gaze on Dessa's body in the first part of the novel. Ruth is first introduced to Dessa's scars through men's accounts—Nehemiah's, Harker's, and Nathan's, signaling Dessa's lack of control over her own being. She first views the marks in a mirror, startled by the contrast between Dessa's white European-style undergarments and black African skin. She is literally and metaphorically incapable of reading their message for herself until her sympathy rises. Once again, a black text, representing the experience of a person of African descent, has been unreadable to a white person. Yet, since this scene immediately precedes the first sexual encounter between Ruth and Nathan, readers might argue that the episode also helps her to see and accept blackness.

The interruption is reversed when Dessa walks in on the two and refuses to call Ruth by her proper name, indicating her unwillingness to understand the scene before her. In an assertion echoed by Morrison's *Playing in the Dark,* Dessa notices that Nathan's skin brings out the whiteness of his surroundings. Once again, she focuses almost exclusively on whiteness, remembering, "Nathan sprawled in whiteness, white sheets, white pillows, white bosom. All he did was make them look whiter. He wasn't nothing but a mark on them. That's what we was in white folks' eyes, nothing but marks to be used, wiped out. Hadn't I seed it in Mistress, in that white man's eyes under the tree? We wasn't nothing to them" (185). Dessa equates Nathan's body on the sheets with marks or writing, but she does not perceive this as empowering. She argues that Nathan's black presence on the sheets may be erased or used just as the man of European descent interprets and thus controls Dessa's story on the page. But Nehemiah's text cannot comprehend (in any sense of the word) Dessa's story and, similarly, this passage is elusive and ambiguous. In this case, the two double negatives in the vernacular, "he wasn't nothing" and "we wasn't nothing" suggest in fact that the African Americans *are* something, and that their marks or presence are necessary. Instead of using the black body for the inscription of the cruelty of whiteness, the former slave mistress needs the runaways to create her own life story.

This interdependence is emphasized in the scene in which Mr. Oscar forces his way into Ruth's bedroom. Dessa chases him away with pillows, turning whiteness against itself. Afterwards, she realizes that Ruth resembles "a ghost in that white nightgown" (219), because her personhood has been invisible to the white man. In his eyes, Ruth leaves no mark against the linens; indeed, she is "white as a sheet" (240) and blends in. This scene is critical in Dessa's emergence as a leader and in her growing understanding of the similarities between herself and the white woman. Significantly, the two women resume sharing a bed thereafter, as they had at home.

The images of whiteness, blackness, scarring, and blankness come together later in the climactic scene at the sheriff's office, a scene which also brings to a close the motif of commodification in the novel, even though it is not precipitated by the false slave trades themselves so much as by Dessa's presence on the streets. When Nehemiah finds and grabs Dessa, she does not recognize him immediately, so unimportant has he become to her, and, in a reversal of the novel's opening, she perceives him as animal-like with a pointed beak (248). What she finally recognizes is the emptiness of his eyes in which she finds "no reflection" of herself (248), appropriately, as the white man does not really see her. She passes out when he hits her, losing herself to darkness rather than memory, coming to in the sheriff's office.

In the ensuing scene, language and vision repeatedly come into play, sometimes paralleling and other times opposing each other, so that ultimately one cannot count on any congruence between them. Dessa claims never to have seen the white man before (243). According to Nehemiah, who wields the written text of the runaway slave poster, the sight of Dessa's genitals will prove his accusations. She must counter his version of her own story. And Dessa must find a way to draw attention away from her own verbal slip when she calls Ruth by her real name instead of the one she has adopted as part of her disguise. With Ruth's arrival, the interplay becomes even more complex as the code of white womanhood intersects with racial tensions and "ironically turns out to be a space for agency" (Sievers 108).

Even though Aunt Chole plays a minimal role in the narrative, she is critically important. Dessa is frightened to have this woman see her scars, while the white people in the room argue about taking Chole's word. However, the aged woman is an eruption of the past and linked to an African heritage. Her eyes are "milky" white and she might be blind (254), but she seems to have insight into the situation. Instead of accepting Dessa's lie that she was scarred in a fire as a child, she takes the small, almost worthless coin, feels only Dessa's back, and announces "I ain't seed nothing on this gal's butt. She ain't got a scar on her back." Typically, Nehemiah scorns this pronouncement as a lie, but in fact, the old woman speaks the truth. Since she never allowed Dessa to lift her skirts, Aunt Chole has seen nothing on Dessa's genitals. And to continue reading the double negatives, if she had looked, all she would have seen was Dessa's body, the scars now part of it rather than on it.[3]

The disruption of English and the slipperiness of vision come to the fore again when Nehemiah threatens to produce the account of Dessa's rebellion based on his interviews with her. While the ancient black woman saves Dessa from the first challenge, Ruth's child Clara rescues her this time, signifying on the potential of the rising generation of whites to collaborate with African Americans.[4] When Clara scatters Nehemiah's text, the sheriff finds illegible scratches on the pages he grabs, and the ones Ruth holds are blank (255).

One could argue that the two have simply collected Nehemiah's notes (from which he prepared the journal entries in part 1) and pages on which he has yet to write, but it is significant that neither one finds any coherent narrative. Kristine Holmes views this as a sign of the "futility" of the white man's efforts: "If the slaveholder's text constitutes a bodily violation of the black woman, then it is akin to a rape, which in the context of slavery often took the form of miscegenation. Nehemiah's text as miscegenation produces something blank and indecipherable—a sterile, impotent, 'mulatto' text" (137). Holmes is astute in comparing violation to rape; nevertheless, her interpretation goes too far and yet not far enough. First, Nehemiah is not a slaveholder, though he aspires to that class. Second, while there is a connection between bodily violation and inscription, Holmes disempowers black women by assuming that the result will be miscegenation. A reading open to African influences would acknowledge the women's ability to prevent conception through roots and other medicine, producing nothing at all. This would suggest that Nehemiah's narrative never existed.

Was the account in the journal then the white man's invention or wild recollections from notes even he was unable to decipher? Or, since we later discover that Dessa is recounting the story, was it her imagining of how Nehemiah perceived her? Sherley Anne Williams herself has commented that in the creation of the story, Dessa's voice came to her first, and that "the white man was created out of Dessa's need, to serve Dessa's purpose" ("The Lion's History" 250). In either case, the resolution empowers the black woman. In the former, it would appear that Nehemiah has indeed been mad throughout, that the text is corrupt. If the latter is true, the text inscribes Dessa's shifting self-perception and growing sense of autonomy as she moves from seeing herself primarily from a white person's point of view to understanding herself and her agency. It is therefore completely apposite that on leaving the sheriff's office she tells Ruth, "my name Dessa, Dessa Rose. Ain't no *O* to it" (256). She is neither a zero, a nothing, or an other (Henderson 133). The white woman accepts this as the two walk on the boardwalk, grinning and sharing the laughter of the Medusa, in which they had indulged only once previously, after vanquishing the rapacious Oscar with mere pillows, rendering him a zero, a nothing, an other.

In a final twist, the entire narrative is revealed to be Dessa's account for her children and grandchildren. Its accuracy is undercut by Dessa's assertion that her mind "wanders" as memories fade. She claims to have dictated her adventures so the children can read them, but then comments that "this *the childrens have heard from our own lips*" (260). Presumably, her story is accurate because it has been written from her speech without a white intermediary. Nevertheless, with memory coming into play, any claims to authority or authenticity for the written text remain unstable. As Deborah McDowell notes, too, "controlling a text of slavery, or any other text for that matter, especially a written one, is no guarantee of freedom. Triumph over language does not translate directly into triumph over social and material circumstances" ("Negotiating Between Tenses" 160). The closing of Williams's novel remains as ambiguous as the final chapters of *Beloved* and *Jubilee,* not only because of the elusive nature of the account, but also because the protagonists face continuing prejudice in the West and, instead of remaining with Nathan, Ruth returns to the East, signaling that such interracial relations cannot last.

Despite these ambiguities, the mesh of images discussed above illustrate Dessa's development through the course of the novel as she rises from being penned (in both senses of the word) to taking leadership over those around her and functioning like an *aje.* Dessa's actions further underscore this point. Dessa's first violent act, her attack on the master out of grief and rage for the loss of Kaine, is individual and it brings retribution only on her. Yet Dessa is unvanquished. Even though she has been beaten terribly and held in a sweatbox, she stands with dignity before the slave trader (143). In the coffle uprising, she takes on superhuman qualities, jumping on the trader Wilson and beating him. Her behavior inverts Hurston's reference to black women as the mules of the world (*Their Eyes Were Watching God* 29) since Dessa refuses to be a mule to the black runaways (198–99). Instead, she rides the white man "like you would a mule. . . . Oh, she was something" (153). Nathan's final comment contrasts all of the remarks about "nothing" in the text, and indeed, after this incident, Dessa incurs the name of "devil woman." Five men are killed in the attack and Wilson loses an arm; little wonder, then, that he fears Dessa and attributes her escape to evil—the "devil merely claimed his own" (69).

As with the *aje*, Dessa's power is seen as both benevolent and maleficent, as she learns when others in the community adopt Wilson's terminology to indicate "their derision of slave dealers, whose only god was money, and their delight that a 'devil' had been the agency of one's undoing" (52). Indeed, Cully, Nathan, and Harker rescue her because they hold her in such awe, and Ruth's curiosity is piqued by rampant rumors. News spreads until Dessa becomes an almost mythical person and Harker hears accounts of her feats "at one of the places he was sold, but this was like a hoodoo story to the peoples, a conjure tale" (249). The fact that Dessa's accomplishments are linked to magic and the supernatural suggests that the other blacks cannot conceive of one of their own being so powerful. Yet one of the most important signs of Dessa's growing power is her acceptance of the name of "devil woman" at the closing of the novel.

Indeed, although Dessa is dependent in the early days of her stay at the Glen, she quickly becomes a target of respect and fear through her disruption of Ruth's conception of "mammy," her objections to Nathan's relationship with Ruth, and her role in the false slave trades. The other black women consider Dessa's vocal objection to the interracial romance to be a sign of her unnatural power, but all these accounts of her power make Dessa uncomfortable: "I didn't no ways look like I could do all that" (192).

Even though Dessa focuses on the tremendous physical strength she shows in times of crisis, much of the respect she earns derives from her increasing self-assertion. When Nathan sells himself, Dessa becomes Ruth's guide and strength; in the epilogue, she is clearly central to the community and its matriarch. Dessa shares the maternal qualities of African female leaders to the extent that she contemplates killing her son before birth, much as Sethe murders Beloved to protect her from the slave catchers. As she undertakes leadership in her own community, she increasingly resembles the *Sowei* rather than the *aje*.

Dessa's ascension is closely linked to her relationship with Harker, the trickster. Harker has studied the ploys of his white master, a gambler, and learned to use them for his own ends, gaining power in an economy that treats men like him as commodities (in his early accounts, Nehemiah keeps referring to the runaways in terms of their cash value). While

Dessa's strength lies in her energy and directedness, Harker tends to be indirect, cunning, even devious. For him, breaking Southern rules for blacks is nothing but an exciting mental challenge. He sends Ruth to Nathan for an account of Dessa's past, and he is the only runaway with the courage to keep leaving the sanctuary of Ruth's farm. Even though he seeks Dessa out early in the novel and seems to prefer her, he defers declaring his love, waiting until Dessa is isolated by her resistance to Ruth's affair with Nathan. He turns the deadly serious business of slave sales into a game. He is literally double tongued, speaking some French as well as English. Harker uses language in other ways as well, being somewhat familiar with writing, and, like Frederick Douglass, he knows how to turn slave passes to good use. More importantly, "he could cipher" with his own marks, diminishing the power of white people's writing and its representations of African Americans. He is also suspicious of paper currency, though he respects gold (212). With his facility in moving between European-American and African-American culture, he is an incarnation of Esu, a liminal being and the guardian of thresholds (Gates, *Signifying Monkey* 26). His sexuality is evident in his lovemaking with Dessa; even then he mocks dominant notions of female attractiveness by telling her that the scars improve her value (208).

When Harker urges his companions to enter the slave trade, he, too, begins a complicated and risky dance in the marketplace, turning it from a place directed by whites into a more liminal space in which the African can play with and disrupt the system of authority. In scripting lines for Ruth and the others, he speaks for them and pulls them together. The market is literally the place where the characters mask themselves and perform elaborate rituals to raise the funds they need to survive in freedom. Like the market in Gelede ritual, the slave exchange is visited by beings from other places—ghosts, memories of lost relatives, ancestral spirits. For the slaves who pass through, it, too, is a liminal space. When Ruth and her cohort begin using trade for their own purposes, they are turning the very economy that has commodified them to their own benefit, empowering themselves. Significantly, Dessa begins to use currency during this period of time, and it is equally appropriate that her son's nickname is Mony. Instead of being part of the slave economy, to be traded like cash, he will be able to earn his own way and to use cash. He is better than money, and he is the key to future generations, parented by the strong African influence of Kaine and the female power of Dessa, and stepfathered by the trickster, Harker.

Dessa Rose moves from a world where the heroine is powerless and facing death to a universe where she has power and family; from a place where Africanisms seem extinct to an enactment of an Africanist ritual; from a narrative in which blacks are passive subjects to a celebration of orality and authentic voice. The novel brings together the issues of voice, violence, and mediation discussed in the previous two chapters while showing more strongly how Africanisms remained present in ante- and post-bellum society, and how contemporary authors can reinscribe them in history.

9

African (Re)Sisters

Rhetoric, Representation, and Liberation
in Alice Walker's Works

In an earlier chapter, I indicated the way Africa functions at once as a point of origin for the reinscription of history and as a rich source of tropes and literary imagery for Alice Walker. When *Possessing the Secret of Joy* is considered together with Walker's nonfiction work, *Warrior Marks: Female Genital Mutilation and the Sexual Blinding of Women*, written in collaboration with Pratibha Parmar, readers may become aware that Walker's project is more complex and far-ranging than it initially appears.

Walker's rhetorical strategies and generic experiments create a complicated picture of African societies that contradicts the preconceptions and stereotypes dear to many Americans, white and black. But this is not unusual for Walker, who has alternately been recognized as a writer of courage and a woman whose "activism becomes an invasive practice imbued with unequal power relations" (Grewal and Kaplan 13). Consistently, Walker has addressed issues that many would prefer to leave in obscurity or explain away in terms of cultural relativism—rape, incest, sexism among blacks, and more recently, female excision. As Barbara Christian remarked in "Alice Walker: The Black Woman Artist as Wayward," "Walker's peculiar sound . . . seems to have much to do with her contrariness, her willingness at all turns to challenge the fashionable belief of the day, to re-examine it in the light of her own experiences and of dearly won principles which she has previously challenged and absorbed. There is a sense in which the 'forbidden' in the society is consistently approached by Walker as a possible route to truth" (458). Walker's risk-taking is particularly apparent when readers consider that her writing exposes the "forbidden" in several, overlapping senses: she explores what men decree should remain secret, and what is taboo among women, either because it is considered immoral or because it is too painful to discuss. Even as she exposes the engendering of the "forbidden," Walker is preoccupied with how the concept maintains and reinforces oppressive social structures as well as conventional literary genres. She seeks to transform this secrecy into a source of power, agency, and creativity.

Walker uses two approaches in her attack on female genital mutilation in Africa. In *Possessing the Secret of Joy*, Walker presents the controversies surrounding genital excision through the story of a fictive African woman, Tashi. The discontinuous narrative consists of Tashi's accounts, interspersed with chapters by her husband and others. In this sense, the novel most resembles other books I have discussed, such as Gloria Naylor's *Mama Day*, Toni Morrison's *Beloved*, or Sherley Anne Williams's *Dessa Rose*. Engaged in an endeavor analogous to other women writers' treatment of slavery, Walker gives readers a heroine who performs acts of resistance and self-creation. She acknowledges black women's historical subjection by multiple others (black and white, male and female), while transforming oppression into power.

In *Possessing the Secret of Joy*, Walker gives voice to a character who *represents* the silenced; in contrast, in *Warrior Marks*, Walker allows women who might otherwise be silenced to speak. *Warrior Marks* is a nonfiction record of Walker and Parmar's activities while making a film on the surgical procedure. While the film version of *Warrior Marks* is generally better known than the book, my analysis will be restricted primarily to the text, partly for reasons of consistency. I have discussed the texts and not the film versions of *Beloved, The Women of Brewster Place*, and *The Color Purple*. More importantly, the book includes many of the features of contemporary novels about slavery discussed in the last three chapters: the narrative is multivocal and unstable, invoking questions of power, authenticity, and violence. Like *Dessa Rose, Beloved*, and *Jubilee*, the text examines the concept of history and the link between violence, visibility, and vision. A compendium of letters, narratives, interviews, poems, financial accounts, photographs, and scientific explanations (complete with diagrams), *Warrior Marks* also resembles the self-consciously generic mixes of early slave narratives. Walker stands in for the text's sponsor or editor, helping to fund the enterprise and find a publisher. Moreover, the strategies of the speakers (Walker, Parmar, and others) for dealing with genital mutilation are reminiscent of those found in slave narratives, such as *Incidents in the Life of a Slave Girl* by Harriet Jacobs.

This is not to imply that the enslavement of Africans by white men is equivalent to female genital mutilation within African communities. The differences in cultural and power relations should be obvious. Whereas chapter 5 focused on Walker's use of Africa and Africanisms, the purpose of this chapter is to study the modes of rhetoric and representation that Walker employs in the inscription of a particularly painful aspect of history (present as well as past). In this context, Walker's recent works are distinctive in their recapitulation of rhetorical strategies, tropes, and other techniques that have characterized African-Americans' reappropriation of the discourse of slavery.

Discussion of Walker's narrative and rhetorical strategies reveals both the benefits and dangers of such an approach. While in chapter 4 I explained mostly the ambiguities and difficulties in the work, in this chapter I will offer a reading that focuses on the more positive aspects of Walker's achievement. For instance, Mary Daly claims that excision and infibulation have remained "unspeakable" not only because they are "inexpressibly horrible" (154), but also because of the strictures "against saying/writing the truth about them, against *naming* them" (155). Walker, however, aims to break the silence by naming the names.

Walker gives voice to the silenced and revises a fictive past when a peripheral character in *The Color Purple* resurfaces as the heroine of *Possessing the Secret of Joy*. Although Tashi's surgery is alluded to in the earlier novel, I have shown how the second work provides a more explicit account, deepening readers' understanding of the event and its consequences. Walker's familiarity with Africa thus enables her not only to reinterpret her own experiences but also to rewrite the stories of characters in ways that illuminate larger issues, much as Naylor's revisions of the stories of the men of Brewster Place deepen readers' understandings of her characters.

Walker's revision of Tashi's story in *Possessing the Secret of Joy* begins with the statement, "I did not realize for a long time that I was dead" (3) so that what follows, up to Tashi's second death, is essentially a posthumous narrative. Because Tashi and other girls who undergo excision are said to die and be reborn as women, Walker's novel may be considered a form of ghostwriting, accompanied by issues of mediation, voice, and authenticity. Furthermore, the text returns repeatedly to the death of

Tashi's sister Dura, an incident revealed in psychoanalysis to be almost as traumatic as Tashi's own excision. Both presences—Dura and Tashi's childhood self—linger in the text and are used in part as justification for the murder of M'Lissa, the excisor.

Their function resembles that of Beloved in Morrison's eponymous novel. Like Beloved, the dead instigate the resolution of the plot, which, although it is ambiguous, involves some re-formation of the community of women. Moreover, in *Beloved* and *Possessing the Secret of Joy,* the ghosts of the maimed, murdered children haunt and torment the living, sucking their lifeblood. The past that will not remain repressed contains a troubling history of violence and subjection, and of women being compelled to collude with their oppressors (Sethe's role in killing Beloved is a particularly chilling example of what a woman will do under duress).

Another congruence in the representation of slavery and of excision may be found in the practice of blaming the victim, and again Walker is able to reappropriate discourse surrounding her subject. Female slaves were accused of deliberate eroticism when their bodies were displayed at slave sales; similarly, they were accused of looseness when in fact they were raped. Harriet Jacobs's long defense of her seduction by Sands provides an apposite example of a slave woman believing that she is to blame for a situation in which her body is little more than a commodity. Just as the discourse of slavery lacked resources to describe the experiences of black women, genital excision has been justified on the grounds that women are sexually unclean and promiscuous without it; infibulation literally tightens them for the enjoyment of men. Mary Daly has catalogued the manner in which such arguments are turned against women (153–77).

Such parallels between narratives about slavery and Walker's recent work occur on many other levels as well. Another is the silence that surrounds violence against black women; as Houston Baker has noted in *Workings of the Spirit,* until relatively recently, the rape of slave women on ships has largely been neglected by historians, who have focused on the male slaves relegated to the hold, rather than on the women who were kept above deck (124–25). For Baker, "access" is a key term in the violation of women's bodily boundaries: "'Access' translates as 'rape'—a violent, terrorizing abuse of African women sanctioned by ownership and enslavement" (124). Similarly, the secrecy surrounding genital mutilation has until recently kept the procedure out of history books. Genital mutilation, especially when accompanied by infibulation, is also best described as concerning "access" and ownership; a husband must reopen his wife's vagina after marriage.

For Walker and others like her, writing about the procedure in works of fiction and nonfiction redresses the imbalance in the history books, while fighting for its eradication is nothing less than reasserting women's physical boundaries and ownership of their bodies. Walker is aware of the way history erases the original reasons for oppression, substituting explanations that blame the victims. In the case of excision, the original reason, controlling women and their sexuality, has literally been washed off. "Bathing" has become a euphemism for the procedure, which has been described as a necessary form of feminine hygiene (*Possessing* 246). Ultimately, in challenging traditional explanations and justifications for the ritual, Walker's works explicitly deconstruct the very concept of history. By delving into such concerns and exposing the abuse of language, Walker is able to reveal the complexities of the issues, drawing international attention to oppressive lies. Annemarie Bean and others argue that in doing so, Walker is presumptuously casting herself as rescuer of African women, when in fact many African women are involved in movements against excision (334).[1] There is an inherent danger in Walker and Parmar's approach of reifying images of Africa as uncivilized, but the book does include African women's organizations, and the publicity following its publication has created pressure against female genital mutilation.

As Walker has indicated, the struggle against excision is linked to vision as well, for the eye/I is the organ through which women experience the world, one that implies a boundary between self and other. Walker's transformation of the forbidden into a source of energy is apparent if readers follow her changing descriptions of being blinded and her exploration of blinding as a metaphor for female genital mutilation. In "Beauty: When the Other Dancer Is the Self," an essay in the collection *In Search of Our Mothers' Gardens,* Walker offers her first account of the accident. Shot in one eye by her brother, she is sworn to secrecy and ordered to say that a piece of wire flew up and hit her: "If I do not say this is what happened, I know my brothers will find ways to make me wish that I had" (387). The incident is described as critical in Walker's developing awareness of herself in a culture that values a particular kind of beauty: "it had taught me of shame and anger and inner vision" (393). As an adult, Walker realizes that she loves and accepts the scar when her daughter points out that there is a "world" in the eye (393).

Just as Sethe's and Vyry's scars take on various meanings in the course of their narratives, the "world" in Walker's eye takes on a different, more literal sense, as she learns to "read" her scarred pupil through an African lens. In *Warrior Marks*, she transmutes her experience, describing her blinding as part of her growth in a society that seeks to control the sexuality of women: "What I had, I realized only as a consciously feminist adult, was a patriarchal wound" (17). Moreover, she compares her blinding to the genital mutilation of African girls: "No one would think it normal to deliberately destroy the pupil of the eye. Without its pupil, the eye can never see itself, or the person possessing it, reflected in the eye of another. It is the same with the vulva. Without the clitoris and other sexual organs, a woman can never see herself reflected in the healthy, intact body of another. Her sexual vision is impaired" (19). Although the two readings of Walker's blinding are similar, the latter emphasizes the sexual nature of the wound, the complicity of men, and the African roots of the suffering. In *Warrior Marks*, Walker adds that she eventually accused her mother of buying the gun used to shoot her. Walker also suggests that, like African women, she has been "blamed" for her own "sexual mutilation" (18). By writing the book, she has learned to "turn" the wound into a "warrior mark," from which she can "fight back." The wound, rather than her daughter, has become a "guide" (17–18).

Walker's connection between blinding and sexual mutilation echoes the celebrated passage in *The Souls of Black Folks* in which Du Bois describes "double-consciousness" as "this sense of always looking at one's self though the eyes of others, of measuring one's soul by the tape of a world that looks on in amused contempt and pity" (16–17). For Walker, the eye/I without a pupil cannot be literate; it resembles the slave who cannot read or comprehend events, the slave whose experience cannot be verbalized and is never acknowledged by whites. As Dessa Rose cannot see herself in Nehemiah's eyes, the blinded eye in Walker's works cannot see its own reflection, especially in faces full of contempt. Nor can it view others. The blinded must therefore rely on others' impressions, just as the young Alice Walker loses self-confidence when she sees that others are repelled by her eye. Only after a long process of self-seeking can the "loss of sight" lead to "the deepening perceptive powers of inner vision" (Warren and Wolff 4)—and that process does not work for everyone, even though Dessa Rose comes to recognize her own selfhood.

Ultimately, Walker's distinctive mining of individual experience for images that become resonant and symbolic (such as her wounded eye or her mother's garden), together with her conscious use of Africanisms, creates a way of seeing, virtually an epistemology, that permeates her very style. It is distinctive in the way she begins with a personal link— her own blinding and the pain of female genital mutilation—and then reverses it so that the surgery can be described as a sexual blinding. The equivalence of Walker's personal experience with the suffering of African women causes controversy that echoes the pain in Audre Lorde's response to Daly; however, the second part of the analogy is less problematic. Just as the suffering caused by an eye injury has yielded its own insights, Walker's consciousness of sexual blinding has deepened her vision of social relations. The internal nature of female genital mutilation, as opposed to the more visible scars left by Walker's blinding, mirrors the secrecy that has surrounded the surgery.

In addition to secrecy, issues of spectatorship and voyeurism appear in multiple forms in Walker's analysis of female genital mutilation, and her treatment of these issues once again resembles what we have found in texts about slavery. Abolitionists commonly included a slave exhibit in their lectures to demonstrate the actuality of the suffering inflicted on Africans. In this way, the black body became a rhetorical device at the disposal of white liberals: "His or her body, in all of its marked and visible clarity of wounding, made affective the metaphors of moral suasion propounded by white abolitionists. . . . The fugitive slave was a silent, partially naked body turning to a predominantly white audience. The silent, fugitive slave's body became an erotic sign of servitude in the social, liberational discourse of white abolitionists and their predominantly white audiences. Gasps and moans (of empathy? reassurance? relief?) followed" (Baker, *Workings of the Spirit* 13).

A similar effect is created by recent films, articles, and books, including Walker's, giving illustrations and graphic descriptions of genital mutilation. But these works, especially those using the first person, such as *Possessing the Secret of Joy*, are also important in reclaiming rhetorical as well as physical space, just as slave narratives by Jacobs, Douglass, and others "flesh out a tale of slavery" through "craft . . . [to] tell his [or her] own horrendous tale rather than serve as an illustration or mere exhibit" (Baker, *Workings of the Spirit* 14). If violence turns the body into a living expression of suffering, appropriately it is language that must reclaim the domain of the physical.

Reference to Jacobs's slave narrative may elucidate the accusations of voyeurism invoked by Walker's texts. As noted in an earlier chapter, Harriet Jacobs faced a similar problem when her editor, Lydia Maria Child, encouraged her to include graphic physical descriptions of rape and violence against slave women. In *Jubilee*, Margaret Walker provides more explicit descriptions to expose the way in which whites inflict their culture on black bodies. In the first half of *Jubilee*, narrative discontinuities follow violence against blacks; their growing power is recorded when the discontinuities follow violence against whites. Through this reversal, Margaret Walker turns the scars on her heroine's body into a subversive kind of power.

As with accounts of violence against female slaves, it appears almost inevitable that descriptions of genital mutilation might be perceived by some readers as voyeuristic and titillating. As noted above, Walker initially described the mutilation only minimally in *The Color Purple*. In *The Color Purple*, Tashi's excision is marked by a narrative discontinuity similar to the ones in *Jubilee*; she undergoes the procedure while the other characters are in England. Its effects are apparent in Tashi's weight loss, combined with her "listless, dull-eyed and tired" demeanor (213), but the procedure itself is not described. In *Possessing the Secret of Joy*, Walker follows Jacobs's lead, again focusing primarily on the effects of the violence, rather than on the procedure itself. Significantly, the most explicit description of Tashi's surgery is offered not by her, but by her husband, who comes to treat her shortly afterward. The only excision discussed in detail is M'Lissa's, appropriately, as she perpetuates this process that yields African men control.

Furthermore, just as Jacobs repeatedly includes an imaginary reader and appeals to that individual's responses, Walker includes Jung as an outside respondent. As described previously, Jung is a source of deep ambivalence in *Possessing the Secret of Joy*, with his claim of a metaphorical equivalence in all human suffering. The wide-eyed delight he expresses in his single chapter, together with his naive pleasure at Africans' responses to him, sounds almost parodic. Walker inserts a subtle marker indicating the difference between Jung and the Africans he encounters.

When Jung is called "out" of his name, he is pleased, whereas many blacks know that this is often neither a compliment nor an "acknowledgment" of "something characteristically theirs" (85). Instead, it is a power play, a refusal to recognize them as individuals. Jung is happy, too, because he has repeatedly been thanked for saying that "Europe is the mother of all evil" (85), without understanding the profoundly misogynist nature of the remark. Here, Walker echoes Mary Daly, who attacks Jung's "way of discrediting women who are mothers" (253–54). The portrait of Jung is a mirror held up before certain white readers, similar to Jacobs's act of envisioning a white northern woman reader.

Moreover, there is an obvious element of voyeurism in Jung's descriptions of Tashi and Adam. Together with his niece Lisette, Jung stands in for the white reader who may be fascinated, horrified, yet oddly excited by the descriptions of a mutilated black woman's body. His (and readers') spectatorship opens an arena for controversy in discussing this text; although all perusers of novels may be compared with voyeurs, the explicitness of Walker's work is especially problematic. As Jung's position suggests, like pornography and slavery, *Possessing the Secret of Joy* and *Warrior Marks* perpetuate a power relation in which spectators (male or female) witness the oppression and suffering of women. Gay Wilentz has echoed this concern in light of the novel's topic ("Healing the Wounds of Time" 16). Given American society's curious (in every sense of the word) mingling of eroticism with discussions of violence directed at African-American women, these concerns seem particularly pertinent. But bell hooks offers a different and useful perspective in an article on *The Color Purple,* which she feels "subverts the pattern" (458) of sadistic pornography: "Her intent is not to titillate sexually, but to arouse disgust, outrage, and anger at male sexual exploitation of females" (459). By adopting such strategies, Walker aims to reappropriate both the image and the flesh, the word and the spirit.

Indeed, the issue of suggestiveness and titillation resides not only in visual images, but also in language. In particular, Walker suggests throughout *Possessing the Secret of Joy* that language itself is implicated in the oppression of women. A country that defines a liberator as one who assents to the practice of excision, a society that finds confirmation of manhood in the suffering of women, rebels who call themselves members of a resistance movement while oppressing women—all of these are expressions not only of the power of language, but more specifically, of those who define. Their definitions have a way of veiling the suffering of women, in the same way that euphemisms such as "bathing" among the Olinka and "tonsillectomy" among Americans negate the violence of genital mutilation. In fact, just as Walker indicates that American women have been circumcised, Harriet Lerner notes that the English language perpetuates the physical violence of clitoridectomy when the term *vagina* is used to refer to all female sexual organs, effectively excising external ones: "The widespread practice of mislabeling female genitalia is . . . astounding in its implications. . . . we do the job [of excision] linguistically—a psychic genital mutilation, if you will. Obviously the two crimes are not equivalent. But language can be as sharp and as swift as the surgeon's knife. What is not named does not exist" (54). In this case, by hiding the extent of the procedure, language facilitates its continuation, perpetuating the cruelty.

The power to name in this novel is not used solely to oppress females; when the Italian woman speaks of the "secret of joy" (in the quotation preceding the text), she obscures the suffering evident in the faces of many Africans, male and female. In her description, a self-serving illusion, similar to the myth of the smiling slave, conveniently substitutes for pain. For most of the novel, Walker's inclusion of the epigraph seems ironic, a signification on the way whites use language to suit their ends. But in the conclusion, Mbati succeeds in redefining both "the secret of joy" and the term "resistance" (281), rendering them equivalent. Thus, Walker proposes that (re)appropriating language is one solution to the oppression of females; when women name acts of violence as such, the world can no longer ignore or condone them (and in fact, this seems to be one of Walker's major goals in writing this book, a goal shared by Toni Morrison in *Beloved* and Margaret Walker in *Jubilee*). As Janette Turner Hospital has noted in a review of *Possessing the Secret of Joy*, "the breakers of taboos must always redefine the terms" (11).

The task of "redefining" is complicated by readers' unfamiliarity with those very "terms." Inevitably, Walker's intent is pedagogical; she wishes to educate readers who might otherwise discount the procedure as belonging to less "advanced" peoples, or seek to condone it out of a belief in cultural relativism. These possibilities create complicated problems in representation; once again, Walker's approaches are illuminated through references to other (re)sister authors.

In narratives pertaining to women slaves, abolitionists as well as ex-slaves draw repeatedly and deliberately on analogies to the lives of their readers. As discussed above, such appeals play a role in the narrators' careful negotiations of issues involving eroticism and voyeurism. But they serve other rhetorical purposes as well. Speakers make comparisons between their lives and the existences of imagined readers to indicate at once a common humanity as well as a difference in situation. For instance, Harriet Jacobs appeals to readers in her description of New Year's Day:

> O, you happy free women, contrast *your* New Year's day with that of the poor bond-woman! With you it is a pleasant season, and the light of the day is blessed. . . . Children bring their little offerings, and raise their rosy lips for a caress. They are your own, and no hand but that of death can take them from you. But to the slave mother New Year's day comes laden with peculiar sorrows. She sits on her cold cabin floor, watching the children who may all be torn from her the next morning. . . . She may be an ignorant creature, degraded by the system that has brutalized her from childhood; but she has a mother's instincts, and is capable of feeling a mother's agonies. (16)

Jacobs relies on the physical for effectiveness, contrasting the contact of the caressing "rosy lips" of the white child with the cold cabin floor from which the black woman must *watch* her children, until she is deprived of the sight.

More importantly, Jacobs's passage gains effectiveness in its subtle rhetorical movement. The passage begins with a sight that might be familiar to the reader, comforting even. With the intrusion of death, which is more than an abstraction—a frighteningly concrete hand that deprives the helpless mother of her infants—Jacobs begins to develop a contrasting scene, of a slave mother fearing the immediate loss of her children. Through this development, the reader experiences a kind of deprivation and empathy for the slave woman. At the end of the passage, when Jacobs refers to "a mother's instincts," she reminds readers of their commonalities, reinforcing the movement toward empathy.

Similarly, a frequent strategy in works regarding female genital mutilation in Africa—and especially in Walker's texts—is to draw parallels between the lives of African women and their counterparts elsewhere. Walker, too, chooses carefully when to emphasize similarity and when to stress difference; consequently, the sequences vary in *Possessing the Se-*

cret of Joy and *Warrior Marks* as Walker deals with complex issues of representation. In the end, language repairs the integrity of the eye/I, which has been violated by the spectatorship of outsiders.

As discussed in chapter 4, the risk in Walker's approach is that she will "reinforce Western stereotypes of 'Africa'" (Wilentz, "Healing the Wounds of Time" 16). Walker's depiction of rural African society does present the practice of female excision as evidence of rampant sexism that suppresses women's physical pleasure for fear that it might disrupt the economy of power relations. And she is concerned about the stereotypes. The problem is not only one of intent, but of readership as well; according to Cynthia Ward, Walker's audience must beware of succumbing to "a feminist reading [that] reinscribes the image of Africa as the dark continent where 'primitive' cultural practices must be guided into productive paths by enlightened Europeans [or Americans]" ("What They Told Buchi Emecheta" 85). In fact, it is questionable whether such readings may be described as feminist, since the "image of Africa as the dark continent" is largely the creation of white male imperialists. The practice of excision is objectionable to many feminists internationally, not because it is "primitive," but because it causes women to suffer.

On the other hand, some readers who refuse to consider the procedure as part of an "unenlightened" society may accept the surgery as part of a beneficent concept of tolerance and respect for others. Indeed, as repugnant as the tradition may be to many readers of the novel, certain anthropologists have represented excision in other ways, focusing on the way women turn the procedure to empower themselves. A look at the functions of excision among Sande women, as described by Sylvia Ardyn Boone, suggests that the surgery is crucial to Sande initiation; it is the point at which, through the experience of pain (emblematic of the suffering of adulthood), the initiate "dies" into the society, leaving her childish self behind (Boone 65). No woman is considered fully adult until she has undergone the surgery. The ordeal is not intended to be pleasant; it is a source of anxiety for the girls and their families.

Boone argues that the pain and ensuing inability to experience pleasure are symbols of womanhood and its responsibilities. Ultimately, the pain may be transformed into a source of power. While the facts of male circumcision are common knowledge, clitoridectomy constitutes a "mystery" (65) from which men and children are excluded. The silence surrounding the operation is not the result of denial; instead, just as the act of excision renders female genital sexuality internal and hidden, its se-crecy is an expression of the potency of women's buried knowledge. Childhood among the Mende is often difficult and cruel, but assumption into Sande after the excision and infibulation gives a young woman pro-tection and status. Dorkenoo and Elworthy comment as well on the fact that "any physical suffering is preferred to the social ostracism experi-enced by an uncircumcised girl" (26).

This interpretation of the ritual minimizes the impact of excision and its role in the subjection of women, making Sande appear more autono-mous than it is. At the same time, it reinscribes women's silence in the confines of a patriarchal tradition. In either case, promoting such relativ-ism is problematic. As Diane Carman, a columnist for the *Denver Post*, has noted, many condone such practices because they fear that confront-ing the distasteful or objectionable in other societies might be "miscon-strued as disrespectful of their culture, *or at least to the men who define it*" (emphasis added) (E1). Underlying this trepidation, then, is an atti-tude similar to that described above: respect and fear for patriarchy in all its forms, and an acceptance of patriarchy as defining other cultures. In fact, societies around the world are rarely completely discrete or unified, as apparent in the many contradictions in *Possessing the Secret of Joy*. Those who wield the power determine the public visage of the culture and claim to speak for it as a whole. Foreigners who accept that visage as the only face of the nation are complicit in the oppression of those who think (but may not speak) otherwise.

Françoise Lionnet offers a useful conceptual basis for discussing these issues when she suggests that "there is a distinction to be made between *cultural* and *moral* relativism." The former can lead to a kind of "antiethnocentrism [that] can have the unfortunate consequence of un-dermining feminist political solidarity," so that, for instance, a Western feminist might hesitate to take a stand against excision for fear that she would be reinforcing preconceptions of Africa as being less "civilized." In making this choice, she would implicitly be condoning and even support-ing a form of oppression against women. Lionnet proposes instead "to continue speaking of community, and to attempt to find a common theo-retical and ethical ground from which to argue for political solidarity without either objectifying the 'other' woman or subsuming collective goals under the banner of sameness" (20).

Possessing the Secret of Joy instigates consideration of these dilemmas in prolonged conversations among different characters. These conversations enact the conflicts and, similar to the passage from Harriet Jacobs's narrative cited above, they force readers to move from the comfortable (stereotypic views of Africa or inherited notions of cultural tolerance) to the risky. Like Jacobs, Walker delays encouraging readers to notice commonalities; like Sherley Anne Williams, she problematizes the commonalities and renders them crucial to the text. For example, I have noted that midway through the novel, Walker introduces accounts of slave women being excised (188) as well as the story of the white woman who suffered the procedure in the twentieth century (186–87). As a result, readers are forced to consider a continuity in the experiences of African and American women, as well as similarities in their societies. This point is emphasized in the text when Tashi asserts that Americans look like her (213).

In *Warrior Marks,* Walker reverses the movement, beginning—rather than ending—the book with passages describing the similarities between female genital mutilation in Africa and other procedures in the United States, such as cosmetic surgery. At first glance, the analogy seems flawed. Cosmetic surgery tends to be external, while genital excision and infibulation are not visible to the world. Although one could argue that societal forces leave some women little choice regarding face-lifts, liposuction, and similar operations, there is a significant difference between the infliction of genital surgery on young girls and "elective" surgery on adult, relatively affluent women.

Nevertheless, Walker's argument resembles the reasoning of other well-known feminists, including Mary Daly and Gayatri Spivak. Spivak in particular recognizes that the ritual presents problems for feminist scholars. In "French Feminism in an International Frame," she argues that European and American feminists must allow and account for cultural differences, but ultimately, her reasoning is somewhat contradictory. In taking the clitoridectomy as "a metonym for women's definition as 'legal object as subject of reproduction'" (183), she suggests that "the arena of research here is not merely remote and primitive societies," because "an at least symbolic clitoridectomy has always been the 'normal' accession to womanhood and the unacknowledged name of motherhood" (181). She proposes that the emphasis on motherhood and a uterine reproductive economy in Western cultures functions as an act of excision, denying female pleasure. Spivak's reading of the ritual removes its physicality, linking it symbolically and metonymically to abstractions pertaining to Western society. Moreover, in slipping from actual clitoridectomies to symbolic ones, Spivak risks excising a disturbing feature in the body of cultural practices, returning it to the realm of what is unspeakable and unspoken.

On the other hand, to argue that no equivalence exists leads to a kind of essentialism. In *Gyn/Ecology*, Daly takes a slightly different approach, one that is closer to Walker's underlying aims. In her second (and significantly, middle) passage, Daly includes chapters on various forms of physical and psychological cruelty against women: Indian suttee, Chinese foot binding, African genital mutilation, European witch burnings, and American gynecology. In these chapters, she develops the argument that the oppression of women is global, and that it involves the infliction of physical pain.

In the early pages of *Warrior Marks*, Walker negotiates between the abstract "symbolic" equivalent invoked by Spivak and the actuality of the mutilation of women, as described by Daly. She refuses to excise the bodies of women, especially black women, from discussion. Walker retains a physical dimension by making a persuasive case for the resemblance between genital mutilation and other wounds, such as those occurring in her blinding or cosmetic surgery. She draws on resemblances between African-American women's "mutilation of hair" and genital excision (13–14), noting an economic parallel in the fact that starving women on both continents will undergo tremendous deprivation for the social acceptance brought by mutilation (14). For Walker, "genital mutilation has been spread over the entire body" (9), and she feels urgency in emphasizing the analogy because "otherwise there will be a tendency for Westerners to assume that genital mutilation is more foolish and 'barbaric' than the stuff they do" (10). In this way, Walker reappropriates the argument concerning barbarism, turning it to her own uses.

By beginning with an explanation of the resemblances between female excision and American practices, she engages Western readers in a text that includes far more explicit discussions than does *Possessing the Secret of Joy*. Moreover, this explanation of the resemblances between excision and other procedures appears in a letter to her collaborator in the film and book; as such, it bears more resemblance to the letters, testimonials, and editorial statements preceding the accounts of ex-slaves (and *Dessa Rose*) than to the narratives themselves. Victims of slavery or excision are in a different position from editors or compilers; appropriately, they may choose to delay difficult parts of their arguments as a defensive and protective gesture. The editor, on the other hand, stands at some distance, mediating between the subject and the audience. In that role, she may begin by pointing out commonalities. By invoking this parallel, Walker sets up another level of resemblance between her account of excisions and slave narratives, one that is inextricable from her exploration of the theme of authority and some critics' disparagement of her manipulations of the voices of African women.

Walker's method entails giving primacy to the didactic purposes of her books. For example, one could argue that *Possessing the Secret of Joy* is not a novel, given that the numerous characters lack extensive development and seem to change little, while the plot is rudimentary. In her review for the *New York Times Book Review,* Janette Turner Hospital argues that the "work sits uneasily within the category of 'the novel'" (11). And in her review for the *Women's Review of Books,* Gay Wilentz comments that Walker "has taken . . . liberties" in her depictions of African cultures, moving the Olinka from West Africa in *The Color Purple* to East Africa in the more recent novel (16). This criticism goes to the heart of contemporary debates concerning literary genres. If Walker's book is "just" a novel, while internal consistency is important, the text need not conform to realistic or actual cultures and languages. But if Walker is claiming to present the "truth" of Africa, then her "liberties" are indeed problematic. They force readers to ask other important questions about truth-telling: Who decides what is the "truth" of Africa? Can there be a single "truth" about Africa? Is it acceptable to take liberties to liberate others? And haven't novels always told their own truths?

Ultimately, the account is about itself as much as anything else, as Walker explores the boundaries between nonfiction and fiction. The versions of events given by the different characters complicate the story; appropriately, as the major subject of the text—female excision—is something that has long remained unvoiced. Additionally, until the very end, readers remain unsure whether Tashi is guilty of killing M'Lissa. First, she tells Olivia that she is innocent and that M'Lissa died naturally, framing the one who turned against her. But later Tashi says that she lied. Given Tashi's propensity for telling tales, the truth is never evident.

In a way, it does not matter whether Tashi is guilty, for as she asserts on the first page of the novel, she has already died once at M'Lissa's hands. A second execution is meaningless. Moreover, Tashi's exposure of the viciousness of the surgery may destroy the practice of M'Lissa, essentially killing her. Yet a third explanation is possible. M'Lissa asserts that the *tsungas*, or female circumcisers, are doomed to die at the hand of one they initiated. Earlier, she claims that Tashi was sent for by the rebels. If this is the case, then Tashi is stripped of her agency and independence; she is merely a pawn of fate. This explanation serves M'Lissa well and deters Tashi for some time, but it is not privileged by Walker or given any more validity than Tashi's accounts.

Walker thus indicates that there is no such thing as unmediated truth. In doing so, she points to a central dilemma in contemporary anthropology—that of the value of participant-observers. Tashi is able to give an insider account of a ritual that is ordinarily privileged information, yet she has also been hospitalized for insanity and depression, conditions that might affect or confirm the validity of her perceptions. On a different level, the whole novel becomes problematic, because all the speakers are fictive. Readers are thrust in the position of judging the accuracy of the accounts of a variety of nonexistent characters, of privileging some voices as "truer" than others. This, in turn, forces them to examine their notions of authority.

In this way, even as Walker questions a pervasive African tradition, she offers a Foucauldian critique of constructions of knowledge. She is especially skeptical of the discursive formations that support the epistemological categories created by the elite in power. The book's multivocal narrative, together with the folktales interspersed throughout, reinforces the theme that truth can appear in many forms, and that history or science need not be told in "facts." Tashi's story about her mother and the leopard explains far more about her youth and sense of abandonment than an exact account would. In contrast, later sections of the narrative yield a wealth of factual information on female genital mutilation, its history, and its effects, drawn from a range of scholarly sources acknowledged at the end of the novel. In essence, Walker is suggesting that science need not only be told "scientifically," any more than history must be told "historically."

Walker questions the nature of such discourses and offers her own approach. As a result, the novel goes beyond simply challenging traditional conceptions of its genre. Janette Turner Hospital "wishes [that] Ms. Walker had opted for a different literary form, a new kind of polemic rather than a variation on the traditional novel" (12). In saying so, Hospital overlooks the fact that the work stands as an example of that new form, a genre that is circular rather than following a linear narrative. Walker has created a supple prose form, dense, multivocal, and inflected with repeated images and allusions. Tashi herself is known for her manner of talking around matters: "the way she talked evaded the issue" (6). She opens the novel with an apparent non sequitur: "I did not realize for a long time that I was dead. And that reminds me of a story: There was once a beautiful young panther . . ."(3). The text follows a similarly elliptical path, working around its subject with the story of the panther, an account of Olivia and Adam's arrival among the Olinka, the memory of the infibulation and subsequent death of Tashi's older sister, records of Tashi's psychoanalysis, and various other chapters, before the cause of Tashi's own grief and the reason for her trial are revealed. As the story becomes clear, the reader is introduced slowly to Tashi's misery and the complexity of the involvement of others.

This elliptical structure is appropriate to Walker's goals, although it, too, raises some problems. The circular, spiraling nature of the narrative, which keeps adding to our understanding of events, imitates the shape of a termite nest, which is a central metaphor in the novel. This motion implies that the text is gendered, since the flatness of the termite hill is presented as the original excision of mother earth (174). At its center is a hole, an absence, that can be circled but not felt. Stories pass before readers as "generations" pass through the queen termite, for she is a hole, not a (w)hole, following her excision by God: "only a tube through which generations of visionless offspring pass, their blindness perhaps made up for by their incessant if mindless activity" (233). Significantly, Walker employs imagery pertaining to vision/sight once more; here the stories are "visionless offspring," to be interpreted by readers, who must put together the various parts of the text and construct meaning from them. Similarly, readers of the first part of *Dessa Rose* must put together the scraps of narrative rising from the black woman's dark cell.

The circular structure of *Possessing the Secret of Joy* forces readers to take active roles, thrusting them into the minds of the speakers and engaging them in puzzles presented by conflicting statements. In essence, they must imagine what lies in the center of the termite nest. Yet

Walker's courageous gesture of stripping Africa of its "otherness" in this manner is problematic. As the Western reader begins to enter the depths of Olinka culture, instead of finding the resemblances iterated in *Warrior Marks*, she becomes increasingly aware of a distance created by multiple possible forms of difference—cultural, geographic, religious, racial, and sexual. This consciousness of difference is revealed to be resistance generated by the discomfort of confronting the forbidden on so many levels. This impulse eventually must yield to a different form of resistance, which consists of delaying or combating the urge to pass judgment. Only by resisting the tendency to habitual or early closure can one arrive at a fuller and clearer understanding of the truth. Readers are not expected to be comfortable or to identify with characters.

Similarly, even though it resembles novels about slavery, *Warrior Marks* cannot be situated in any convenient and conventional generic category. The multivocal text, containing accounts of filmmaking by both Walker and Parmar, breaks all the "rules" about repetition in literature. Diary entries are juxtaposed with poems and interviews, statistics, photographs of relevant sites and individuals, and discussions of the finances of the project. A brief interview with musical celebrity Tracy Chapman toward the end of the text functions as a testimonial to the importance of its subject. The book closes with a list of contact groups and a bibliography, rendering its advocacy role apparent as well.

Situated in the midst of the text is a marker suggesting an approach to understanding its structure: readers are given a description, complete with photographs, of the film crew's visit to Gorée Island and the House of Slaves. According to Parmar, Walker and another African-American crew member are welcomed by the curator as "distant cousins" or "long-lost relatives" (214). The assertion on the part of a "Third World" woman gives the comparison more validity than if it had come from Walker, from whom it might represent self-interest. The visit to the House of Slaves is clearly a return home; the journey traced throughout the book, then, is also a return, an internal journey that recognizes—and asserts—the kinship in the sufferings of African and African-American women. Appropriately, then, Walker has chosen a genre that resembles the one created by slaves to express and authenticate their experiences. The long discussions of the project's finances, for instance, which seem extraneous to the book's argument on excision, take their place along with the explanations of economics in slave narratives such as Olaudah Equiano's and in neo-slave narratives, such as *Dessa Rose*. As Houston Baker has shown in *Blues, Ideology and Afro-American Literature*, Equiano is preoccupied with the cost of buying himself, a preoccupation that "inscribes these economics as a sign of its 'social grounding'" (33). Similarly, Walker's crew at every turn must negotiate the costs of traveling, gaining interviews, and buying equipment, all of which would be less burdensome to a commercial crew making a less didactic film. Like Equiano, they learn the extent to which their enterprise (and I use the word deliberately) of encouraging African women to liberate themselves from the suffering of excision echoes the costs of freeing slaves.

Finally, *Warrior Marks* shares another quality of early slave narratives—a concern with authenticity. This concern is apparent in the inclusion of interviews with a midwife-circumciser, victims of excision, activists, and others. These interviews are important because they involve fewer layers of mediation than one would find in a third-person account. The interviews de-authorize the writer, rendering her a collaborator in the project, and empowering many who would otherwise remain voiceless.

At the same time, the nature of the book reminds readers that truth may be variable and endlessly self-serving. In doing so, it creates a problem—that of circularity. For if each version of the truth serves the teller (or the editor), then one must assume that Walker's portraits of the dangers and suffering of excision are themselves biased. Walker's subtlety lies in offering multivocal works, in which readers are encouraged to evaluate the differing voices. In doing so, she disempowers those who have traditionally held narrative authority, and decenters the importance of narrative itself. As with so many of the novels discussed in this book, the way of telling becomes as important as what is told. These issues of authenticity, mediation, and African influences are increasingly important in literature by African-American female authors. These writers seek to recover their history in complex accounts of the relationships involving their African heritage, their people's enslavement, and their contemporary existence. Because of the complexity of the issues and the varied ways in which authors deal with them, these subjects will no doubt continue to occupy writers and readers for years to come.

10

A Call Finds Its Response

African Women and African-American Women Writers

This book began with a relatively short voyage—to Naylor's Willow Springs, an island off the coast of the United States. Although the geographical distance could be measured by many Americans in hundreds of miles, the spiritual journey involved a pilgrimage to Africa. Time travel was necessary, too, in exploring the distinctively female heritage of African-American women.

This book ends on an island as well—Gorée Island, off the coast of Africa, the point of departure for slaves in their journey to forced labor, cultural oppression, and spiritual silencing. If the island in the first chapter of this work is a metaphor and metonym for Africa, the House of Slaves represents America. And, just as the House of Slaves was the departure point for so many Africans, slavery itself was the beginning of a journey for African Americans.

Both sections of this book, then, chart a journey back, one that involves not just physical locations but also the other tiers of geography, consisting of spiritual or cultural spaces. These spaces gain representation in language through the narratives of contemporary African-American women who seek to authenticate and reappropriate the stories of their forebears.

I wrote this book because I wanted to read it, and it hadn't been written yet. In the beginning, I knew just enough about Sande to recognize its traces in *Mama Day* but could not find sufficiently detailed critical works that supported and developed the idea of gendered Africanisms in fiction by contemporary African-American women. In my exploration of the subject, I discovered that there was nothing coincidental about the transmission of female traditions, and that it was not stretching to trace these traditions in the novels I was reading. Moreover, I learned quickly that new interpretations of novels emerged when I adopted a more Africanist perspective. The scene in the Clearing in *Beloved* looked entirely different, and power relations in *Mama Day* took another cast when analyzed in the context of the Sande society.

I also found that to understand the traditions fully, it was important to analyze books that examined the contact between African and Euro-centric cultures in the antebellum era. This illuminated recurrent themes pertaining to voice and silencing in current novels by black women in America. While African continuities might initially be less apparent in such neo-slave narratives, these works are suffused with a sense of otherness derived from the heroines' African heritage. This otherness becomes evident in scenes depicting the infliction of violence, ideals of motherhood, and the special powers of characters such as Dessa Rose, Beloved, and the speaker in *Family*.

I could have analyzed other books, too, such as Paule Marshall's novels, which resemble Kincaid's fiction in tracing African retentions through the Caribbean. Other themes I discuss, such as motherhood, are apparent in Marshall's novels as well. Yet Jamaica Kincaid's treatment of alienation is a better example of what I wished to prove. Moreover, one of the more subtle themes of this book is the way Africa and Africanisms are embedded in notions of geography and movement. Kincaid's use of small places to express cultural conflict is essential to this purpose. Another text I considered including was *Voodoo Dreams,* by Jewell Parker Rhodes. This novel is notable in the way it covers the nineteenth century *and* is pervaded with Africanisms, but it is less well known than the books I have discussed at length. In retelling the story of New Orleans sorceress Marie Laveau, Rhodes addresses themes of voice and authenticity, since it is not clear whether the conjure woman is genuine or a fraud. While there may be uncertainty about Laveau's sorcery, there is no doubt about the Dahomeyan influences in *Voodoo Dreams,* including references to the serpent god Damballah, a liminal being linked to transformation and change. The heroine's drowning and resurgence from the water may be interpreted in terms of Sande initiations or the Yoruba goddess Osun as well, even as the book records the clashes between African beliefs and Catholicism.

In contrast to the African retentions and figurative journeys in the preponderance of novels I have discussed, Alice Walker's physical return to the African continent marks a different movement. In traveling to Africa, Alice Walker brings America with her; in describing how African women respond to her and her colleagues, she implies that the Africans will invent America and, correspondingly, African-American culture. Walker's books are important because they remind us that there is another contact zone as well—in Africa. People of European descent have long attempted to impose themselves on the indigenous societies of the subcontinent; arguably, assimilated African Americans such as the missionaries in *The Color Purple* or Alice Walker have done so as well. Many Europeans and Americans continue to act as if there is little of value to be gained from African cultures.[1] Yet an increasingly global economy has led to new cultural mixtures and forms of hybridity. The appropriation by Africans of African-American dance steps and musical rhythms has become a commonplace of cultural criticism. A dance step performed on a street in Lagos or Dakar may resemble one in Los Angeles or the Bronx. Yet rap, jazz, and other American genres now popular in Africa are themselves derived from African art forms.

Similarly, works of African-American women writers are beginning to affect African literature and the lives of African women. I believe that the next necessary critical task is to attend to these African readings. It is time for us in America to learn about African women's reactions to the novels discussed in this text, so that we may more precisely locate the fiction in terms of African cultures. I have cited articles and books by a number of Africans residing in the United States and Europe, and several, especially Femi Ojo-Ade's edited collection, *Of Dreams Deferred, Dead or Alive: African Perspectives on African-American Women Writers,* offer crucial insights. But we need to hear from the women who have less contact with Western culture as well. Somewhere in Africa, a woman is reading or hearing the story of *Mama Day* or *Sula.* How does she interpret this narrative? What cultural references resound for her? Will her voice be heard across the diaspora? Cynthia Ward has offered a model for such a reading in her article, "Reading African Women Readers," in which she admonishes against essentializing African women. Ward argues instead for acknowledging not only that African women in different settings interpret narratives in various ways, but also that African literary critics may be "too acculturated, too assimilated, too educated" (78), and therefore should not be privileged. The understandings of rural or illiterate women who have little or no contact with the West are significant, too. And how can they make the world's elite aware of their stories?

If we are truly committed to the notion of the journey back, we must make efforts to hear women on the subcontinent and to learn from them as well. So, a circle dance comes to completion. A call finds its response. Paradoxically, the journey continues . . . back.

Notes

1. Otherness and the Black Mask

1. Rody's use of the term "indigenous" is odd here, because most of the characters under discussion are no more indigenous than the Europeans who brought their ancestors from Africa to the Americas. However, like indigenous populations, they have not been acculturated by the Europeans.

2. Defining the *aje* as a witch is not entirely accurate, but there is no better alternative in English. Therefore, I follow the lead of Babatunde Lawal (30) and Margaret Drewal (177) in using this analogy.

3. Significantly, Naylor herself grew up around female healers who used herbs and other forms of alternative medicine, and her mother believed in the supernatural. In contrast, her father scoffed at this notion (Tharp 119). Thus, as a girl, Naylor may have seen the conflicts between Mama Day's beliefs and George's rationalism enacted in her own home.

2. Metaphor and Maternity in *Mama Day*

1. For a discussion of Naylor's text as magic realism, see Elizabeth T. Hayes, "Gloria Naylor's *Mama Day* as Magic Realism."

2. Snakes take on a more ominous significance in Jewell Parker Rhodes's *Voodoo Dreams*, where they are associated with the serpent god, Damballah, and the African references are based on the culture of Dahomey.

3. As Virginia Fowler points out, Naylor's novel revises Toni Morrison's *Tar Baby*, where Son represents Afrocentrism while Jadine is cut off from her ancestral cultures. In rewriting Morrison, Naylor "insists on the restorative powers for black Americans of the past and of female and African-derived traditions" (103).

3. Clearing Space: Dramas of Liminality and Initiation in Morrison's Novels

1. "Outdoors" in *The Bluest Eye* contrasts "Out There" in *Paradise*. The latter is not a marginal space, but one totally beyond the moral and geographical boundaries of the community. Its very existence forces men to seek and create towns of their own, shunning the unknown, where "space, once beckoning and free, became

unmonitored and seething; became a void where random and organized evil erupted when and where it chose—behind any standing tree, behind the door of any house, humble or grand. Out There where your children were sport, your women quarry, and where your very person could be annulled . . . where every cluster of whitemen looked like a posse, being alone was being dead" (16).

2. Significantly, Gloria Naylor alludes to Sula's family when she names two of Mama Day's relatives Peace. Yet the ferocious survival instinct that characterizes Morrison's matriarch is not evident in either Peace from Willow Springs. Miranda's eldest sister, Peace, dies young. Then, "there is no peace" (36)—Mama Day's mother, who is also named Peace, retreats into her mourning, and Miranda must assume the responsibilities of the household.

3. Sharon Holland describes the spirit as a *bakula* from Zaire traditions. Although the *bakula* rises from the river like Beloved, it is white and invisible, and Beloved, though clothed in white, is black and visible. The *abiku* offers a more appropriate comparison, especially since Beloved dies as an infant, and the *abiku* are spirits of dead children.

4. This critique of young people who adopt and sometimes invent Africanisms is another iteration of the conflict in Alice Walker's story "Everyday Use" in the collection *In Love & Trouble*. In her story, Walker questions what kinds of traditions are authentic expressions of African-Americans' heritage as well as how that heritage should be valued.

5. Paired characters are apparent in Morrison's earlier novels as well. Examples include Howard and Buglar in *Beloved*, in addition to the indistinguishable Deweys in *Sula* .

4. Mother as Colony, Colony as Mother

1. Here, Kincaid reverses the practice of hyphenating the names of peoples; she hyphenates *Scots-man*, but avoids adding a suffix to *African*. In this way, she subverts traditional power structures that allow the colonizers to mark others as different from themselves (as when European-Americans are referred to simply as *Americans*, whereas Americans of Asian descent become *Asian-American*). Moreover, by hyphenating after the word *Scots*, Kincaid draws attention to gender. Ironically, the Scots have been a colonized people as well.

2. Significantly, Kincaid's book, *My Garden*, frequently employs metaphors of conquest and domination instead of those pertaining to fertility and cultivation. Presumably, if this is an Eden, it is an Eden after the fall; if it is a Western garden, it shows the meaningless perversion of space that could grow food and healing herbs into a place of decoration.

8. "We Wasn't Nothing": Leadership and Vision in *Dessa Rose*

1. Another example of the way Nehemiah's preconceptions limit his understanding is his futile search for the maroon colony. Because he cannot believe that a white

person would harbor escaped slaves, he misses Ruth's estate, which shelters the runaways he seeks.

2. In *Beloved*, however, Amy compares Sethe's marks to a tree (15–16), and Paul D describes them as "the decorative work of an ironsmith" (179; perhaps a reference to Ogun). These descriptions also reveal the viewers' inability to deal with the full pain of the whipping; Amy's choice of the tree naturalizes the scars, and Paul's reference to the ironsmith takes allusions of branding and hardness and turns them into adornment. After Paul has had sex with Sethe, he perceives the ugliness of her scars. Kristine Holmes offers a negative reading of this circumstance (139–40), but in fact, Paul's shifting perceptions indicate that with growing intimacy, he sees the marks for what they are.

3. This ironic use of the word "nothing" anticipates George's search of the chicken house at the end of *Mama Day*. In language "nothing" itself has a presence and becomes visual, much as the supposed "nothing" of African-American experience takes form in the writings of the authors discussed in this book.

4. Likewise, Deborah McDowell notes that at the novel's conclusion, Dessa has to hug Clara instead of Ruth. McDowell argues that "Throughout the novel their children have functioned both to mediate and mollify the differences between them and to symbolize the possibilities of a new order" ("Negotiating Between Tenses" 160).

9. African (Re)Sisters

1. See, for instance, Dorkenoo and Elworthy's work or the first-person account, *Do They Hear You When You Cry*, by Fauziya Kassindja.

10. A Call Finds Its Response

1. One example is a 1996 exhibit at the National Portrait Gallery in London titled "David Livingstone and the Victorian Encounter with Africa." A less Eurocentric museum might have named the exhibit "David Livingstone and the African Encounter with Victoria," or even "The African Encounter with David Livingstone and Victoria."

Works Cited

Adams, Monni. *Designs for Living*. Cambridge: Harvard University Press, 1982.

Alcoff, Linda. "The Problem of Speaking for Others." *Cultural Critique* 20 (1991): 5–32.

Allen, Paula Gunn. "Kochinnenako in Academe: Three Approaches to Interpreting a Keres Indian Tale." In *Feminisms: An Anthology of Literary Theory and Criticism*, ed. Robyn R. Warhol and Diane Prince Herndl, 746–64. New Brunswick, N.J.: Rutgers University Press, 1997.

Awkward, Michael. "Roadblocks and Relatives: Critical Revision in *The Bluest Eye*." In *Critical Essays on Toni Morrison*, ed. Nellie Y. McKay, 57–68. Boston: G. K. Hall, 1988.

Baker, Houston A., Jr. *Blues, Ideology, and Afro-American Literature: A Vernacular Theory*. Chicago: University of Chicago Press, 1984.

———. *The Journey Back: Issues in Black Literature and Criticism*. Chicago: University of Chicago Press, 1980.

———. *Workings of the Spirit: The Poetics of Afro-American Women's Writing*. Chicago: University of Chicago Press, 1991.

Bass, Margaret Kent. "Alice's *Secret*." *College Language Association Journal (CLAJ)* 38.1 (1994): 1–10.

Bean, Annemarie. "Disclosures, Silences, Agency: African Female Genital Circumcision." *Women & Performance* 7–8 (1995): 324–28.

Beaulieu, Elizabeth Ann. *Black Women Writers and the American Neo-Slave Narrative: Femininity Unfettered*. Westport, Conn.: Greenwood, 1999.

Bledsoe, Caroline. "The Political Use of Sande Ideology and Symbolism." *American Ethnologist* 11 (1984): 455–72.

Bonetti, Kay. "An Interview with Margaret Walker Alexander." *Missouri Review* 15 (1992): 111–31.

Boone, Sylvia Ardyn. *Radiance from the Waters: Ideals of Beauty in Mende Art*. New Haven: Yale University Press, 1986.

Buckman, Alyson R. "The Body as a Site of Colonization: Alice Walker's *Possessing the Secret of Joy*." *Journal of American Culture* 18.2 (Summer 1995): 89–94.

Buckner, B. Dilla. "Folkloric Elements in Margaret Walker's Poetry." In Graham, ed., q.v., 139–47.

Busia, Abena P. B. "Words Whispered over Voids: A Context for Black Women's Rebellious Voices in the Novel of the African Diaspora." In *Black Feminist Criticism and Critical Theory*, ed. Joel Weixlmann and Houston A. Baker, 1–41. Greenwood, Fla.: Penkevill, 1988.

Butt-Thompson, Captain F. W. *West African Secret Societies*. New York: Argosy Antiquarian, 1969.

Carby, Hazel. "Ideologies of Black Folk: The Historical Novel of Slavery." In McDowell and Rampersad, eds., q.v., 125–43.

———. *Reconstructing Womanhood: The Emergence of the Afro-American Woman Novelist*. New York: Oxford University Press, 1987.

Carman, Diane. "Women's Rights Take 2nd Place to Diplomacy in Tokyo." *Denver Post*, 10 July 1993, E1.

Chesnutt, Charles W. *The Conjure Woman*. Ann Arbor: University of Michigan Press, 1969.

Chick, Nancy. "The Broken Clock: Time, Identity, and Autobiography in Jamaica Kincaid's *Lucy*." *College Language Association Journal (CLAJ)* 4.1 (1996): 90–103.

Child, Lydia Maria. *The Romance of the Republic*. Boston: Ticknor and Fields, 1867.

Chodorow, Nancy. *The Reproduction of Mothering: Psychoanalysis and the Sociology of Gender*. Berkeley: University of California Press, 1978.

Christian, Barbara. "Alice Walker: The Black Woman Artist as Wayward." In Evans, ed., q.v., 457–77.

———. "An Angle of Seeing: Motherhood in Buchi Emecheta's *The Joys of Motherhood* and Alice Walker's *Meridian* (1984)." In *Black Feminist Criticism: Perspectives on Black Women Writers*, ed. Barbara Christian, 211–52. New York: Pergamon, 1985.

———. "Trajectories of Self-Definition: Placing Contemporary Afro-American Women's Fiction." In Pryse and Spillers, eds., q.v., 233–48.

Collier, Eugenia. "Fields Watered with Blood: Myth and Ritual in the Poetry of Margaret Walker." In Evans, ed., q.v., 499–510.

Collins, Patricia Hill. *Black Feminist Thought*. New York: Routledge, 1991.

Cooper, Carolyn. "'Something Ancestral Recaptured': Spirit Possession as Trope in Selected Feminist Fictions of the African Diaspora." In *Motherlands: Black Women's Writing from Africa, the Caribbean, and South Asia*, ed. Susheila Nasta, 64–87. New Brunswick: Rutgers University Press, 1992.

Cooper, J. California. *Family*. New York: Anchor Doubleday, 1991.

Creel, Margaret Washington. *"A Peculiar People": Slave Religion and Community-Culture among the Gullahs*. New York: New York University Press, 1988.

Cudjoe, Selwyn. "Jamaica Kincaid and the Modernist Project: An Interview." In *Caribbean Women Writers*, ed. Selwyn Cudjoe, 215–32. Wellesley, Mass.: Calaloux, 1990.

Cullen, Countee. "Heritage." In *On These I Stand: An Anthology of the Best Poems of Countee Cullen*, 24–30. New York: Harper and Brothers, 1947.

Daly, Mary. *Gyn/Ecology: The Metaethics of Radical Feminism*. Boston: Beacon, 1990.

Davies, Carole Boyce. "Mother Right/Write Revisited: *Beloved* and *Dessa Rose* and the Construction of Motherhood in Black Women's Fiction." In *Narrating Mothers: Theorizing Maternal Subjectivities*, ed. Brenda O. Daly and Maureen T. Reddy, 44–57. Knoxville: University of Tennessee Press, 1991.

DeKoven, Marianne. "Postmodernism and Postutopian Desire in Toni Morrison and E. L. Doctorow." In Peterson, ed., q.v., 111–30.

de Lauretis, Teresa. "The Violence of Rhetoric: Considerations on Representation and Gender." In *The Violence of Representation: Literature and the History of Violence*, ed. Nancy Armstrong and Leonard Tennenhouse, 239–58. New York: Routledge, 1989.

de Weever, Jacqueline. *Mythmaking and Metaphor in Black Women's Fiction*. New York: St. Martin's Press, 1991.

Demetrakopolous, Stephanie. "Maternal Bonds as Devourers of Women's Individuation in Toni Morrison's *Beloved*." *African-American Review* 26 (1992): 51–60.

Diedrich, Maria. "Mastering American Destiny: The Ante-Bellum Slave Narrative." In *Reconstructing American Literary and Historical Studies*, ed. Gunther H. Lenz, Harmut Keil, and Sabine Bröck-Sallah, 254–67. New York: St. Martin's Press, 1990.

Deidrich, Maria, Carl Pedersen, and Justine Tally, eds. *Mapping African America: History, Narrative Formation, and the Production of Knowledge*. Hamburg: Lit Verlag, 1999.

Dieke, Ikenna. "Walker's *The Temple of My Familiar*: Womanist as Monistic Idealist." In *Critical Essays on Alice Walker*, ed. Ikenna Dieke, 127–39. Westport, Conn.: Greenwood, 1999.

Dorkenoo, Efua, and Scilla Elworthy. *Female Genital Mutilation: Proposals for Change*. London: Minority Rights Group, 1992.

Drewal, Margaret Thompson. *Yoruba Ritual: Performers, Play, Agency*. Bloomington: Indiana University Press, 1992.

Du Bois, W.E.B. *The Souls of Black Folk*. Cutchogue, N.Y.: Buccaneer Books, 1976.

Edwards, Lee. *Psyche as Hero: Female Heroism and Fictional Form*. Middletown, Conn.: Wesleyan University Press, 1984.

Erickson, Peter. "'Shakespeare's Black?': The Role of Shakespeare in Naylor's Novels." In Gates and Appiah, q.v., 231–48.

Evans, Mari, ed. *Black Women Writers, 1950–1980: A Critical Evaluation*. New York: Anchor Doubleday, 1984.

Ferguson, Moira. *Jamaica Kincaid: Where the Land Meets the Body*. Charlottesville: University Press of Virginia, 1994.

———. "A Lot of Memory: An Interview with Jamaica Kincaid." *Kenyon Review* 16 (1994): 163–88.

———. "*Lucy* and the Mark of the Colonizer." *Modern Fiction Studies* 39 (1993): 237–59.

Fowler, Virginia. *Gloria Naylor*. New York: Twayne, 1996.

Fraser, Celeste. "Stealing B(l)ack Voices: The Myth of the Black Matriarchy and *The Women of Brewster Place*." In Gates and Appiah, q.v., 90–105.

Gates, Henry Louis, Jr. *Figures in Black: Words, Signs, and the "Racial" Self*. New York: Oxford University Press, 1987.

———. Introduction. In Gates, ed., *Reading Black, Reading Feminist*, q.v., 1–17.

———. *The Signifying Monkey: A Theory of African-American Literary Criticism*. New York: Oxford University Press, 1988.

———, ed. *Reading Black, Reading Feminist: A Critical Anthology*. New York: Meridian, 1990.

Gates, Henry Louis, Jr., and Kwame Anthony Appiah. *Gloria Naylor: Critical Perspectives Past and Present*. New York: Amistad, 1993.

Genepp, Arnold Van. *The Rites of Passage*. London: Routledge and Kegan Paul, 1960.

Gilbert, Sandra M., and Susan Gubar. *The Madwoman in the Attic: The Woman Writer and the Nineteenth-Century Literary Imagination*. New Haven: Yale University Press, 1979.

Graham, Maryemma, ed. *Fields Watered with Blood: Critical Essays on Margaret Walker*. Athens: University of Georgia Press, 2001.

Grewal, Inderpal, and Caren Kaplan. "*Warrior Marks*: Global Womanism's Neo-Colonial Discourse in a Multicultural Context." *Camera Obscura* 39 (September 1996): 4–33.

Gwin, Minrose C. "*Jubilee*: The Black Woman's Celebration of Human Community." In Pryse and Spillers, eds., q.v., 132–50.

Hall, R. Mark. "Serving the Second Sun: The Men in Gloria Naylor's *Mama Day*." In Stave, ed., q.v., 77–96.

Hamilton, Cynthia S. "Revisions, Rememories and Exorcisms: Toni Morrison and the Slave Narrative." *Journal of American Studies* 30 (1996): 429–45.

Handley, William R. "The House a Ghost Built: Nommo, Allegory, and the Ethics of Reading in Toni Morrison's *Beloved*." *Contemporary Literature* 36 (1995): 676–701.

Harris, Trudier. *The Power of the Porch: The Storyteller's Craft in Zora Neale Hurston, Gloria Naylor, and Randall Kenan*. Athens: University of Georgia Press, 1996.

Hayes, Elizabeth T. "Gloria Naylor's *Mama Day* as Magic Realism." In *The Critical Response to Gloria Naylor*, ed. Sharon Felton and Michelle C. Louis, 177–86. Westport, Conn.: Greenwood, 1997.

Henderson, Mae Gwendolyn. "Speaking in Tongues: Dialogics, Dialectics, and the Black Woman Writer's Literary Tradition." In Gates, ed., *Reading Black, Reading Feminist*, q.v., 116–42.

Hirsch, Marianne. *The Mother/Daughter Plot: Narrative, Psychoanalysis, Feminism*. Bloomington: Indiana University Press, 1989.

Hite, Molly. *The Other Side of the Story: Structures and Strategies of Contemporary Feminist Narrative.* Ithaca: Cornell University Press, 1989.

Hogue, W. Lawrence. *Discourse and the Other: The Production of the Afro-American Text.* Durham, N.C.: Duke University Press, 1986.

Holland, Sharon P. "*Bakulu* Discourse: The Language of the Margin in Toni Morrison's *Beloved*." *LIT* 6 (1995): 89–100.

Holloway, Joseph. *Africanisms in American Culture.* Bloomington: Indiana University Press, 1990.

Holloway, Karla F. "Acknowledgment of Womanself." In *New Dimensions of Spirituality: A Biracial and Bicultural Reading of the Novels of Toni Morrison* by Stephanie A. Demetrakopoulos and Karla Holloway, 67–81. New York: Greenwood, 1987.

———. "*Beloved*: A Spiritual." *Callaloo* 13 (1990): 516–25.

———. *Moorings & Metaphors: Figures of Culture and Gender in Black Women's Literature.* New Brunswick, N.J.: Rutgers University Press, 1992.

Holmes, Kristine. "'This is flesh I'm talking about here': Embodiment in Toni Morrison's *Beloved* and Sherley Anne Williams' *Dessa Rose*." *LIT* 6 (1995): 133–48.

hooks, bell. "Writing the Subject: Reading *The Color Purple*." In Gates, ed., *Reading Black, Reading Feminist,* q.v., 454–70.

Horvitz, Deborah. "Nameless Ghosts: Possession and Dispossession in *Beloved*." *Studies in American Fiction* 17 (1989): 157–68.

Hospital, Janette Turner. "What They Did to Tashi." Rev. of *Possessing the Secret of Joy,* by Alice Walker. *New York Times Book Review,* 28 June 1992, 11–12.

Hurston, Zora Neale. *Their Eyes Were Watching God.* Urbana: University of Illinois Press, 1978.

Irigaray, Luce. *Speculum of the Other Woman.* Trans. Gillian C. Gill. Ithaca: Cornell University Press, 1985.

Ischinger, Anne Barbara. "The African Connection: Toni Morrison's Bonds with West African Women Writers." In Diedrich, Pedersen, and Tally, eds., q.v., 129–44.

Jacobs, Harriet. *Incidents in the Life of a Slave Girl, Written by Herself.* Ed. Jean Fagan Yellin. Cambridge: Harvard University Press, 1987.

Johnson, Charles. *Being & Race: Black Writing since 1970.* Bloomington: Indiana University Press, 1988.

Jones-Jackson, Patricia. *When Roots Die: Endangered Traditions on the Sea Islands.* Athens: University of Georgia Press, 1987.

Juhasz, Suzanne. *Reading from the Heart.* New York: Viking, 1994.

Kanneh, Kadiatu. *African Identities: Race, Nation and Culture in Ethnography, Pan-Africanism and Black Literatures.* New York: Routledge, 1998.

Karcher, Carolyn L. "Lydia Maria Child's *A Romance of the Republic*: An Abolitionist Vision of America's Racial Destiny." In McDowell and Rampersad, eds., q.v., 81–103.

Kassindja, Fauziya. *Do They Hear You When You Cry*. New York: Delacorte, 1998.

Kelley, Margot Anne, ed. *Gloria Naylor's Early Novels*. Gainesville: University Press of Florida, 1999.

Kieti, Nwikali. "Homesick and Eurocentric? Alice Walker's Africa." In Ojo-Ade, ed., *Of Dreams Deferred*, q.v., 157–70.

Kincaid, Jamaica. *Annie John*. New York: Plume, 1985.

———. *At the Bottom of the River*. New York: Plume, 1992.

———. *The Autobiography of My Mother*. New York: Plume, 1997.

———. *Lucy*. New York: Plume, 1991.

———. *My Brother*. New York: Farrar, Straus and Giroux, 1997.

———. *My Garden*. New York: Farrar, Straus and Giroux, 1999.

———. *A Small Place*. New York: Plume, 1988.

King, Nicole. "Meditations and Mediations: Issues of History and Fiction in *Dessa Rose*." *Soundings* 76 (1993): 351–68.

Kraft, Marion. *The African Continuum and Contemporary African-American Women Writers: Their Literary Presence and Ancestral Past*. New York: Peter Lang, 1995.

Krumholz, Linda. "Dead Teachers, Rituals of Manhood and Rituals of Reading in *Song of Solomon*." *Modern Fiction Studies* 39 (1993): 551–74.

Lauret, Marie. *Alice Walker*. New York: St. Martin's Press, 2000.

Lawal, Babatunde. *The Gẹ̀lẹ̀dẹ́ Spectacle*. Seattle: University of Washington Press, 1996.

LeClair, Thomas. "The Language Must Not Sweat" [interview with Toni Morrison]. *New Republic*, 21 March 1981, 25–29.

Lerner, Harriet G. *The Dance of Deception: Pretending and Truth-Telling in Women's Lives*. New York: Harper Perennial, 1994.

Levy, Helen Fiddyment. "Lead on with Light." In Gates and Appiah, q.v., 263–84.

Lewis, Vashti Crutcher. "African Tradition in Toni Morrison's *Sula*." *Phylon* 48.1 (1987): 91–97.

Lionnet, Françoise. "Dissymmetry Embodied: Feminism, Universalism, and the Practice of Excision." In *Borderwork: Feminist Engagements with Comparative Literature*, ed. Margaret Higonnet, 19–41. Ithaca: Cornell University Press, 1994.

Lorde, Audre. *Sister Outsider*. Freedom, Cal.: The Crossing Press, 1984.

Loriggio, Francesco. "Regionalism and Theory." In *Regionalism Reconsidered: New Approaches to the Field*, ed. David Jordan, 3–27. New York: Garland, 1994.

MacGaffey, Wyatt. "The Eyes of Understanding: Kongo Minkisi." In *Astonishment and Power*, 19–103. National Museum of African Art. Washington, D.C.: Smithsonian Institution Press, 1993.

Mahlis, Kristen. "Gender and Exile: Jamaica Kincaid's *Lucy*." *Modern Fiction Studies* 44 (1998): 164–83.

Marshall, Paule. *Brown Girl, Brownstones*. New York: Feminist Press, 1981.

Martin, Jacky. "From Division to Sacrificial Reconciliation: Toni Morrison's Novels." *Obsidian II* 5.2 (Summer 1990): 80–99.

Mathieson, Barbara. "Memory and Mother Love in Morrison's *Beloved*." *American Imago* 47 (1990): 1–21.

Mbalia, Doreatha Drummond. *Toni Morrison's Developing Class Consciousness*. Selinsgrove, Pa.: Susquehanna University Press, 1991.

McBride, Dwight A. "Speaking the Unspeakable: On Toni Morrison, African American Intellectuals and the Use of Essentialist Rhetoric." In Peterson, ed., q.v., 130–52.

McDowell, Deborah E. "Negotiating Between Tenses: Witnessing Slavery after Freedom—*Dessa Rose*." In McDowell and Rampersad, eds., q.v., 144–63.

McDowell, Deborah E., and Arnold Rampersad, eds. *Slavery and the Literary Imagination*. Baltimore: Johns Hopkins University Press, 1989.

Michie, Helena. "Mother, Sister, Other: The 'Other' Woman in Feminist Theory." *Literature and Psychology* 32.4 (1986): 1–10.

Miller, J. Hillis. *Fiction and Repetition*. Cambridge: Harvard University Press, 1982.

Mistron, Deborah. *Understanding Jamaica Kincaid's* Annie John. Westport, Conn.: Greenwood, 1999.

Morrison, Toni. *Beloved*. New York: Plume, 1987.

———. *The Bluest Eye*. New York: Washington Square Press, 1970.

———. "City Limits, Village Values: Concepts of Neighborhood in Black Fiction." In *Literature and the Urban Experience*, ed. Michael C. Jaye and Ann Chalmers Watts, 35–43. New Brunswick: Rutgers University Press, 1981.

———. *Jazz*. New York: Plume, 1992.

———. *Paradise*. New York: Plume, 1997.

———. *Playing in the Dark*. Cambridge: Harvard University Press, 1992.

———. "Rootedness: The Ancestor as Foundation." In Evans, q.v., 339–45.

———. *Song of Solomon*. New York: Signet, 1977.

———. *Sula*. New York: Plume, 1973.

———. *Tar Baby*. New York: Signet, 1983.

Murdoch, H. Adlai. "Severing the (M)Other Connection: The Representation of Cultural Identity in Jamaica Kincaid's *Annie John*." *Callaloo* 13 (1990): 325–40.

Nagel, James. "Desperate Hopes, Desperate Lives: Depression and Self-Realization in Jamaica Kincaid's *Annie John* and *Lucy*." In *Traditions, Voices, and Dreams: The American Novel Since the 1960s*, ed. Melvin J. Friedman and Ben Siegel, 237–53. Newark: University of Delaware Press, 1995.

Naylor, Gloria. *Bailey's Cafe*. New York: Harcourt Brace Jovanovich, 1992.

———. *Linden Hills*. New York: Penguin, 1985.

———. *Mama Day*. New York: Vintage, 1989.

———. *The Men of Brewster Place*. New York: Hyperion, 1998.

———. *The Women of Brewster Place*. New York: Penguin, 1982.

Ojo-Ade, Femi. "Africa and America: A Question of Continuities, Cleavage, and Dreams Deferred." In Ojo-Ade, ed., *Of Dreams Deferred*, q.v., 1–27.

———, ed. *Of Dreams Deferred, Dead and Alive: African Perspectives on African-American Writers*. Westport, Conn: Greenwood, 1996.

Olney, James. "'I Was Born': Slave Narratives, Their Status as Autobiographies and Literature." In *The Slave's Narrative*, ed. Charles T. Davis and Henry Louis Gates, Jr., 148–75. New York: Oxford University Press, 1985.

Otten, Terry. *The Crime of Innocence in the Fiction of Toni Morrison*. Columbia: University of Missouri Press, 1989.

Page, Philip. "Circularity in Toni Morrison's *Beloved*." *African-American Review* 26 (1992): 31–39.

Peach, Linden. *Toni Morrison*. New York: St. Martin's Press, 1995.

Pérez-Torres, Rafael. "Knitting and Knotting the Narrative Thread—*Beloved* as Postmodern Novel." In Peterson, ed., q.v., 91–109.

Peterson, Nancy J., ed. *Toni Morrison: Critical and Theoretical Approaches*. Baltimore: Johns Hopkins University Press, 1997.

Pryse, Marjorie. "Introduction: Zora Neale Hurston, Alice Walker, and the 'Ancient Power' of Black Women." In Pryse and Spillers, eds., q.v., 1–24.

Pryse, Marjorie, and Hortense J. Spillers, eds. *Conjuring: Black Women, Fiction, and Literary Tradition*. Bloomington: Indiana University Press, 1985.

Randle, Gloria T. "'Knowing When to Stop': Loving and Living Small in the Slave World of *Beloved*." *College Language Association Journal (CLAJ)* 41.3 (1998): 279–302.

Reardon, Patrick T. "'The Wind' Done For? 'Unabated Privacy' Wins Round over Public Interest." *Chicago Tribune*, 2 May 2001, 5:3.

Rhodes, Jewell Parker. *Voodoo Dreams*. New York: Picador, 1995.

Rigney, Barbara Hill. *The Voices of Toni Morrison*. Columbus: Ohio State University Press, 1991.

Roberts, John W. *From Trickster to Badman*. Philadelphia: University of Pennsylvania Press, 1989.

Rody, Caroline. *The Daughter's Return: African-American and Caribbean Women's Fictions of History*. New York: Oxford University Press, 2001.

Rose, Gillian. *Feminism and Geography: The Limits of Geographical Knowledge*. Minneapolis: University of Minnesota Press, 1993.

Ryan, Judylyn. "Contested Visions/Double Vision in *Tar Baby*." In Peterson, ed., q.v., 63–87.

Sale, Maggie. "Call and Response as Critical Method: African-American Oral Traditions and *Beloved*." *African-American Review* 26 (1992): 41–50.

Samuels, Wilfrid. "Liminality and the Search for Self in Toni Morrison's *Song of Solomon*." *Minority Voices* 5 (1981): 59–68.

Sievers, Stefanie. *Liberating Narratives: The Authorization of Black Female Voices in African American Women Writers' Novels of Slavery*. Hamburg: Verlag, 1999; Rutgers: Transaction Publishers, 1999.

Simmons, Diane. *Jamaica Kincaid*. New York: Twayne, 1994.

Sitter, Deborah Ayer. "The Making of a Man: Dialogic Meaning in *Beloved*." *African-American Review* 26 (1992): 17–29.

Smith, Barbara. "Toward a Black Feminist Criticism." In *The New Feminist Criti-*

cism: Essays on Women, Literature, and Theory, ed. Elaine Showalter, 168–85. New York: Pantheon, 1985.

Soyinka, Wole. "The critic and society: Barthes, leftocracy, and other mythologies." In *Black Literature and Literary Theory*, ed. Henry Louis Gates, Jr., 27–58. New York: Routledge, 1990.

Spears, James. "Black Folk Elements in Margaret Walker's *Jubilee*." *Mississippi Folklore Register* 14 (1980): 13–19.

Spillers, Hortense J. "Changing the Letter: The Yokes, the Jokes of Discourse, or, Mrs. Stowe, Mr. Reed." In McDowell and Rampersad, eds., q.v., 25–61.

———. "Cross-Currents, Discontinuities: Black Women's Fiction." In Pryse and Spillers, eds., q.v., 249–61.

Spivak, Gayatri Chakravorty. "French Feminism in an International Frame." *Yale French Studies* 62 (1981): 154–85.

Stave, Shirley. "Re-Writing Sacred Texts: Gloria Naylor's Revisionary Theology." In Stave, ed., *Gloria Naylor*, q.v., 97– 117.

———, ed. *Gloria Naylor: Strategy and Technique, Magic and Myth*. Newark: University of Delaware Press, 2001.

Stewart, Michelle Pagni. "Moynihan's 'Tangle of Pathology': Toni Morrison's Legacy of Motherhood." In *Family Matters in the British and American Novel*, ed. Andrea O. Herrera, Elizabeth M. Nollen, and Sheila R. Foor, 237–53. Bowling Green, Ohio: Bowling Green State University Popular Press, 1997.

Tally, Justine. "*Paradise* and the Production of History." In Diedrich, Pedersen, and Tally, eds., q.v., 203–19.

Tharp, Julie. "The Maternal Aesthetic of *Mama Day*." In Stave, ed., *Gloria Naylor*, q.v., 118–31.

Thomas, H. Nigel. *From Folklore to Fiction: A Study of Folk Heroes and Rituals in the Black American Novel*. Westport, Conn.: Greenwood, 1988.

Thompson, Dorothy Perry. "Africana Womanist Revision in Gloria Naylor's *Mama Day* and *Bailey's Cafe*." In Kelley, ed., q.v., 89–111.

Thompson, Robert Farris. *Flash of the Spirit: African and Afro-American Art and Philosophy*. New York: Vintage, 1984.

Traore, Ousseynou. "Creative African Memory: Some Oral Sources of Toni Morrison's *Song of Solomon*." In Ojo-Ade, ed., *Of Dreams Deferred*, q.v., 129–41.

Traylor, Eleanor. "Music as Theme: The Blues Mode in the Works of Margaret Walker." In Evans, ed., q.v., 511–24.

Tucker, Lindsey. "Recovering the Conjure Woman: Texts and Contexts in Naylor's *Mama Day*." *African-American Review* 28 (1994): 173–88.

Turner, Victor W. *From Ritual to Theatre: The Human Seriousness of Play*. New York: Performing Arts Journal Publications, 1982.

———. *The Ritual Process: Structure and Anti-Structure*. Chicago: Aldine, 1969.

Twain, Mark. *Pudd'nhead Wilson*. New York: Penguin, 1986.

Ty, Eleanor. "Struggling with the Powerful (M)Other: Identity and Sexuality in

Kogawa's *Obasan* and Kincaid's *Lucy*." *International Fiction Review* 20.2 (1993): 120–26.

Uchendu, Victor. *The Igbo of Southeast Nigeria*. New York: Holt, Rinehart, and Winston, 1965.

Walker, Alice. *The Color Purple*. New York: Washington Square Press, 1982.

———. *In Love & Trouble*. New York: Harcourt Brace Jovanovich, 1973.

———. *In Search of Our Mothers' Gardens*. New York: Harcourt Brace Jovanovich, 1983.

———. *Possessing the Secret of Joy*. New York: Simon and Schuster, 1992.

———. *The Temple of My Familiar*. New York: Pocket Books, 1989.

Walker, Alice, and Pratibha Parmar. *Warrior Marks: Female Genital Mutilation and the Sexual Blinding of Women*. New York: Harcourt Brace, 1993.

Walker, Margaret. *Jubilee*. New York: Bantam, 1988.

Wall, Wendy. "Lettered Bodies and Corporeal Texts in *The Color Purple*." *Studies in American Fiction* 16 (1988): 83–97.

Wallace, Michele. "Variations on Negation and the Heresy of Black Feminist Creativity." In Gates, ed., *Reading Black, Reading Feminist*, q.v., 52–67.

Wallerstein, Edward. *Circumcision: An American Health Fallacy*. New York: Springer, 1980.

Ward, Catherine C. "*Linden Hills*: A Modern *Inferno*." In Gates and Appiah, q.v., 182–194.

Ward, Cynthia. "Reading African Women Readers." *Research in African Literatures* 27.3 (Fall 1996): 78–86.

———. "What They Told Buchi Emecheta: Oral Subjectivity and the Joys of 'Otherhood.'" *PMLA* 105 (1990): 83–97.

Warren, Nagueyalti, and Sally Wolff. "'Like the Pupil of an Eye': Sexual Blinding of Women in Alice Walker's Works." *Southern Literary Journal* 31.1 (Fall 1998): 1–16.

Washington, Mary Helen. "'The Darkened Eye Restored': Notes Toward a Literary History of Black Women." In Gates, ed., *Reading Black, Reading Feminist*, q.v., 30–43.

White, Deborah Gray. *Ar'n't I a Woman? Female Slaves in the Plantation South*. New York: Norton, 1985.

Whitt, Margaret Earley. *Understanding Gloria Naylor*. Columbia: University of South Carolina Press, 1999.

"Wild Spirits, Strong Medicine: African Art and the Wilderness." *The BlockLetter* [Newsletter of the Mary and Leigh Block Gallery of Northwestern University], November 1989, 1–5.

Wilentz, Gay. *Binding Cultures: Black Women Writers in Africa and the Diaspora*. Bloomington: Indiana University Press, 1992.

———. "Healing the Wounds of Time." Rev. of *Possessing the Secret of Joy*, by Alice Walker, and *Bailey's Cafe*, by Gloria Naylor. *Women's Review of Books* 10.5 (February 1993): 15–16.

Williams, Sherley Anne. *Dessa Rose*. New York: Berkley, 1987.

———. "The Lion's History: The Ghetto Writes B[l]ack." *Soundings* 76 (1993): 245–60.

———. "Some Implications of Womanist Theory." In Gates, ed., *Reading Black, Reading Feminist*, q.v., 68–75.

Woidat, Caroline M. "Talking Back to Schoolteacher: Morrison's Confrontation with Hawthorne in *Beloved*." In Peterson, ed., q.v., 181–200.

Index

Amy K. Levin is director of Women's Studies and an associate professor of English at Northern Illinois University. She is author of *The Suppressed Sister: A Relationship in Novels by Nineteenth-Century British Women*. Currently, she is completing a book manuscript on museums, narrative, and culture.

Books of related interest from University Press of Florida

Gloria Naylor's Early Novels, edited by Margot Anne Kelley (1999)
The Apocalypse in African-American Fiction, by Maxine L.
    Montgomery (1996)
Zora in Florida, edited by Stephen J. Glassman and Kathryn Lee
    Seidel (1991)